# The GRAIN MERCHANTS

# The GRAIN MERCHANTS

## An Illustrated History of the
## MINNEAPOLIS GRAIN EXCHANGE

**DAVE KENNEY**

Foreword by
**WALTER F. MONDALE**

AFTON HISTORICAL SOCIETY PRESS

The Minneapolis Grain Exchange is grateful to the following corporate, foundation, and individual donors for helping to fund the publication of

# THE GRAIN MERCHANTS : *An Illustrated History of the Minneapolis Grain Exchange*

## CORPORATE OR FOUNDATION DONORS

### PLATINUM
Archer Daniels Midland Company

### GOLD
Cargill, Incorporated
CHS Inc. and Country Hedging, Inc.
ConAgra Trade Group
General Mills Foundation
The Wallin Foundation: Winston R. and
    Maxine H. Wallin

### SILVER
AGP, in honor of all the men and women who, throughout the centuries, have dedicated their labor to the growth and development of agriculture in Minnesota and the nation
Bay State Milling Company
Cargill Investor Services, Inc.
Commodity Specialists Company, in memory of
    Philip J. Lindau Sr. and James H. Lindau
de Rosier, inc.
Faegre and Benson Foundation
Miller Milling Company
Rahr Foundation
The Southways Foundation
The Wallin Foundation: Bradford W. Wallin in
    memory of Kenneth P. "Bud" Boe

### BRONZE
BNSF Foundation
Bunge North America
Chicago Mercantile Exchange
CLD Pacific Grain, LLC
FC Stone, LLC
Frontier Futures, Inc.
Futures Industry Association

Galt Commodities, Inc.
Garfield Clark and Associates
Great Lakes Commodities, LLC
J. P. Morgan Futures Inc.
Kellogg Commission Company Fund of the
    Minneapolis Foundation
Keystone Corporation/Brian McGuire, in memory
    of William S. Katz
Lansing Grain Company, LLC
Mastel Grain Company
Mayco Export
National Grain Trade Council
New York Board of Trade
Rabobank International
The Scoular Company
Wilson Trading Company

## INDIVIDUAL DONORS

### GOLD
Mark G. and Anne Bagan, Lindsay, Alyssa,
    Shaley, and Drayton
John G. and Patricia Dill
Kent and Beth Horsager

### SILVER
Mr. and Mrs. W. Brooks Fields Jr., in memory of
    Allan L. Burdick Sr., Frank H. Murrin, and the
    "Mullin brothers" (Jim & Ed)
Charles A. Gallup
Cliff W. Larson Jr.
Malcolm McDonald
Howard I. McMillan Jr., Tammis A. McMillan, and
    John M. Ringer, in honor of their four-
    generation grain family
Truxtun and Adrienne Morrison, in memory of
    Frank H. Peavey, Frank T. Heffelfinger, and
    H. Terry Morrison

Carter K. Ohrt
Anthony C. Owens
J. Peter Ritten, in memory of Louis N. Ritten and
    Charles E. Ritten
Robert Schachter
W. Shelley Walsh

### BRONZE
Gregory and JoAnn Bagan & family
Jesse Marie Bartz, in memory of Martin Bartz and
    Tommy Hartness
Layne G. Carlson/Carlson Ag Enterprises
Richard A. Coonrod
Austin Damiani
David P. Darr
April Egan
James D. Jr. and Michele Facente & family
Martin F. Farrell
L. Scott Hackett
Michael P. Halpert, in honor of Samuel R. Halpert
T. Bradley and Pattie Hays
Scott Hedin
Burton M. Joseph
Mike Krueger/The Money Farm
Cliff W. Larson III
Steve and Donna Lennartson
Raymond F. Lottie
The Robert McWhite Family
MGEX Staff Members
The Michael James Mullin and Karin Mullin Winter
    families, in memory of James F. Mullin
Billie Jo Norris
Daniel Roemer
Kevin Sallstrom
Sandra S. and Storm Sullivan
Wendy Warren Wood, in memory of
    John Patton Wood

Library of Congress Cataloging-in-Publication Data

Kenney, Dave, 1961-
The grain merchants : an illustrated history of the Minneapolis Grain
Exchange / by Dave Kenney ; foreword by Walter F. Mondale.—1st ed.
    p. cm.
Includes index.
ISBN-13: 978-1-890434-74-8
ISBN-10: 1-890434-74-4
1. Minneapolis Grain Exchange—History—Pictorial works.  2. Grain trade—
Minnesota—Minneapolis—History—Pictorial works.  3. Commodities exchanges—
Minnesota—Minneapolis—History—Pictorial works.
I. Title.
HD9038.M5K46 2006
332.64'413109776579—dc22

2006013200

Printed in China

Edited by Michele Hodgson

Designed by Mary Susan Oleson

Production assistance by Beth Williams

Printed by Pettit Network, Inc., Afton, Minnesota

*Afton Historical Society Press*

W. Duncan MacMillan        Patricia Condon McDonald
*President*                *Publisher*

P. O. Box 100, Afton, MN 55001
800-436-8443
aftonpress@aftonpress.com
www.aftonpress.com

# CONTENTS

A timeless scene on the Minneapolis Grain Exchange trading floor: Traders in trading jackets bid and offer as they keep a sharp eye on market fluctuations. From left: Don Wilson (arm in air), Cliff Larson III (in red smock), and Patrick Commerford (center, in blue smock).

# FOREWORD

ALONG WITH IRON ORE, TIMBER, and other natural resources, grain is an enduring contributor to Minnesota's economy. As a U.S. senator, vice president, and ambassador to Japan, I have seen our state's grain industry continue to grow within a regional, national, and international marketplace. One remarkable constant in that growth has been the Minneapolis Grain Exchange, whose 125th anniversary in the fall of 2006 is truly cause for celebration.

The state's grain industry took off in the 1860s, when Minneapolis flour mills flourished with the rise in Minnesota's production of hard red spring wheat. The growth was mutually beneficial to several enterprises. To transport settlers to the farmland and the wheat to the mills, for instance, a network of railroads began to expand, some built by railroad barons like James J. Hill, others built by the millers themselves. Recognizing the need for credit to finance the burgeoning grain market, millers also helped underwrite the state's fledgling banking industry. When millers invented techniques that processed spring wheat into a finer, more desirable flour, it revolutionized the milling industry, fetching higher prices than winter wheat and, in 1880, making Minneapolis the nation's leading flour producer. As the grain merchants prospered, so did the city's parks, schools, hospitals, and other philanthropic endeavors. Minneapolis was poised to enter a new phase of growth, but one thing was missing: a central market where buyers and sellers could gather to trade grain.

The Minneapolis Grain Exchange was founded in 1881 as that central market, vaulted into prominence through its connections to the industrialists who were driving the growth of the city and the region. A mere five years later, Minneapolis was the largest wheat market in the United States, and the exchange had established itself as a prominent business with a growing national reputation for ensuring fair trade in grain. By the 1970s, the Minneapolis Grain Exchange had formed a regional stronghold within an international marketplace.

Foreign exports have been a factor in the Minneapolis grain trade since the late nineteenth century, but the primary focus was on the domestic market until the early

1930s, when Minnesota's Cargill built a grain terminal at Albany, New York. Foreign exports grew modestly until the 1940s, then expanded to meet Europe's wartime needs. Foreign trading had a brief, heady run in 1963 and 1964, when Cargill and Continental Grain Company agreed to sell wheat to the Soviet Union. Although the sales were short-lived, the Russians returned to U.S. grain markets in 1972 under President Nixon's policy of détente, which was aimed at reducing superpower tensions while providing mutual economic advantages. The effect on the Minneapolis market was profound, with wheat futures trading at their highest level in nearly ten years.

The volume of futures trading increased steadily until January 1980, when President Carter imposed a grain embargo on the Soviet Union in an effort to force the Russians out of Afghanistan, which the USSR had recently invaded. Futures trading was suspended in four commodities markets, including the Minneapolis Grain Exchange. The exchange's board of directors worried about the long-term implications of the embargo, but within weeks the markets rebounded. A year later, President Reagan lifted the grain embargo and the free market was back in business.

By the early 1990s, business once again picked up. In 1991, the Minneapolis Grain Exchange was the fastest-growing futures market in the country. In fact, as the exchange entered the twenty-first century, the futures market seemed to be breaking records every few months. The annual vol-

ume for 2005—over 1.4 million futures and options contracts traded—was more than twenty-five times larger than the volume in 1971, the year before the Russian grain deals.

Of the $22 billion in total goods and services exported by Minnesota in 2004, $2 billion were in agricultural goods, according to the U.S. Department of Agriculture. Minnesota is the seventh largest exporter of agricultural commodities and related food products, accounting for 4.6 percent of national exports in this category. Traders come to the Minneapolis Grain Exchange from all parts of the globe, from Canada to Japan to Australia, via major firms like Cargill, Archer Daniels Midland, ConAgra, General Mills, and Cenex Harvest States.

The Minneapolis Grain Exchange has surely stood the tests of time, some of them severe: the invasion of "bucketshop" gambling dens, a fire that nearly destroyed its headquarters, competition from farmers' cooperatives, the stock market crash and the Great Depression, government price controls, the Russian grain embargo, the farm crisis of the 1980s. Through it all, the exchange has endured. This cornerstone of our state's economy has not only exceeded its founders' expectations, it has earned its place many times over as a regional powerhouse within a global marketplace. It is a dynamic institution worthy of Minnesota's heartiest congratulations for 125 years of outstanding achievement.

*Walter F. Mondale*

VICE PRESIDENT OF THE UNITED STATES
1977–1981

# ACKNOWLEDGMENTS

ONLY A FRACTION of the world's population has even the most basic understanding of how commodities markets work. Thankfully, the Minneapolis Grain Exchange is teeming with people who willingly share their knowledge with neophytes like me.

The list of contributors to the publication of this history begins with the Grain Exchange's 125th Commemoration Commission Committee: chair Martin Farrell, John Dill, Burton Joseph, Howard I. McMillan Jr., Robert B. McWhite Sr., Jean Niklason, Bradford Wallin, special adviser Malcolm McDonald, and Grain Exchange board chair Charles Gallup. Each was supportive throughout, but we might never have accomplished our goals had it not been for Grain Exchange chief of staff Jesse Marie Bartz. Jesse was my main sounding board and a joy to work with. Thanks too to the Hennepin History Museum for serving as the project's fiscal agent.

I also owe a debt of gratitude to those who helped me understand the ins and outs of the business, including Grain Exchange president and CEO Mark Bagan, former president and CEO Kent Horsager, John Comford, Al Gloe, Mike Mullin, Leo Odden, Helen Pound, Howard Smith, Mort Sosland, and many others who fielded random questions with patience and good humor. Research associate Matt Carhart tracked down information and photos that eluded me and helped me avoid historical pitfalls. Deborah Morse-Kahn performed research and did oral-history interviews before I was brought into the project. The work she did made my job much easier than it might otherwise have been.

The Grain Exchange supplied many of the book's images. Other organizations that contributed artwork include the Minnesota Historical Society; the Special Collections Department of the Minneapolis Public Library; DeAnn M. Dankowski, Minneapolis Institute of Arts; Patricia Maus, Northeast Minnesota History Center, University of Minnesota–Duluth; Susan Larson-Fleming, Hennepin History Museum; Cathy McLane, The Blake School; Cori Becker, Archer Daniels Midland; Hans Schaub, The Minneapolis Club; Bruce Bruemmer, Cargill; Rachel Hermansander, ConAgra Mills; and Marti DeMoss, ConAgra Foods. Charlie Gallup and Brad Wallin deserve special thanks for lending images from their personal collections.

My manuscript was transformed into this handsome volume by the talented team at Afton Historical Society Press: publisher Patricia McDonald, editor Michele Hodgson, designer Mary Sue Oleson, and production assistant Beth Williams. I can't pretend to know how they did it. Suffice it to say that I put my words in good hands. —D. K.

# INTRODUCTION

**IT'S 9:29 ON A TUESDAY MORNING.**
Several dozen people have staked out positions along the rim of a large indentation in the floor, a sunken octagon of wooden steps about twenty feet across. Some stare intently at the big, black electronic board that looms above them on the nearest wall. Others gaze at nothing in particular, affecting nonchalance. One strains his neck, hoping to catch the attention of a colleague in a nearby cubicle. Another tries out a joke, a burst of laughter greeting the punchline. Most members of this crowd display what appears to be a confused sense of fashion. They wear brightly colored smocks with big pockets. Loud prints—red and black checkerboards, blue and white flowers, even stylized pizza slices—are especially popular.

At precisely 9:30, a bell clangs.
Pandemonium erupts.

For anyone unfamiliar with the surroundings, the chorus of shouts and yelps is incomprehensible. Every once in a while, the din dies down enough to make out words that sound somewhat familiar.

"Deece four and a half!"
"Four Deece!"
"Deece four and a half!"
"A quarter!"
*"Sold!"*

This is the beginning of another day of controlled chaos at the Minneapolis Grain Exchange, one of the nation's fourteen commodities exchanges. The colorfully clad traders are here to buy and sell wheat futures—contracts to deliver a certain amount of wheat during a certain upcoming month. Until 1:15 p.m. each weekday, bids and offers are shouted or signaled via an "open outcry" auction system as trades are made. In the transaction just completed, for example, the seller announced that he wanted to sell five thousand bushels of December wheat ("Deece") for three dollars seventy-four and a *half* cents a bushel. The buyer countered with a bid of three dollars and seventy-four cents *even*. In the end, they split the difference and agreed to a price of three dollars seventy-four and a *quarter* cents a bushel. The deal was done with a pointed finger and a nod—a gentlemen's agreement. The paperwork comes later. It's the way business has been done here for 125 years.

The Minneapolis Grain Exchange opened in 1881 as a regional cash marketplace to promote fair trade in wheat, oats, corn, and all the other grain that farmers of the Upper Midwest produce. Before the development of this centralized marketplace, regional farmers had no way of knowing if they were receiving the best price for their grain. Since most of them harvested and sold their crops at the same time, the glut of grain into the market set the supply-and-demand curve askew. Futures trading moderated those market fluctuations.

These days, most of the activity at the Grain Exchange takes place in or around the futures pit. For many years, however, the real action was on the other side of the trading floor: the cash grain side. There, dozens of buyers and sellers gathered around hulking wooden tables to haggle over actual shipments of grain. Most of the tables were cluttered with stacks of pans brimming with samples drawn from railcars. Buyers fingered the grain, rolled it in the palms of their hands, and held it up to the natural light streaming through the tall, arched windows on the east end of the room. Now the cash grain tables are mainly relics, reminders of a time when samples from nearly every shipment of grain originating in the Upper Midwest eventually made their way to the exchange's trading floor.

Yet the twenty-first-century cash market still provides a valuable service for Minneapolis Grain Exchange members, with an average of one million bushels of corn, wheat, barley, oats, rye, flax, and soybeans changing hands daily. For the most part, however, millers, exporters, elevators, farmers, and speculators look to the exchange as the only designated contract market for hard red spring wheat, one of the world's most highly prized grains. An average of more than five thousand futures and options contracts representing twenty-five million bushels are traded here daily, including several electronically

traded agricultural index contracts. Billions of dollars of trades are completed here every year. The Minneapolis Grain Exchange provides the facilities for and oversight of trading, yet it does not participate in trading, nor does it establish prices. That is the business of its members. Memberships, or seats, on the exchange are bought and sold between individuals and firms.

It's been 125 years since Minneapolis's first generation of business leaders founded what would become one of the premier grain markets in the world. In the decades since its creation, the Minneapolis Grain Exchange (known originally as the Minneapolis Chamber of Commerce) has produced countless success stories. As might be expected from an institution that attracts risk-takers, it has also witnessed its share of unfulfilled dreams. Through it all, the trading floor has served as a kind of commercial and civic nucleus, a place where some of the city's most important business gets done by dozens of individuals who share an enduring vision: to promote fair trade of the Upper Midwest's agricultural riches within a national and international marketplace.

*They are the grain merchants.*
*This is their story.*

*Mark Bagan,* PRESIDENT AND CEO

*Charles Gallub,* CHAIR

MINNEAPOLIS GRAIN EXCHANGE
May 2006

**Bird's-eye view of downtown Minneapolis, with the milling district in the center foreground, circa 1880s.**

# CHAPTER ONE

To 1895

# Creating an Open Market

## Tuesday, November 15, 1881

The sun had just set behind the modest Minneapolis skyline, ushering in the end of another business day. The city was beginning its nightly transformation. As gaslights winked on, the bustling downtown streets and sidewalks emptied of their daytime crowds. The bowler-topped gentlemen, the hoop-skirted ladies, the stooped and exhausted workers of the city's mills and factories— all had begun to seek refuge in homes extravagant to humble.

The temperature during the day had barely reached double digits, and signs of looming winter were unmistakable. On the east side of downtown Minneapolis, chunks of ice already clogged the Mississippi River, forcing several sawmills above St. Anthony Falls to

close for the season. Workers prepared to install wood-burning stoves in the horse-drawn streetcars that plied Hennepin and Washington Avenues. Police reported a rash of overcoat thefts, including one allegedly perpetrated by a "traveling vagabond" known as Mississippi Red Jr. On the positive side, the cold snap had frozen the miles of mud that comprised the city's street system. Pedestrians could now cross busy intersections, confident that they wouldn't lose their shoes in suction-inducing goo.[1]

Yet despite the hour, despite the cold, parts of Minneapolis continued to stir. The corner of Hennepin and Washington, for example, came to life briefly as scores of well-bundled men and women converged on the Academy of Music and headed inside. Haverly's

Mastodon Minstrels were in town for a return engagement, and the ticket holders were looking forward to a raucous evening of song and dance performed in black face. Little did they know that, because of a railroad baggage mix-up, much of the traveling troupe would be performing without costumes.

One block away, at the corner of Hennepin and Third Street, a much smaller contingent of Minneapolis residents was gathering at Security State Bank. Unlike the crowd just

**The Security State Bank Building, circa 1885. It was the birthplace of the Minneapolis Chamber of Commerce. Established by Hugh, Thomas, and William Harrison in 1877, Security operated as an independent financial institution until 1915, when it merged with First National Bank of Minneapolis.**

down the street, the group of men here had business, not entertainment, on their minds.

About three dozen men had crammed into the bank's small basement meeting room. The roster included not only prominent businessmen from Minneapolis, but civic leaders. There was the city's current mayor, Alonzo Rand, as well as a former mayor (and then president of Security Bank), Hugh Harrison. Charles Loring of the Galaxy flour mill on Eighth Avenue South was there. So were Otis Pray, Minneapolis's most successful mill builder, and John Coykendall, whose wholesale dry-goods store on Washington Avenue North was among the city's largest. It was an impressive cross section of some of Minneapolis's most influential bankers, millers, merchants, manufacturers, and railroad executives, most of whom had exhibited over the years an uncommon interest in promoting the long-term economic and civic vitality of the city. These men had come together for the first official meeting of a new organization called the Minneapolis Chamber of Commerce.

They would rather have called their new organization the Minneapolis Board of Trade, but that name was already taken. The existing Minneapolis Board of Trade was a club of local businessmen who had formed an association in 1872 to "facilitate and promote the commercial, mercantile and manufacturing interests of the city of Minneapolis." When George Rogers, a commission man, and his fellow grain exchange boosters asked the Board of Trade to relinquish the name, the board refused. Rebuffed, the men were forced to adopt their second choice: the Minneapolis Chamber of Commerce.

Nineteen years later, as the Board of Trade teetered on the brink of insolvency, its members blamed their problems, in part, on their predecessors' stubborn refusal to give up the contested name. "Now it is the Board of Trade people who have made overtures," the *Minneapolis Journal* reported on December 17, 1900. "They have expressed a willingness to give a quit claim deed to the name if the grain men so desire." But the grain men did *not* so desire. They would hold onto the name, Chamber of Commerce, for another forty-seven years.

As most of the men gathered in the crowded bank room knew, the group's name was a tad misleading. While most chambers of commerce acted as an umbrella organization encompassing all of the city's business interests, the Minneapolis Chamber of Commerce's founders had created it to serve a specific function: to operate as an open market, a place where like-minded businessmen could meet to buy and sell grain.

No grain was traded during that first meeting; that wouldn't happen for another few weeks. Instead, the men who ventured to the corner of Hennepin and Third were there to officially join what, at the moment, appeared to be a dubious undertaking. A close look at the group's make-up revealed the primary challenge facing the newborn chamber. Of the forty or so men gathered in the bank's basement, only four were millers. The rest were either prominent city leaders who had built their reputations in businesses outside the grain trade or members of a relatively obscure class of Minneapolis entrepreneurs: commission men struggling to make their living as middlemen in the grain trade. Most of the city's most powerful millers—men with names like Pillsbury, Washburn, Crosby, and Dunwoody—were absent, which meant that the men in attendance were planning to create an open market for grain without even the tacit approval of Minneapolis's biggest grain buyers. Folly? Perhaps, but as the Tuesday evening turnout at Security State Bank demonstrated, the idea still enjoyed substantial and influential support. Two years earlier, the Minneapolis Board of Trade—which, ironically, performed most of the functions of a typical chamber of commerce—had declared that the

**Alonzo Cooper Rand was president of the Minneapolis Gaslight Company, a mayor of Minneapolis (1878–1882), and, along with general merchandiser John Coykendall, a charter member of the Chamber of Commerce.**

**On July 12, 1885, Rand and Coykendall chartered the *Minnie Cook* for a leisurely excursion with their families on Lake Minnetonka. A sudden storm capsized the steamboat and all of the passengers, including five children, drowned. The funeral at Lakewood Cemetery was one of the biggest events in Minneapolis's early history. Chamber of Commerce members passed a special memorial resolution in which they paid tribute to Rand and Coykendall, who, despite their lack of experience in the grain trade, had helped bring the chamber into being.**

time was "not far distant when Minneapolis [would] become a market to which grain [would] be shipped and sold." As far as the members of the new Chamber of Commerce were concerned, that time had arrived.[2]

Scouring logs at the sawmill of Minneapolis lumberman C. A. Smith, circa 1885.

Minneapolis's first gristmill was six decades old when James Fairman completed this painting, *Old Government Mills at Falls of St. Anthony,* circa 1890.

## Before the Chamber

It had taken Minneapolis several decades to grow into a city capable of dreaming the kind of grandiose civic dreams entertained by the Chamber of Commerce's charter members. The city had started out as not one frontier settlement, but two: St. Anthony, which had been established on the east side of the Mississippi in the late 1830s, and Minneapolis, which had had its start on the river's west bank about a decade later. (They merged in 1872.) Both communities depended on the waterpower generated by St. Anthony Falls to propel their economies and sustain their growth. Their first major industry was lumber milling; the first significant sawmill began operating in 1848. Others soon followed, and by 1856, the mills of St. Anthony Falls were producing up to 100,000 board feet a day. It was at about that time that Minneapolis and St. Anthony witnessed the rise of their second major industry: flour milling.[3]

The grinding of flour at the falls dated back to 1823, when soldiers erected a small gristmill for nearby Fort Snelling, which overlooked the confluence of the Mississippi and Minnesota Rivers. But the area's flour industry didn't begin in earnest until the mid-1850s, when a group of local businessmen built the Island Mill, the first true merchant flour mill at the falls, near the lower end

In 1848, Seth Eastman painted the untamed wilderness of *The Falls of Saint Anthony*.

Nine years later, in 1857, Ferdinand Reichardt painted a more civilized view of *St. Anthony Falls*.

Cadwallader C. Washburn, circa 1880. A former U.S. congressman and governor from Wisconsin, Washburn built his first flour mill at St. Anthony Falls in 1866. After an explosion destroyed his mammoth "A" mill in 1878 (see opposite page), he rebuilt his operations to take advantage of the latest technologies. Innovations such as the middlings purifier revolutionized the milling industry and allowed Washburn (and his imitators) to produce high-quality white flour from spring wheat.

of Hennepin Island. Over the next decade or so, the falls area became home to a small collection of modest milling operations. The Cataract, Union, Arctic, and Model Mills stood on the west side; the River, Summit, and St. Anthony Mills sat on the east side. At that point, the flour they produced had a dubious reputation. Knowing that some buyers might refuse to accept flour from the "land of wild rice and beaver skins," a young steamboat billing clerk named James J. Hill helped brand some early Minneapolis flour barrels with the words "Muskingum Mills, Troy, Ohio" before they were shipped downstream.[4] By 1866, there were eight mills clustered around St. Anthony Falls, producing 172,000 barrels of flour a year—an impressive output for such a young industry, but not nearly in the league

of established milling centers such as Buffalo, New York, and St. Louis, Missouri. It wasn't until the 1870s, when millers like Cadwallader C. Washburn and Charles A. Pillsbury built seventeen immense mills, each brimming with the latest milling technology, that Minneapolis established itself as one of the nation's premier flour-producing centers.[5]

Minneapolis rose to flour-milling prominence for reasons other than its access to waterpower generated by the falls. Many of the city's first flour millers were lumbermen who had made their fortunes operating sawmills at the falls. The money they accumulated turning white pine into lumber provided much of the capital needed to establish the city's first merchant flour mills. Banking

Interior of the first Washburn "A" Mill, circa 1874.

# THE DAILY GRAPHIC

## AN ILLUSTRATED EVENING NEWSPAPER

### 39 & 41 PARK PLACE

| VOL. XVI. | All the News. Four Editions Daily. | NEW YORK, FRIDAY. MAY 10. 1878. | $12 Per Year in Advance. Single Copies, Five Cents. | NO. 1603. |

NEW BRIDGE CONNECTING EAST AND WEST MINNEAPOLIS.　　SAW AND LUMBER MILLS.　　HENNEPIN ISLAND.　　ELEVATOR.　　GREAT WASHBURN MILL "A." MILL "B." ST. ANTHONY'S FALLS.

GENERAL VIEW OF THE MINNEAPOLIS FLOURING DISTRICT.

REMOVING WHEAT FROM THE RUINS.

SCENE OF THE EXPLOSION.

RUINS OF THE GREAT WASHBURN MILL.

SCENES OF THE FATAL EXPLOSION AND CONFLAGRATION AMONG THE GREAT FLOURING MILLS AT MINNEAPOLIS, MINN.

## THE GREAT FIRE IN MINNEAPOLIS.

[FROM PHOTOGRAPHS BY W. H. JACOBY.]

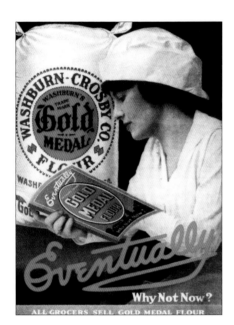

Washburn-Crosby's "Eventually . . . Why Not Now?" slogan, seen here in a 1916 advertisement, proved so popular that it was copied by non-flour firms worldwide. It was adapted to promote everything from Harley-Davidson motorcycles to banking services.

was an essential ingredient in the milling industry's growth as well. Recognizing the need for credit, millers were among the primary organizers and controllers of Minneapolis's early banks, including First National Bank (later First Bank System and U.S. Bancorp) and Northwestern National Bank (later Norwest Corporation and Wells Fargo and Company). In the 1870s, Minneapolis millers also introduced two technological advances—the middlings purifier and the gradual-reduction milling process—that transformed the state's hard red spring wheat into the world's most desirable flour.

The flour made from spring wheat—the only wheat that grew well in the state—had always been considered inferior to flour made from softer, winter varieties. Spring wheat's brittle bran husk shattered during milling, producing a flour speckled with unappealing dark flecks. Still, spring wheat did have one big advantage over winter wheat: it was rich in gluten, the nutritious substance that makes bread dough rise.

Getting rid of the undesirable flecks first required a gradual-reduction milling process, which involved replacing the mill's traditional grindstones with steel rollers that did "more work with less power, lasted much longer, and yielded more

flour." The middlings purifiers then removed the unwanted bran flecks and produced a fine, white flour that consumers preferred. Together, the two new techniques revolutionized the milling industry. Minneapolis's spring wheat flour now fetched much higher prices than winter wheat flour. In 1880, Washburn-Crosby's three brands of flour won the gold, silver, and bronze medals at a prestigious international millers convention, and Minneapolis replaced St. Louis as the nation's leading flour producer.[6]

Spring wheat was the raw material that fueled Minneapolis's flour mills, and the development of the milling industry closely paralleled the expansion of wheat farming in Minnesota and the Upper Midwest. When Minneapolis's first merchant mill, the Island Mill, opened in 1854, its owners had a hard time finding enough locally grown wheat to keep the mill running. In fact, for a few years, they had to import grain from Wisconsin and Iowa. But soon the situation began to change as more and more settlers set up farms and planted wheat, especially in southeastern Minnesota. By 1860, just two years after achieving statehood, Minnesota was producing significantly more wheat than the mills at St. Anthony Falls were capable of processing. Most of the wheat went to local mills in towns like Winona, Northfield, and Preston, or was sent

**Wheat harvest in Glyndon, Minnesota, circa 1878.**

by steamboat down the Mississippi River to St. Louis and points farther east. Minnesota farmers traveled mainly by horse and wagon during these years, and they had no convenient way to move their grain to Minneapolis. As a result, flour milling at the falls languished.[7]

Minneapolis's flour-milling industry might have remained a small-scale proposition had it not been for a series of government initiatives that encouraged settlement on Minnesota's prairies during the 1860s and 1870s. In 1862, the U.S. Congress passed and President Abraham Lincoln signed into law the Homestead Act, which entitled individual settlers and their families to claim as many as 160 acres of free land, provided they lived on their claims for at least five years. The legislation was especially popular in Minnesota. By 1880, settlers had claimed more than sixty-two thousand homesteads, accounting for nearly one-seventh of the state's land. The other initiative that did the most to stimulate settlement in Minnesota was the subsidizing of the railroads. Beginning in the 1860s, the federal government granted millions of acres of public land to

**Oliver Dalrymple's "bonanza" farm of thirty thousand acres—depicted here in _Dakota Territory—The Great Wheat Fields in the Valley of the Red River of the North—Threshing by Steam on the Dalrymple Farm, Formerly a Barren Prairie,_ as sketched by George Ellsbury—made the Minnesota farmer the largest grower of wheat in the world. He employed five hundred to six hundred men; his farming equipment included 150 seven-foot self-binding harvestors, 150 gang plows, 70 eleven-foot gang drills, and 12 extra-large steam threshing outfits, which together turned out 2,000 to 2,500 bushels of wheat each day.**

various railroads to encourage the expansion of rail lines across sparsely populated regions, including Minnesota and the Dakotas. The railroad companies, in turn, sold most of that land at bargain prices to settlers. This arrangement benefited the railroads in two ways: it generated funds needed to cover construction costs, and it created more business for the companies by ensuring that people lived and worked along the lines. The results of these and other land initiatives were stunning. Minnesota's population, which stood at 172,000 in 1860, ballooned to 440,000 in 1870 and 780,000 in 1880. Most of the new Minnesotans settled in rural areas, and many of them raised wheat.[8]

During the early days of settlement, corn was the most popular crop in Minnesota, and for good reason. Corn fed the livestock as well as the family. But by 1860, wheat had displaced corn as the state's top crop. Wheat grew well in the rich soil that lay beneath the heavy carpets of sod covering the open grasslands. Breaking the prairie was a thankless job, but for those farmers who persevered, the reward was often bushel upon bushel of golden grain. The numbers told the story. Between 1850 and 1880, Minnesota's annual wheat production jumped from four-teen hundred bushels to more than thirty-four million bushels. In the years to come, the dangers of one-crop farming would become painfully clear, but at this stage in the state's history, farmers depended almost entirely on wheat.[9]

As wheat production increased, the system for moving grain to market grew increasingly complex. Through much of the 1860s, frontier farmers had to travel long distances over roadless terrain to sell their wheat for cash. Often they would find a willing buyer—a storekeeper or a local miller. But sometimes they would return to the farm with their load after failing to make a sale. Small cash wheat markets devel-oped in a few Minnesota towns, including Chatfield and Winona, but they couldn't handle by themselves the burgeoning flow of grain that was coming in from the prairies. The demand for wheat was begin-ning to grow in Minneapolis, where milling capacity was steadily increas-ing, but the farmers of southern and western Minnesota still had no reli-able way to get their grain there.[10]

Once again, the railroads played a major role. Many of the trains that began carrying people and supplies

to previously unsettled parts of Minnesota during the 1860s also hauled back to Minneapolis the farmers' most important cash crop: wheat. Rails linked Minneapolis with Anoka in 1864 and Elk River in 1865. The following year trains be-gan running between Minneapolis and Faribault. By 1870, about one thousand miles of railroad criss-crossed Minnesota. By 1880, the state's railroad network had tripled. And while the paths they took rarely followed a straight line, nearly all railroads in Minnesota led one way or another to Minneapolis's fast-expanding milling district:[11]

**A switch engine moves freight cars between the mills at Seventh Avenue and Eighth Avenue, circa 1890.**

**James Stroud Bell was born in 1847 in Philadelphia, where his father was a miller and established a flour commission business that represented the Washburn-Crosby Company in Pennsylvania. In 1879 the younger Bell moved to Minneapolis to become general manager of Washburn-Crosby, where he was named president ten years later. Lionized as the greatest merchant miller of his era during his presidency of more than twenty years, James Stroud Bell oversaw the capacity of Washburn-Crosby mills grow from ten thousand barrels to almost forty-five thousand barrels a day. The company was a major tenant of the Chamber of Commerce for many years.**

Speaking of the commercial interests of the city, it may be mentioned that thirteen railroads now center there, giving the city unsurpassed facilities as a receiving and distributing point. It is the northwestern terminus of the Chicago, Milwaukee & St. Paul system; and it is here that this company has recently decided to erect the great machine shops for its trans-Mississippi department. . . . With the rapid expansion of the Northern Pacific railroad westward through Montana and the building of the Canada Pacific through the fertile plains, 300 miles farther north, the field within which the merchants and manufacturers of Minneapolis are to find their market becomes simply imperial.[12]

As the 1880s got under way, it appeared that Minneapolis was poised to enter a new phase of growth, driven largely by wheat and flour. Milling capacity at the falls continued to expand. Farmers were producing more and more grain each year. And the railroads were connecting the city with wheat-producing regions throughout the Upper Midwest. All the necessary pieces seemed to be in place. All, that is, except for one: Minneapolis still had no central market where buyers and sellers could gather to trade grain.

In 1881, as the charter members of the Chamber of Commerce stepped back into the chilly November evening, they had high hopes that their new organization might serve as the catalyst that would transform Minneapolis into a great American metropolis. Many outside the group were skeptical, but at least one knowledgeable observer was intrigued. "The inevitable logic of events already points to Minneapolis as a leading wheat market and center of distribution of the large spring wheat crop of Minnesota and other wheat growing districts of the magic northland," wrote the editor of the *Northwestern Miller,* a trade publication. "If the new organization . . . carries out the programme [sic] of its incorporators," he added, "it will be largely instrumental in advancing the commercial and industrial interests of this city."[13]

## The Millers' Monopoly

George D. Rogers was no head-in-the-clouds youngster when he arrived in Minneapolis in 1873. "The Colonel," as he was almost universally known, was a forty-four-year-old veteran of the Civil War and an experienced businessman. Before the war he had made his living as a farmer and miller in Wisconsin. Afterward, he settled in Calmar, Iowa, about twenty miles south of the Minnesota border, and went into business as a grain buyer and shipper. He did well in Iowa. Before long he had established strings of grain warehouses along several railroad lines. But Rogers wasn't satisfied. He monitored developments in the grain business, and he could tell that the center of the Upper Midwest grain trade was shifting to Minneapolis. In 1873, he sold most of his operations in Iowa and headed north.[14]

Rogers set up shop at the corner of Fourth and Washington, at the edge of the city's milling district, fully expecting to duplicate in Minneapolis the success he had enjoyed as a grain commission agent in Iowa. But he soon discovered otherwise. Despite its growing reputation as a mill city, Minneapolis had hardly any grain traders—maybe a dozen— and most of them were merchants who dealt in grain "on the side." The situation didn't seem to make

sense, but it didn't take long for Rogers to figure out what was going on. Independent grain merchants were rare in Minneapolis because the city's millers enjoyed a virtual monopoly over the buying and selling of wheat.[15]

It had been this way for at least six years. In 1867, the owners of most of the city's mills had formed the Minneapolis Millers' Association, a loose-knit consortium that purchased wheat for all the mills with the expressed goal of preventing "dangerous competition." The organization dissolved after two years, but by all accounts the millers continued to make the most of their wheat purchases through an informal buying pool. In 1875, they reconstituted the association "with a view

James Ford Bell, son of James Stroud Bell, worked his way up through the Washburn-Crosby Company as a carpenter, electrician, clerk, bill collector, and salesman to become president in 1925. With millers facing hard times and declining profits, James Ford Bell achieved an economy of scale by masterminding the merger of Washburn-Crosby and four other mills in 1928 to create General Mills, this country's largest milling company.

A friend and underwriter of the arts, including the Minneapolis Institute of Arts, Bell was also committed to the University of Minnesota, where he served as regent, built the James Ford Bell Library to house his rare books, and supported the museum now named for him: the James Ford Bell Museum of Natural History.

*Minneapolis from the University of Minnesota Campus* by Alexis Jean Fournier, circa 1888. The view includes St. Anthony Falls, which powered the city's mills.

to securing to its members the advantages of cooperation in the purchase of wheat to supply their mills"—in other words, to keep grain prices down. The revived Millers' Association assigned a general agent to supervise a platoon of local buyers in farming towns around the state and to distribute the wheat to each mill, according to its milling capacity, once it arrived in Minneapolis. The association's buying territory included nearly all of Minnesota's wheat-growing areas except for the far southeast corner of the state and the still largely unpopulated Red River Valley to the northwest. Members were allowed to buy grain from within the association's territory only if they did so through the general agent. All of the city's biggest mills were represented in the association, and the men who ran them were happy with the arrangement.[16]

But the Minneapolis millers were not the only people interested in buying Minnesota wheat. One-crop farming was driving down the quality and yields of grain in more established wheat-growing regions such as southern Minnesota, Iowa, and Wisconsin, and the millers in those areas were desperate to secure fresh supplies of hard spring wheat from newer farms to the west and northwest of Minneapolis. The few commission men based in Minneapolis did everything they

could to help these country mills find the grain they needed, but the system was rigged against them. The Millers' Association's stranglehold on the wheat supply proved nearly impossible to break.[17]

It didn't take George Rogers long to figure out how the system worked. Soon after arriving in Minneapolis, he walked down to the rail yards adjacent to the milling district to inspect three cars of No. 1 wheat that a client had shipped from the southern Minnesota town of Luverne. He took samples of the wheat to the Millers' Association to find out what price it would fetch. Rogers assumed that the quality of the grain would matter most to the association's agent. Instead, the agent was primarily concerned with where the grain came from. If it was harvested from an area within the association's purchasing territory, he could not buy it. As it turned out, the millers did have an agent in Luverne. The agent walked away. "Nothing was left for me to do but ship it to Chicago," Rogers recalled.[18]

But the travails of Rogers's shipment of Luverne wheat didn't end there. The railroad that had carried the wheat to Minneapolis refused to transfer its cars to a Chicago line. That meant that Rogers had to hire a crew to shovel the entire shipment of wheat into three new railcars so that it could continue on its journey

to Illinois. Just as the workers were about to begin transferring the grain, the Millers' Association's agent showed up on the loading deck and offered to buy the wheat at the price Rogers had quoted the day before. Rogers refused:

"Pay me two cents a bushel more to cover my expenses and take the wheat," I told him. "Ridiculous," he answered, and I ordered the men into the cars. Before the first shovel full of wheat had left the car he paid the price, and explained that the association was acting to prevent "dangerous competition." That's the kind of a market we had in those early days.

The experience with the Luverne wheat helped convince Rogers that Minneapolis needed an open market where buyers, sellers, and middlemen like himself could trade grain and neutralize the millers' monopoly. As it was, the Minneapolis mills consumed more than 95 percent of all the wheat shipped into the city. Rogers believed that a true open market for grain would encourage wheat production throughout the Upper Midwest and stimulate economic growth in Minneapolis. At first, his fellow grain traders resisted the idea. "Time and again they answered my urgent pleas for a grain exchange by declarations that only cities located at lake or seaports with water transportation

were entitled to an exchange," he later recalled. As time went on, though, the city's few commission men started coming around. In early 1881, Rogers and several of his colleagues approached the Minneapolis Board of Trade and proposed that it set up a grain exchange. The board declined. But the idea was planted, and it was sprouting increased interest elsewhere.[19]

That summer, Rogers and seven other Minneapolis businessmen met in a tiny, ten-foot-square room on the second floor of the Security State Bank Building to discuss his grain exchange proposal. The city's merchants and bankers were beginning to warm to the proposition that such an exchange could propel Minneapolis into the ranks of the nation's most prosperous cities. "It became apparent to business men who knew something about grain that Minneapolis must have something better if the city was to become a real market for the grain that Minnesota was growing in greater quantities each year," recalled one of the chamber's early members, William T. Fraser. These men were coming to believe that a grain exchange could serve three indispensable functions: as a distribution market for Minnesota's expanding wheat surplus; as a parallel market for grains such as corn, oats, and flax; and as a platform where legitimate futures trading could take place.[20]

**The Chamber of Commerce held its first trading sessions on the third floor of the Johnson, Smith, and Harrison Building in Minneapolis.**

As the weeks progressed, a consensus developed that a new organization—not a restructured board of trade—was the answer. George Rogers kept pushing. Finally, on October 19, 1881, the Colonel's dream came true when twenty-one Minneapolis business leaders signed a document officially incorporating the Minneapolis Chamber of Commerce as an organization devoted to the buying and selling of "all products," to the "principles of justice and equity in trade," and to the acquisition and dissemination of "valuable commercial information." A month after signing the document, the incorporators—and an equal number of new members—

gathered in the basement of the Security State Bank for the chamber's first official meeting. "[The chamber's] formation is one of the first steps toward making Minneapolis an open wheat market," the *Northwestern Miller* reported, "[one that's] independent of the control which the millers' association has so long exercised."[21]

## Making a Market

As the *Northwestern Miller* intimated, the founding members of the newly minted chamber had a lot of work ahead of them. They had filed the necessary paperwork with the secretary of state and set forth their goals. They had even raised a few hundred dollars and placed the cash in a "treasury." But that was about it. If the chamber's founders hoped to establish a viable grain exchange, they would need to do a lot more than that. At the very least, they needed to find a place where buyers and sellers could do business—a place more suitable than the basement of the Security State Bank.

C. W. Johnson, one of the new members who had crammed into the bank basement for the first meeting, had just the place in mind. Johnson was a partner in a printing company called Johnson, Smith, and Harrison. The building where he did business was a handsome four-story structure at the corner of Third Street South and First Avenue South, and its third floor was vacant. Why not set up the fledgling grain market there?

The chamber's home in the Johnson, Smith, and Harrison Building was not spacious, but it didn't have to be, at least not at first. During the first few weeks of the organization's existence, few members bothered to show up, and those who did rarely conducted business there. Trading was relegated to one hour, from 11:30 a.m. to 12:30 p.m. While the *Minneapolis Tribune* reported that sales in early December were "brisk," and that a "good deal of merchandise" changed hands, the chamber's initial trading numbers verged on pathetic. On December 9, for example, traders at the chamber exchanged a grand total of four railcars of "No. 2 wheat" at $1.12 to $1.19 a bushel. By contrast, the figures for the week ending December 3 showed that fifty-six cars of wheat—about half of it being top-quality "No. 1"—had been "inspected into store and mill," presumably through the Millers' Association.[22]

As winter took hold, trading "on 'change" gradually increased and skeptics began to take notice. Applications for membership arrived by the dozens. Sensing that demand was rising quickly, the chamber's board voted to increase the membership fee from $25 to $250, effective March 1, 1882. By the time the

new fees kicked in, the chamber had received about five hundred new membership applications.[23]

The number of new members was impressive, but even more striking were some of the names on the list: John Crosby, William Dunwoody, John Pillsbury, John Washburn, C. J. Martin, J. A. Christian, L. Christian, Charles Hardenberg—all of them powerful executives from local milling companies who had, over the past decade, established a virtual grain trading monopoly through the Minneapolis Millers' Association. Most would continue to do their wheat buying through the association, but all of them were intrigued enough by the action on the chamber's trading floor to fork over the membership fee. If nothing else, it allowed them to keep a close eye on the competition.

With its membership now topping five hundred, the Chamber of Commerce had suddenly outgrown its quarters on the third floor of the Johnson, Smith, and Harrison Building. Additional space on the first floor helped alleviate the overcrowding, but most members knew it was just a temporary fix. In April, the chamber appointed a search committee to find a piece of property, not too far from the milling district, on which the organization could erect a building more suited to its peculiar needs.[24]

In 1877 John Crosby joined Cadwallader Washburn in Minneapolis to create the Washburn-Crosby Company. Three years later, at the first International Millers Exhibition in Cincinnati, Ohio, Washburn-Crosby's flour was judged the best in the world and awarded a gold medal. From then on, the company called its finest product Gold Medal Flour.

An avid outdoorsman for whom "the unspoiled beauty and recreational opportunities in Minnesota provided restful leisure," Crosby often entertained guests of the company by taking them fishing on Lake Minnetonka.

**William Hood Dunwoody, circa 1893. Dunwoody was a top executive at Washburn-Crosby who oversaw the dynamic growth of the company's export trade during the late 1800s. On his death in 1914, he left $3 million to establish Dunwoody Institute (later Dunwoody College of Technology) in Minneapolis. Dunwoody envisioned a school "where youth, without distinction on account of race, color or religious prejudice, may learn the useful trades and crafts, and thereby fit themselves for the better performance of life's duties."**

The search for a new home triggered what was, at that point, the young chamber's most intense political skirmish. Everyone knew that, once the decision was made, real estate values in the neighborhood surrounding the chosen site would immediately jump. Many of the chamber's members possessed substantial real estate holdings in downtown Minneapolis, so they, along with others outside the organization, had a vested interest in selecting the site. In the end, the choice came down to two parcels. The search committee recommended a site at Fourth Avenue South and Third Street, which was to be donated by a group of local businessmen that included several prominent chamber members. But a substantial minority of members preferred a second location on the northeast corner of Hennepin and Fourth. Partisans on both sides of the debate jockeyed for support throughout the summer. Finally, in mid-August, the chamber met for a final vote. In the words of one newspaper reporter, the rooms on the third floor of the Johnson, Smith, and Harrison Building "were packed with a seething mass of crowded humanity." When the votes were counted, the committee's recommendation was approved. The Chamber of Commerce accepted the donation of two lots on the corner of Fourth Avenue and Third Street, and agreed to construct

a building on it to cost no less than $100,000.[25] In his first annual report, Chamber of Commerce secretary C. C. Sturtevant could barely contain his enthusiasm:

The result of the competition for location was eminently satisfactory to most of the members of the Chamber, as it was the means of giving them lots ample for all their purposes, located on one of the best business streets in the city, only three blocks from the new post office site, very near the milling district and admirably fitted for their purposes, and last, but not least, as a donation.[26]

With a site selected, the chamber moved quickly to develop plans for its new home. The design, developed by the architectural firm Hodgson and Son, called for a five-story building of gray stone topped by two majestic towers. It would house a trading hall—fifty-by-ninety feet—and sixty-five offices, most of which were to be rented to chamber members. Construction began in April 1883, but progress was slow. Money was a constant problem. After voting to assess each member $65, the board of directors struggled to raise the rest of the cash needed to cover the building's $175,000 price tag. When an initial attempt to arrange a bond issue failed, and it appeared likely that construction would have to be suspended, several wealthy members stepped in with personal loans. The chamber finally did secure a $100,000 bond issue in November 1883, but only after some of those same wealthy members agreed to ensure the bonds with their own assets.[27]

On June 5, 1884, the Chamber of Commerce held a grand opening for its new home. It was an impressive affair, featuring many familiar faces from the upper reaches of Minneapolis society. "The building was brilliantly illuminated by electricity and gas," the *Northwestern Miller* reported, "and was crowded with representatives of wealth and beauty of the northwest." Guests began arriving at 7:30 p.m., with the men "in full dress, sans gloves, with the conventional badge and button hole bouquet attached conspicuously upon the lapel of the coat. . . . Nearly every lady sensibly wore a short dress." The eighteen-piece Great Western Band from St. Paul provided background music as the gathering throng moved from room to room, taking in the building's polished opulence. (Several members fretted that the corridor railings, being shorter than usual, might pose a hazard to guests; others believed "that after the opening banquet there [would] be little or no danger of people tumbling over them.")[28] The fifty-by-ninety-foot trading room was, by far, the main attraction.

"The floor is of polished hard wood thoroughly seasoned, and is as smooth as glass," the *Miller* gushed. "The walls are of polished ash throughout, with elaborate panels of exquisite design, presenting an appearance that is at once pleasing and unusual." In his welcoming address, the chamber's new president, George A. Pillsbury, praised the organization's founders for their foresight, predicting that the opening of the new building would prove to be a seminal moment in the history of Minneapolis:

The fact stands prominently before the world that Minneapolis today is the second city in wheat in the United States. This is a marvelous statement, especially when I see before me tonight persons who a few years ago beheld an unbroken prairie where the city now stands. Within the four walls of this building business will be transacted which will affect the breadstuffs of the world. The northwest is yet in its infancy, and will expand, and this chamber of commerce will be a mighty factor. . . . The trials and difficulties of a great enterprise have been overcome, and our chamber starts up its grand mission.[29]

Actually, the chamber had started up its grand mission about a month earlier. Several commission men, unwilling to wait for completion of the new trading hall, began buying and

George A. Pillsbury was a prominent citizen and banker in Concord, New Hampshire, where he was twice elected mayor. In 1878 he moved to Minneapolis, where his two sons, Charles A. and Fred Pillsbury, were engaged in flour milling. George Pillsbury became active in Charles A. Pillsbury and Company as well as in civic affairs, rising to mayor of Minneapolis by 1884. George's brother, John S. Pillsbury, became governor of Minnesota.

George Pillsbury adhered to the ideal that a man should do as much good as he could in this life. He did not believe in leaving money to able-bodied offspring, but instead used his wealth to support schools, hospitals, and homes for orphans and the aged.

selling grain at a marble-top table set up unceremoniously in a corridor populated by construction workers. In the years that followed, chamber members would come to disagree about who made the first trade in the building at Fourth and Third, but newspapers of the time were clear on the matter. On May 1, 1884, E. A. Whiting sold a car of No. 2 wheat to fellow commission man G. W. Porter for ninety-two cents a bushel. After struggling for more than two years as an upstart grain market in makeshift quarters, the Minneapolis Chamber of Commerce was finally on its way.[30]

## Getting Down to Business

While the millers and grain traders of Minneapolis could sense a seismic shift in the grain business, the rest of the world seemed oblivious. Only occasionally would observers from the East take note of what was happening in the wheat fields of the Upper Midwest and the fledgling grain market of Minneapolis. And even when they did, they were incredulous. In December 1882, the *Chicago Times* seemed genuinely taken aback at how "the mills of Minneapolis continue to absorb a very large amount of spring wheat, which has the tendency every year to decrease the amount of shipments that formerly found their way to our large grain centers." Minneapolis had only recently—in 1879— broken into the rankings of the ten leading wheat markets in the United States, and those who kept track of such things in New York and Chicago seemed unable to fathom that a city as young as Minneapolis might challenge them for grain-trading supremacy any time soon.[31]

Still, the trends were hard to misread, at least for anyone who was paying attention. By 1881, the year the Chamber of Commerce was formed, Minneapolis had moved to third in the national rankings, with more than sixteen million bushels of wheat received. In the years that immediately followed, receipts continued to increase steadily, but the eastern markets still refused to acknowledge Minneapolis's ascendancy. They "would not credit the figures and could not conceive the possibility of the development of such a market," an early historian of the chamber observed. "It must have seemed to them a fairy tale."[32]

The lack of recognition not only bruised the chamber's collective ego, it also threatened to undermine one of the organization's primary objectives: the dissemination of accurate market information. The wire services, which sent out price quotations and other information from markets like New York, Chicago, and Milwaukee, refused to do the same for Minneapolis, despite its ranking as one of the world's top grain markets, especially in spring wheat. "The associated

press has no use for anything western," the *Northwestern Miller* complained. In December 1882, the chamber appointed a committee to try to persuade the Associated Press to transmit Minneapolis market quotations to the rest of the country. Officials with the wire service listened politely to the chamber's entreaties, but continued to ignore the Minneapolis numbers. Finally, in 1885, the New York Produce Exchange, which had stubbornly refused to include Minnesota production figures in its summaries of the national wheat supply, sent representatives west to get a first-hand look at the Minneapolis market. The delegation was apparently impressed with what it saw. Within weeks, the Associated Press was transmitting Minneapolis market quotations and the New York Produce Exchange was including them in its summaries.[33]

The new building at Fourth Avenue and Third Street was teeming with activity, and in the summer of 1885, members voted to open trading an hour earlier—at 10:00 a.m.—to accommodate the rapid growth in volume. A new "wheat pit" for futures trading was constructed on the floor, and the buying and selling of corn, oats, flax seed, and other small grains was picking up. Arrangements were made to wire the building so that members could send and receive telegraphs directly from the trading room. (The contract went to the North American Telegraph Company, a firm formed by incoming chamber president Charles Loring to compete directly with Western Union.) Nearly every week, the *Northwestern Miller* ran at least one story that described the chamber's increasingly frenzied atmosphere. In July 1885 it reported that "evidence of the life and activity in our chamber of commerce is found in the fact that the elevator carries from 2,000 to 2,500 persons per day."[34]

The chamber also spent a lot of time dealing with one of the grain trade's longest-running headaches: the railroads. The rail companies had been instrumental in the development of the grain market and the flour-milling industry, but they were often difficult to do business with. During the 1870s farmers and millers had complained regularly to the railroads about discriminatory freight charges that frequently made it more expensive to ship grain short distances than it did to ship it long distances. By the 1880s, many of the most egregious rate irregularities had vanished, but problems remained. In the fall of 1884, the Chamber of Commerce stepped into the fray, lodging a formal complaint with James J. Hill's St. Paul, Minneapolis, and Manitoba line. The chamber accused Hill's company of exercising "unfair discrimination" by allowing its trains to deliver wheat directly to mills associated with the Millers' Association (a service that was not available to non-association millers who bought wheat through the chamber). In this case, the chamber received no satisfaction, but the experience marked the beginning of a protracted struggle against the railroads that sometimes included costly litigation.

The increasing activity at the Chamber of Commerce was not lost on the city's millers. The Millers' Association stayed busy (it continued to account for the bulk of the city's grain trade as late as 1885), but its monopoly was crumbling. As more grain poured into Minneapolis from newly settled wheat-growing regions, the city's mills—even with their increased capacities—were unable to make use of the entire supply. Millions of bushels of surplus grain went to buyers elsewhere, and most of that was traded on the chamber's floor. As time went on, the Millers' Association seemed to become less and less relevant. Millers began openly violating the association's rules against purchasing grain outside the buying pool. By

**Looking south on Fourth Avenue South, circa 1885. The first Chamber of Commerce Building stands at the center.**

"Empire Builder" James J. Hill, circa 1873. Hill was born in 1838 in Rockwood, Ontario, Canada. At age seventeen he left home for St. Paul in the Minnesota Territory to work in the steamboat trade; at age twenty-eight, he founded James J. Hill and Company, a transportation and warehousing business; and in 1879 he took over the bankrupt St. Paul, Minneapolis, and Manitoba Railroad. The extension of Hill's rail line (later, the Great Northern) into the wheat-growing regions of the Dakotas and Montana was instrumental in the development of the Minneapolis grain trade.

1883, four of the city's milling companies had abandoned the association to buy their wheat through the chamber. Rumors began to spread that the Millers' Association was on the verge of disbanding. For a while the millers dismissed such speculation, insisting that "the association was never stronger or more harmonious," but the new realities of the grain trade eventually won out. In the fall of 1886, the Minneapolis Millers' Association officially ceased to exist. "The greatest wheat buying organization on earth" was no more.[35]

Five years after holding its first meeting in the cramped basement of a downtown Minneapolis bank, the Minneapolis Chamber of Commerce had emerged as the primary market for the region's grain. At the chamber's annual meeting in October 1886, President Charles

In 1883, James J. Hill's Minneapolis Union Railway Company completed construction of the Stone Arch Bridge over the Mississippi River, depicted here by Lloyd P. Hinton. The bridge connected Hill's St. Paul, Minneapolis, and Manitoba rail line with the new Union Depot passenger terminal and with the existing railway facilities serving the flour mills on the west side of the river. As a result, Minneapolis's millers gained much greater access to wheat grown in the rich Red River Valley, where Hill's railroad was especially strong. The bridge is now a popular pedestrian footbridge.

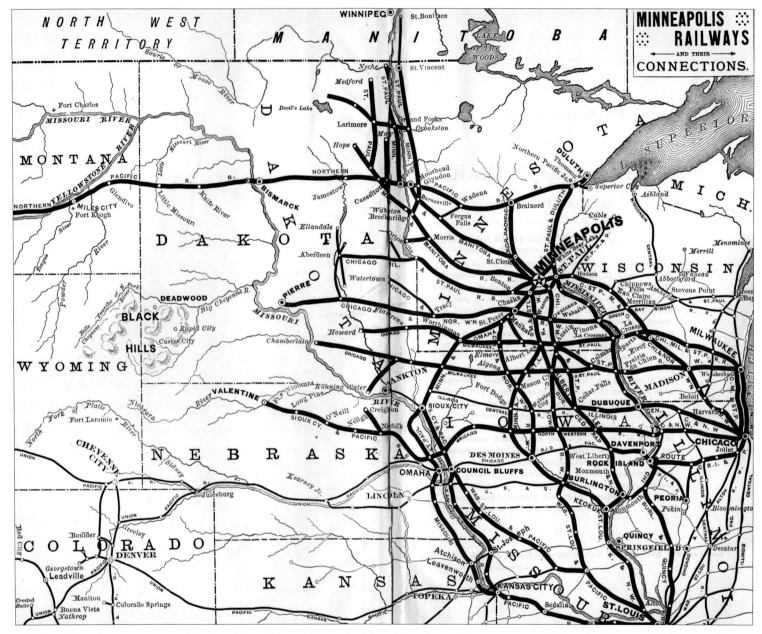

This railroad map appeared in the *Joint Annual Report of the Chamber of Commerce and Board of Trade of Minneapolis, Minn., 1882.*

Loring marked the organization's fifth birthday with a crowd-pleasing announcement:

At a meeting in October last year I stated that Minneapolis was the second largest wheat market in the country, and my belief that it would at no distant day be second to none. I little thought that before January 1886 my prediction would be verified. It gives me great pleasure to announce today that Minneapolis is now the largest wheat market in the United States, having received last year 8,500,000 bushels more wheat

**Charles Loring, circa 1910. Loring was lauded by historian (and prominent Minnesota politician) Joseph A. A. Burnquist as an "early merchant, pioneer flour miller, public-spirited citizen, the father of her park system, and the promoter of much of the work of improving and beautifying Minneapolis."**

than New York and 13,000,000 bushels more than Chicago.[36]

The Chamber of Commerce had now settled comfortably into the business of facilitating the buying and selling of grain. It performed most of its day-to-day work with little or no notice from the general public. But the same could not be said for some of its most prominent members. For better or worse, the public was beginning to identify the chamber with some of the powerful men who did business there. In many cases, the chamber basked in the glow of its members' considerable success, but sometimes it found itself caught in the middle of controversies not of its own making. Public perceptions about the relationships between the chamber and its members—especially the millers and elevator operators—were beginning

to demand more and more attention "on 'change."

## The Millers and the Warehousemen

The demise of the Millers' Association did not, of course, end the millers' involvement in the grain trade. The mill owners still had a vested interest in maintaining a steady supply of high-quality spring wheat, preferably at the lowest prices. Now that their buying pool was gone, they simply shifted their business to the Chamber of Commerce. What they lost in price savings (quotations from the Millers' Association consistently had run one to three cents per bushel lower than the Chamber of Commerce's prices) they gained in quality because they now had more grain from which to choose. And after all, it wasn't as though the millers were new to the chamber's way of doing business. A slew of mill owners had joined the chamber during its first few months of existence, and since then had played a prominent role in the organization's development. In fact, three of the chamber's first four presidents—E. V. White, George Pillsbury, and Charles Loring—were millers.[37]

The men who owned Minneapolis's mills were the young city's top celebrities, rich and famous industrialists whose every move was monitored by the public. The people of Minneapolis marveled as William D.

Washburn built his personal castle, dubbed "Fair Oaks," just south of downtown. (It "fills almost as large a space in the public eye as the Grand Opera House or the Chamber of Commerce," one admirer observed.) They closely followed the political careers of several millers, including Washburn (who ran successfully for Congress), John S. Pillsbury (who served as Minnesota's governor between 1876 and 1882), and Charles Loring (who was nearly elected mayor of Minneapolis in 1882). And they watched in wonderment as these men—already fabulously wealthy and powerful—expanded their corporate empires.[38]

Of all the millers' audacious business moves, none captured the public's imagination as thoroughly as their decision to build their own railroad. Determined to find a more direct route to eastern and foreign markets, a group of millers led by Washburn established and financed the construction of two new roads. The first, the Minneapolis and Pacific, ran west into the wheat fields of Minnesota's Red River Valley, North Dakota, and Canada. The second, the Minneapolis, St. Paul, and Sault Ste. Marie, ran east through Wisconsin to hook up with the Canadian Pacific Railway at Sault Ste. Marie. Together, the two new railroads became known as the Soo Line, and the connection of the Soo with the Canadian Pacific in 1887 was cause for celebration on the floor of the Chamber of Commerce. In its annual report for that year, the chamber crowed that Minneapolis flour could now travel to eastern markets without "the vexatious delays in passing through Chicago, where east-bound cars are often side-tracked for an indefinite period, to the great disadvantage of shippers and consignees."[39]

The millers were not, however, the only chamber members who were busy expanding their operations during this period. Storage elevators were becoming an increasingly important factor in the Minneapolis grain trade, and the "warehousemen," as they were known, were quickly learning to exert their influence inside and outside the chamber.

Grain elevators came in two distinct types. The first, the country elevator, was ubiquitous in the region's wheat-growing districts. Every railroad town had at least one. Farmers brought their wheat to the country elevator and sold it at the going rate (usually the latest Minneapolis price minus shipping costs and margin). The elevator operator then arranged to have the grain loaded into railcars and sent on its way. The second type, the terminal elevator, was generally found in what were known as primary markets—cities like Minneapolis, Duluth, and Chicago, each of

Atlantic "A" was just one of a growing number of terminal grain elevators to sprout up in Minneapolis during the late 1800s.

*Van Dusen Elevator* by Alexis Jean Fournier, circa 1888.

which had its own grain exchange. Terminal elevators stored grain until their owners—millers, shippers, exporters—were ready to use it or ship it. Together, the country elevators and the terminal elevators formed a storage system that helped maintain a steady supply of grain throughout the year.

The elevator system in Minnesota and the rest of the Upper Midwest had developed slowly. Country elevators were the first to appear. They generally went up at the end of railroad lines and were, at first, owned by independent operators. As the railroads stretched out and more land was converted to wheat, some of the more ambitious independents expanded their operations to form lines of elevators, most of which were concentrated along one or two railroads. By the late 1870s, successful line elevator operators like Frank Peavey, George Van Dusen, and brothers W. W. and Sam Cargill were extending their reach far into the wheat-growing areas to the southwest, west, and northwest of Minneapolis.

Even as the network of country elevators expanded, the construction of terminal elevators languished. Minneapolis, the region's largest primary market, had only two terminal elevators through most of the 1870s, and neither was very large. It wasn't until

1879, when the Minneapolis Elevator Company built what became known as Elevator "A," that the city began developing into a true grain storage and shipping center. Over the next decade, companies put up eighteen more elevators on both sides of St. Anthony Falls, pushing the city's total grain storage capacity to more than sixteen million bushels.[40]

By the mid-1880s, many of the strongest line elevator companies had expanded their operations to include both country elevators and terminal elevators. All had purchased seats on the Chamber of Commerce, and most had moved their headquarters to Minneapolis. Some were even moving into other phases of the grain trade. They constituted a new breed of middlemen—"terminal warehousemen who owned country lines and bought, [blended], stored and sold grain in Minneapolis and through agents in other markets." These companies had gathered strength quietly, and the men who ran them were generally newcomers to the city who did not seek or attract public attention as readily as the millers did. But the elevator operators were, like the millers, becoming impossible to ignore.[41]

## Friends and Foes

No one was keeping a closer eye on the millers and warehousemen of Minneapolis than the region's farmers. The millers in particular had long been targets of the farmers' wrath. Many farmers believed, and with ample justification, that the millers had formed the Minneapolis Millers' Association back in 1867 to eliminate competition and suppress grain prices to the detriment of the farmer. It was no surprise, then, that many wheat growers were elated when the Chamber of Commerce formed in 1881 to challenge the millers' monopoly. The farmers considered the chamber their ally. It was a sentiment the chamber was glad to encourage:

The average Granger is suspicious of the equity of the grading and inspection of grain as practiced at terminal points, and prefers consigning his grain to a commission firm to be sold by sample on its merits. Until the organization of this Chamber, this was not practicable, for the reason that there [were] very few firms engaged in that business, and no country orders to fill, leaving the millers about the only purchasers, and they only bought good milling wheat. This difficulty is now obviated. There are on 'change at all times buyers for all samples offered and of all grades.[42]

During its first few years of existence, the chamber made a point of highlighting cases in which its interests overlapped with those of the

farmers. On January 10, 1885, a group called the Minnesota Valley Farmers Association asked the

RIGHT: *Frank H. Peavey* by Alexis Jean Fournier, circa 1890. Peavey's career as a grain storage entrepreneur dated to the mid-1870s, when, in Sioux City, Iowa, he began buying and building country elevators. He moved his operations to Minneapolis in 1885. In the late 1890s, he hired C. F. Haglin (who would later build the new Minneapolis Chamber of Commerce Building) to construct an experimental concrete elevator in nearby St. Louis Park (see page 48). The success of that elevator revolutionized the grain storage business.

BELOW: *Highcroft,* the Wayzata, Minnesota, home of Frank H. Peavey, by Alexis Jean Fournier.

chamber to "unite with the farmers in the country" and petition the state legislature to establish new regulations on the shipping, inspection, weighing, and warehousing of grain. A few days later, the chamber passed a resolution to do just that. Although the chamber's petition was probably not decisive, the legislature did pass a new law creating the Railroad and Warehouse Commission later that year. The legislative victory buttressed the chamber's relations with the farmers and gave the organization something to brag about. "A year's experience is now before us," the chamber noted in its 1886 annual report, "and we do not hesitate to say [the law] has given general satisfaction. . . . All in all, we are satisfied that it has benefited the state largely."[43]

Still, many farmers remained wary of the chamber. The millers, who had colluded to drive down grain prices through the defunct Millers' Association, were now, by all accounts, happily buying their wheat on the chamber's floor. Not only that, the rapidly expanding line elevator companies, with their dominating positions in the country and terminal markets, were likewise becoming an entrenched presence at the chamber. More and more farmers were starting to wonder whether the Chamber of Commerce really was on their side.

As time went by, the relationship between the chamber and the farmers soured. Wheat prices, which had peaked in 1882, were in the middle of prolonged decline, and the farmers found it hard to believe that the chamber wasn't at least partly to blame. Even if it didn't manipulate prices, the farmers reckoned, the millers and warehousemen, who accounted for a good portion of its membership, probably did have something to do with the skid.[44]

By the early 1890s, the farmers' skepticism about the Chamber of Commerce had degenerated into

In 1867, brothers William Wallace Cargill (left, portrait by Edward V. Brewer) and Sam Cargill (below, at his desk), formed a grain-storage company, based in Iowa, called W. W. Cargill and Brother. The firm later moved its headquarters to La Crosse, Wisconsin, and then to Minneapolis, steadily expanding its operations. Under the direction of W. W. Cargill's son-in-law John MacMillan Sr., and later John MacMillan Jr., Cargill grew into the largest privately held company in the United States. By 2006 it was a diversified provider of food, agricultural, and risk-management products and services, employing 124,000 people in fifty-nine countries.

open disdain. Farmers and their sup-porters generally agreed that the 1885 law creating the Railroad and Warehouse Commission had failed to stop the manipulation of grain prices, at least on the local level. There were just too many country elevators, hundreds of them, for the state to regulate effectively. The result, according to one state rail-road commissioner, was a system in which line elevator companies felt free to conspire with each other in an effort to keep prices low:

So in the process of time it had come to be a fact here that the han-dling and marketing of grain on the different lines of road had generally come to be controlled by a few cor-porations, firms or men, who arbi-trarily dictated terms, fixed rates and customs and were able in many instances to drive out of existence the independent buyer, and so establish with or without the aid of the railway companies, a monopoly which touched nearly every produc-er in the state.[45]

As far as the farmers were con-cerned, the old millers' monopoly had been replaced by a new monopoly of elevator operators, and all the obvious culprits had at least one thing in com-mon besides the fact that they ran elevators: they all belonged to the Minneapolis Chamber of Commerce. In 1892, wheat producers, backed by the Farmers' Alliance, the Democratic Party, and a vocal contingent of pop-ulist newspaper editors, launched a verbal war against what they called the "elevator combines." Their pri-mary target was Charles A. Pillsbury, the famous Minneapolis miller who also happened to be a major stock-holder in two of the state's biggest elevator companies. One of the fiercest attacks against Pillsbury came from the *Marshall County Banner,* which referred to the old miller as "a monstrous human devilfish":

Much power has made him mad. He can conceive of nothing stronger than the accursed wheat

**Still standing east of Minneapolis in St. Louis Park; this experimental concrete monolith for grain storage was built in 1899 by Charles F. Haglin for "Elevator King" Frank H. Peavey. Critics called it "Peavey's Folly" and predict-ed that it would burst when filled to the brim. It didn't, and instead it became legendary as the granddaddy of all modern grain terminals in North America.**

**John S. Pillsbury, circa 1887. One of Minnesota's early settlers, Pillsbury was seeking opportunity when he arrived in Minnesota from New Hampshire in 1855. A prescient young man of twenty-seven, he foresaw in the power of St. Anthony Falls the possibilities of a great city on the adjacent banks of the Mississippi.**

**Starting out in the hardware business (until his store burned, leaving him heavily in debt), Pillsbury interested himself in lumber milling and land speculation, and ultimately became active in the milling industry with his nephew, Charles A. Pillsbury. A leading citizen who sat on the boards of several Minneapolis banks and was identified with railroad building, John S. Pillsbury was three times elected governor of Minnesota, serving from 1876 to 1882.**

ring, of which he is the leading spirit. He has ruled the prices and absolutely controlled the markets ever since the Red River valley first blossomed with growing grain. He has filched from the pockets of every wheat grower in Minnesota and the Dakotas to enrich the coffers of a monstrous and gigantic octopus that threatens the prosperity of every wheat raiser in the West.[46]

Pillsbury's friends at the Minneapolis Chamber of Commerce did not appreciate the attacks against their esteemed colleague. Just as the farmers' campaign against the elevator operators was reaching its peak, the chamber, in what must have looked to the farmers like an act of defiance, elected Pillsbury president of the organization. (He served two terms, from 1892 to 1894.) Whatever warm feelings the farmers may have had for the chamber in the years immediately following the demise of the Millers' Association quickly vanished. In the mid-1890s, farmers began banding together to build farmer-owned cooperative elevators in a handful of towns along the rail lines that fed Minneapolis. The cooperative movement was slow to take hold, but its establishment would help define the farmers' relationship with the Chamber of Commerce for years to come. In his final address

as the chamber's president, Charles Pillsbury couldn't resist taking one last shot at his critics. If the farmers couldn't appreciate that "the milling industries represented on this Chamber" helped them get the best possible prices for their wheat, he said, then "they are either too ignorant to comprehend it or too much prejudiced or humbugged to be able to form any intelligent opinion."[47]

## On Fire

The Chamber of Commerce building had opened in 1884 to accolades. It was, in the words of the *Northwestern Miller,* "one of the finest buildings in the state, pleasing and imposing in appearance." Unfortunately, it also contained a significant mechanical-design flaw that was not evident to the untrained eye. On the morning of September 26, 1895, electrical wires in the northeast side of the building's attic short-circuited. The fire that the wires sparked burned for some time before a janitor smelled smoke. By then it was too late. At about 8:30, the ceiling of the fifth-floor hallway collapsed, and glass from the building's skylight shattered and crashed to the ground floor, a hundred feet below. The fire spread quickly, especially on the top floor, where grain traders were dictating memos to their stenographers in preparation for the business day. Panicked office workers scrambled for the stairwells. "I never saw a fire start so quickly," said an evacuated bookkeeper. "I don't see what made it burn so quickly or what made so much broken stuff fall down."[48]

Firefighters, ill-equipped to battle blazes in five-story buildings, managed nonetheless to quell the flames. The building survived, but it was in a sorry state. The trading room was "a sickening ruin." It seemed obvious that the Chamber of Commerce would have to close for the day and possibly for much longer. But the grain traders weren't about to let a few flames get in their way. About an hour after the fire broke out, trading resumed in an empty room in the Corn Exchange Building across the street and continued there for several weeks until the chamber could repair the extensive damage caused by the fire.

It had been fourteen years since a small band of Minneapolis business leaders had gathered in the basement of Security State Bank to inaugurate an open and fair market for the trading of grain. In that time, the Minneapolis Chamber of Commerce had grown from a questionable proposition into a vibrant grain exchange capable of withstanding competition from a millers' monopoly and adapting to rapidly changing markets. Now the

The Corn Exchange Building, designed by architects (Franklin B.) Long and (Frederick G.) Kees, across Third Street from the first Chamber of Commerce Building, circa 1900. Long had worked with C. F. Haglin, a successful Minneapolis engineer and contractor who built the "Peavey's Folly" elevator (see page 48). In 1890, Kees partnered with Serenus Colburn to build the present gray-stone Minneapolis Grain Exchange Building.

Charles Alfred Pillsbury, pictured in his Minneapolis office, circa 1883. With a loan from his father and his uncle (and future Minnesota governor) John S. Pillsbury, Charles Pillsbury founded Charles A. Pillsbury and Company in 1872. He introduced technologies such as steam rollers and dramatically increased production. By the mid-1880s, his mills were producing ten thousand barrels of flour a day. In 1889, he sold controlling interest of the company to a British syndicate that operated under the name Pillsbury-Washburn Flour Mills.

exchange was demonstrating to the world that not even a fire could shake its commitment to the trading of grain.

The fact was that the grain trade—especially the trade of hard red spring wheat—had become an indispensable cog in the economic machinery of the city and the region. In 1880, the year before the Chamber of Commerce was formed, Minneapolis recorded wheat receipts of slightly more than ten million bushels. By 1895, its receipts stood at more than sixty-five million bushels, a sixfold increase. During that same period, the city's flour production—now controlled almost entirely by two large firms, the Pillsbury-Washburn Flour Mills Company and the Washburn-Crosby Company—had increased fivefold.[49] And the storage capacity of Minneapolis's grain elevators had increased exponentially, from one and a half million bushels to nearly twenty-eight million bushels.

The city itself had changed too. Its streets, which in 1881 were little more than muddy and rutted thoroughfares, were now paved with cedar blocks and asphalt. Electric streetcars carried passengers nearly everywhere they wanted to go. A world-class park system was taking shape under the determined leadership of a former Chamber of Commerce president, Charles Loring. And the city's population, which had jumped from 47,000 to 165,000 between 1880 and 1890, was well on its way to breaking the 200,000 mark.

Minneapolis and its fourteen-year-old grain exchange were heading into the twentieth century with plenty of momentum. Their leaders could only hope that they would be able to keep up the pace.[50]

*Rainy Evening on Hennepin Avenue* by Robert Koehler, circa 1910. The artist's wife is pictured with their small son and the family dog.

TOP: Architect's drawing of the "A" flour mill, rendered by L. S. Buffington for Charles A. Pillsbury and Company. BOTTOM: St. Anthony Falls with the Pillsbury "A" Mill in the background, 1897.

*"The Great Harvest at Minneapolis, Sept. 23d—A Wonderful Exhibit of the Progress of the Northwest and the Growth of Minneapolis"* appeared as an illustration in *Frank Leslie's Illustrated Newspaper* on October 10, 1891. Touted as the most prosperous city in the United States, Minneapolis had grown from a backwater of slightly more than 8,000 souls in 1865 to some 200,000 residents less than thirty years later.

# MORE THAN GRAIN
## Social Responsibility

**THE MINNEAPOLIS GRAIN EXCHANGE** has always been well represented in the city's remarkably vibrant philanthropic community. As Minneapolis's grain and flour industries expanded, they generated incredible wealth for a select group of successful entrepreneurs. Those who prospered most soon began looking for ways to give back to the community, including the city's less fortunate residents. In some cases, women took the lead.

In the *Encyclopedia of Biography of Minnesota* (1900), Mahala Fisk Pillsbury, wife of John S. Pillsbury, is glowingly regarded for her philanthropic endeavors: "It would be vain to attempt enumerating the miscellaneous charities dispersed by the hand of Mrs. Pillsbury. Prosperity, in smiling upon her, smiles also upon the poor within the range of her helpfulness, such poor selected always with conscientious discrimination." In 1880, she established a children's home; in 1900 she built a residence for young women, "where those worthy will find a pleasant home at a low expense. Her husband joined her in making a present of the building to the Women's Christian Association, at a cost of several thousand dollars."[51] Founded in 1866 as the

Christian Aid Society of Minneapolis, the WCA was Minnesota's first women's benevolent association. Its general purpose was to "provide for the temporal and spiritual wants of

**Mahala Fisk Pillsbury with her mother, Mrs. Lougee; her daughter, Susan Pillsbury Snyder; and her grandson, John P. Snyder, circa 1888.**

the destitute, irrespective of age and color" and to establish a place where "working women may find board at a moderate price with the influence of a Christian home in Minneapolis."[52] The WCA Foundation continues to award grants to Twin Cities charities.

Kate Dunwoody did her part as well in turning the Women's Christian Association of Minneapolis into one of the city's most enduring charitable organizations. Her husband, William Hood Dunwoody, also rebuilt a hospital in 1910 in gratitude for the medical treatment provided to his wife by Dr. Amos Abbott; Dr. Abbott's hospital is now known as Abbott Northwestern Hospital. In 1914, the Dunwoodys founded Dunwoody Institute, a nonprofit school "where youth, without distinction on account of race, color, or religious prejudice, may learn the useful trades and crafts, and thereby fit themselves for the better performance of life's duties."[53]

In 1905, brothers John S. and Charles S. Pillsbury set an admirable philanthropic

example when they spent $40,000 to build a settlement house to help newly arrived immigrants weave their way into the city's social fabric. Named after their parents, Pillsbury House grew into Pillsbury United Communities, which, by the turn of the millennium, was considered one of Minneapolis's most respected social service agencies. The organization provides educational and recreational services to youth and families in Minneapolis's Powderhorn-Central neighborhood.

In the decades that followed, several of the Grain Exchange's largest member firms set up foundations to share their wealth with the community. Others made social responsibility an integral part of their corporate philosophy. During the 1970s, for example, General Mills launched a series of public-service initiatives, including Stevens Court, a for-profit corporation that provided affordable housing in a fifty-block neighborhood just south of Minneapolis's business district. Verne Johnson, vice president for corporate

**Woman's Boarding Home, the former Dunwoody mansion, at 52 South Tenth Street, Minneapolis, circa 1912.**

**Women listening to the Victrola in the parlor of the Woman's Boarding Home, circa 1918.**

Pillsbury Settlement House, Sixteenth Avenue South, Minneapolis, circa 1910.

planning at General Mills, insisted that good corporate citizenship and good business sense were compatible, saying, "We have to begin seeking out new areas of activity where both goals can be met and where there is a happy confluence of profit and principle."[54]

Stevens Court continued into the twenty-first century, as did the Minneapolis Grain Exchange's commitment to social responsibility. Several prominent Grain Exchange firms, including Cargill, General Mills, and Pillsbury, were among the dozens of companies that joined the Minnesota Keystone Program—an initiative in which participants pledged to commit at least 2 percent of their pre-tax profits to philanthropy.

Stevens Court, Minneapolis, circa 1970s.

## CHAPTER TWO

1895 — 1930

# Building Momentum

## Saturday, October 23, 1897

Of all the beautiful days the people of Minneapolis had enjoyed over the previous week, this one was easily the most stunning. The sun shone bright and warm on grass that was greener than anyone had a right to expect this time of year. And what better place to enjoy the unseasonably lovely conditions, the *Minneapolis Times* rhapsodized, than the crown jewel of the city's growing park system, Loring Park—the tranquil urban oasis named after Minneapolis Chamber of Commerce charter member Charles Loring:

Against the shadowy outlines of the gray-green landscape, gorgeous masses of color stand out in strong relief. Here the island rises from the blue lake, a thicket of yellow maples with an underbrush of scarlet, where the white plumed swans are gathered. On the farther bank stands a row of tall yellow trees, interspersed with the fine, fringing green of willows and banked with vivid scarlet bushes. To the right rises a slope of emerald greensward with a grove beyond, while in the paths lie fluttering heaps of russet leaves, whose fragrance spices the air.[55]

The gorgeous day coaxed so many people outdoors that it seemed the city's entire population now mingled with a single-minded determination to absorb "a store of sunshine for the cold and melancholy days to come." The fact that it was Saturday—a day of rest and relaxation for most of the city's residents—made the fine weather that much easier to enjoy.

Unfortunately for those who made their living in the grain trade, this was not a day off. The nation's commodity markets were six-day-a-week

Couples enjoy a stroll through Loring Park, the jewel of Minneapolis's early park system, circa 1898.

LORING PARK
MINNEAPOLIS.

Designed with meandering walkways and lush flower gardens by landscape architect Horace W. S. Cleveland, Loring Park was named for its champion, prominent miller Charles M. Loring.

affairs, and all serious grain traders knew there was good money to be made on Saturdays—even sunny, seventy-degree Saturdays in late October. So, as lucky weekend revelers strolled along the paths of Loring Park, dazzled by vibrant autumn hues and glinting sunlight, the traders of the Minneapolis Chamber of Commerce gathered a dozen blocks away to find out whether the previous day's advances would hold (they would) and to hear the association's president, L. R. Brooks, deliver what was rumored to be an important state-of-the-chamber address to the members.

It didn't help matters that the chamber's building at Fourth Avenue and Third Street had, in recent years, become one of the last places anyone would want to spend a beautiful October day. The damage caused by the fire two years earlier was just part of the problem. The building was now simply too small to accommodate the business transacted there each day. Trading volume "on 'change" had doubled during the previous six years, and at least a quarter of the chamber's members were now forced to keep offices elsewhere. Space was at such a premium that rental fees ran 50 to 100 percent above the city average.[56] Members joked that "the thinner a man is, the bigger his salary." Others spread rumors that some firms in the building were paying clerks bonuses "every time they lose a pound in weight or can pull up their belts another notch."[57]

The journey from the building's main entrance to the trading floor had, itself, become a daunting task. After descending into "the semi-darkness of a basement, cheerless, bare and depressing," traders crammed into "the most congested and hardest-worked elevators in the city" for a harrowing ascension. After stepping out of the elevator cage, the occupants then proceeded to elbow their way through the congested, smoke-filled lobby toward the trading-floor entrance. Once there, they joined a raucous crowd, "packed

By the late 1890s, the Chamber of Commerce had lost much of its earlier luster. From the outside, it remained an imposing edifice, but inside the atmosphere was becoming increasingly claustrophobic.

Trading floor of the first Chamber of Commerce Building, circa 1895.

almost to suffocation." The air in the room didn't circulate; it stagnated, especially at the center of the floor. When, as occasionally happened, the "foul smells and nauseating odors" became overwhelming, workers were dispatched to the basement to search for dead rats, a common nuisance in the grain business. The building was, in the words of the *Northwestern Miller,* an architectural embarrassment of "glaring crudeness":

The whole place is unspeakably wretched, the atmosphere is nau-seating, the offices small and dingy, and as to healthfulness, the crudest principles of hygiene are entirely disregarded, so that from close attention to business within its walls the unfortunate occupant can reasonably expect to derive any disease from barber's itch to typhoid fever. Amid such unlovely, unkempt, cramped, and unsanitary surroundings is conducted the business of the largest primary wheat market in the world, and the most important group of mills on earth; and therein men live their daily lives and come and go on business

**Twin images of the Minneapolis Chamber of Commerce appear on this stereocard, intended for parlor viewing.**

errands, who are [conducting] enormous enterprises of vital importance, but who imperil their lives without thought by breathing its polluted air and inhabiting its ill-ventilated cells. To this remarkable shrine come annually thousands of visitors from the outside world, knowing the enormous extent of the flour and grain trade here represented, and expecting to be impressed by its outward evidence, only to find that this immense interest does its daily work in a place little better than a kennel.[58]

Clearly, the Chamber of Commerce building, which had opened to rave reviews just thirteen years earlier, had not aged well. And its weaknesses were especially glaring on a day like this, when nearly everybody inside would rather have been somewhere else. When the closing bell rang at 12:30, members closed out their accounts and milled around impatiently, waiting for President Brooks to deliver his annual address. They didn't have to wait long. Brooks quieted the crowd, ran through a quick summary of the previous year's business, and concluded with an announcement that must have cheered every sweaty trader on the jam-packed floor. He noted that previous presidents had acknowledged as early as 1891 that the building at Fourth and Third was too small to handle the chamber's growing business. Now, he said, "your directors

will, with your co-operation, use their best efforts to furnish you with a suitable exchange room and office building before the end of 1898."[59] After enduring years of complaining from its members, it seemed that the Chamber of Commerce was finally on the verge of securing the kind of home that the structure at Fourth and Third never really was: a building worthy of a world-class trading organization. Little did anyone know how difficult it would be to get the building built.

## Real Estate Games

William Henry Eustis was the kind of pull-yourself-up-by-your-bootstraps success that dominated Minneapolis's early business community—the son of a New England wagon-maker who, after a battle with tuberculosis that left one leg shorter than the other, worked his way through law school and entered private practice. He chose to move to Minneapolis, he said, because he craved adventure and was convinced that Minneapolis's future was brighter than that of any other city west of the Mississippi. Eustis was a talented attorney, an astute real estate investor, and a tireless booster of his adopted hometown. In 1892, the people of Minneapolis elected him mayor, and his one term in office was notable for the businesslike efficiency with which he ran city government. He was, in the words of

**William Henry Eustis, circa 1885. Eustis was the driving force in efforts to erect a new Chamber of Commerce building near the original structure. Eustis's interest in the construction project had much to do with his existing real estate holdings, which included the adjacent Corn Exchange Building and Flour Exchange Building. In addition to his real estate interests, Eustis was a leader in Minneapolis's civic affairs. He served one term as the city's mayor.**

Streetcar entrepreneur Thomas Lowry, circa 1895. Lowry was among the Minneapolis business leaders that William Eustis most admired. Eustis believed the city was fortunate to have a group of men—many of whom worked in the grain trade—dedicated to one ultimate goal: "the upbuilding of Minneapolis."

one of his contemporaries, "a man of strong convictions whom neither fear nor favor can swerve from the course which he believes to be right." His firm will, combined with his keen interest in real estate and civic affairs, brought him early on into the orbit of the Minneapolis Chamber of Commerce.[60]

The young attorney had arrived in Minneapolis on October 23, 1881, just four days after George Rogers and company signed the papers officially incorporating the chamber. Eustis set immediately to building up his law practice, but it was slow going. Confident in his abilities, he began cultivating friendships among the city's business leaders, including Charles Loring and streetcar entrepreneur Thomas Lowry (each a chamber member)—men who could help him get ahead. He enjoyed the company of his new friends and mentors, and he was impressed with their commitment to the city's success:

In the first five years of my residence in Minneapolis, there was no social group. Men mingled with a single thought—the upbuilding of Minneapolis. Anybody could get in. There were no limitations. A man's money and a man's brains were needed. The city got both. The economic laws were working for the fellows who invested their money. They knew that their fortunes of the

future depended upon making Minneapolis great. Those who weren't doing their share in boosting the town, of course, benefited also.[61]

Minneapolis was booming, and Eustis wanted a piece of the action. He had brought with him from New York "a small sum of money" saved from his first law practice, and the more he looked for places to invest, the more he gravitated toward real estate. During his first year in town, he purchased a corner lot at Sixth Street and Hennepin Avenue. Soon he added three more properties in the lightly populated Powderhorn Lake area. By early 1884, he was turning his attention elsewhere, to a part of town that looked ripe for development: the neighborhood near the corner of Fourth Avenue and Third Street, where the Chamber of Commerce was building its new home.

Here was a real opportunity, he thought. The new chamber building undoubtedly would inject vitality into what was a moribund section of the city. As the chamber expanded and business traffic increased, real estate values would almost certainly jump. Eustis, knowing the value of personal relationships in business, applied for membership in the chamber. On March 5, 1884, he was unanimously voted in. No one seemed to mind that he was not a miller or an elevator operator or a grain trader. Many of the chamber's early members came from businesses peripheral to the grain trade, so he was in good company. Besides, Eustis had already demonstrated a keen interest in the city's economic development and he was friendly with many of the chamber's members. He fit in well. It was only later that some members would wonder whether he was putting his personal interests above those of the chamber.

As time went by and the chamber outgrew the building at Fourth and Third, Eustis maneuvered to take advantage of the situation. In 1886, he arranged and financed the construction of the Corn Exchange Building, just across Third Street, which immediately became the business home of choice for members who couldn't find office space in the chamber building. A few years later, when the Corn Exchange filled up with tenants, Eustis bankrolled another building—the Flour Exchange—on the west corner of the intersection. By the mid-1890s, he was, by far, the neighborhood's most profitable landlord.

Eustis's real estate interests were now heavily dependent on the chamber. As long as the chamber stayed where it was, his Corn Exchange and Flour Exchange Buildings would remain highly profitable. If the chamber moved, the value of his properties

would plummet. So when chamber president L. R. Brooks announced on that beautiful October Saturday in 1897 that the association would soon construct a new building, Eustis was almost certainly one of the only members who considered it a lousy idea. Over time, his opposition to relocation would prove to be a major factor in the site selection process.

**Eustis's Flour Exchange Building, across Fourth Avenue from the Chamber of Commerce Building, was designed by Long and Kees and built in 1893. It was added to the National Register of Historic Places in 1977.**

With the chamber's board now officially committed to the construction of a new building, nearly everyone "on 'change" assumed that the process would move forward quickly. "There is no doubt but that we will have a new building completed within the year of 1898," Secretary George Rogers declared. "The principal thing to settle is the location." While Rogers acknowledged that site selection would be "a big affair," he and his fellow board members apparently did not anticipate any significant delays. They should have.[62]

The first inklings of trouble came the following Tuesday, during a special meeting on the trading floor. Eustis urged his fellow members to consider his position as owner of the Corn Exchange and the Flour Exchange. He had invested in those buildings, he said, on the assumption that the chamber would remain at its current location for some time to come. Why not enlarge the present quarters, he asked—maybe with an addition on the Fourth Avenue side? His proposal did not go over well. As one reporter noted, most members believed that an addition would merely "provoke comments effecting the dignity and influence of the chamber":

A canvass of some of the members of the chamber developed the fact that, although there was general appreciation of the position assumed by W. H. Eustis, it was not felt that his interests could be so far respected as to result in the chamber remaining in its present quarters. In other words, the most reasonable proposal submitted to the new committee will likely be acted upon favorably. Many of the members of the chamber feel that they are now too far from the banks and clubs of the city, and desire to move uptown.[63]

The neighborhood surrounding the corner of Fourth and Third had, in fact, become something of an embarrassment to the chamber. The area was, in the words of the *Northwestern Miller*, "a calamity," featuring vacant lots and "rows of boarding houses—abodes of poor but doubtless honest people, as well as habitations of sundry clairvoyants and fortune tellers who, for a consideration, foretell with unerring accuracy the course of the markets, yet remain in poverty themselves."[64] If, as nearly every member believed, the chamber needed a new home, wouldn't it make sense to construct a new building in a part of town that reflected the organization's importance to the community?

Despite predictions of an early resolution, the debate over what became known as "removal" dragged on for more than a year as Eustis and his supporters fought off a series of ill-defined relocation proposals. Finally, in the spring of 1899, members approved a plan, proposed by Thomas Lowry, to construct a building adjacent to the city's first "skyscraper"—the twelve-story Northwestern Guaranty Loan, on Second Avenue South between Third and Fourth Streets. The new building, located in the center of the city's business district, would, according to its supporters, "draw around its location a number of other institutions that would have long ago been clustered around the present chamber but for its outside location."[65] But as it turned out, Lowry's plan was just that. He didn't actually own all the land on which he proposed to erect the new building, and when he tried to buy the last parcel, the owner rebuffed him. The plan fell apart, and the chamber was back where it began. "An earnest effort was made

Members hoped to build the new Chamber of Commerce Building next to Minneapolis's first skyscraper, the Northwestern Guaranty Loan (Metropolitan Building). Difficulties in purchasing the land doomed the project.

The demolition of the Metropolitan in 1961–1962 was perhaps the greatest architectural loss in Minneapolis history and sparked the city's contemporary historic preservation movement.

Tiny residences line Fourth Avenue, directly across the street from the site of the future Chamber of Commerce Building (at Fourth Street and Fourth Avenue), 1900. The Northwestern Guaranty Loan Building looms in the background.

to provide new and suitable quarters for your use, though nothing was gained but experience," a frustrated Charles Harrington admitted in his annual presidential address the following October. "Several plans were considered, but none matured, and we are now . . . more crowded in our Exchange room than ever."[66] Eustis could breathe easier. His investments at the corner of Fourth and Third were still safe—at least for the moment.

## Bucket Brigade

The chamber's efforts to secure a new building coincided with another obsession of sorts, one that would cause its leaders no end of frustration during the first several years of the new century. The object of this obsession was nothing new, really. Stock and commodities markets in other, larger cities were quite familiar with it. But the Minneapolis Chamber of Commerce had managed to avoid the problem during its first decade and a half of existence. By the late 1890s, however, the problem had arrived at its doorstep, and most—although, significantly, not all—of its members were convinced that something needed to be done about it. It was a mortal threat to their business, they believed—a threat called the bucketshop.

Definitions varied, but bucketshops were, essentially, gambling dens in which "investors" bet that the market for, say, hard red spring wheat, would go up or down. Unlike legitimate commodity exchanges, bucketshops did not execute trades with the expectation that anyone would ever deliver or accept shipments of the commodity being bought or sold. The trades were fictitious. But they were based on real market quotations from the nation's major exchanges, and, as such, they assumed a kind of legitimacy by association.

To the people who ran the legitimate exchanges, the bucketshops were anathema. On the one hand, they competed directly with brokers who traded on the big exchanges, siphoning millions of dollars from the pockets of unsophisticated investors who didn't much care who executed their trades, so long as the commissions they paid were low. On the other hand, the bucketshops sowed confusion in the public's mind about the distinctions between legitimate speculation, as practiced on the exchanges, and gambling.

The Chicago Board of Trade was the first exchange to try to snuff out the bucketshops. In 1882, it launched a protracted campaign to drive the self-styled "independent exchanges" out of business by cutting off their access to Chicago quotations. It started by persuading the telegraph companies to stop sending market information to the bucketshops. But the bucketshops found other, surreptitious ways to get the information—everything from planting spies on Chicago's exchange floor to tapping telegraph lines. Everything else the Chicago board tried to stop the leak of information failed. Frustrated by its inability to control its own market information, the board turned to the courts. It conducted private investigations of alleged bucketshop operations, and then turned over the information it collected to law enforcement authorities. In 1896 alone, eighty-seven Chicago bucketshops were indicted for engaging in illegal gambling.[67] As the Chicago Board turned up the heat, bucketshop operators started looking elsewhere for quotations. One of the first places they looked was Minneapolis.

For a long while, members of the Minneapolis Chamber of Commerce were content to watch from a distance as the Chicago Board of Trade waged its war on the bucketshops. After all, they figured, the shady business posed little threat to the traders in Minneapolis so long as they relied primarily on Chicago quotations. But the situation began changing in the mid-1890s. Under increasing pressure from the Chicago board and the courts, bucketshops started executing "trades" based on quotations from other commodity markets, especially the Minneapolis

Chamber of Commerce. The men in Minneapolis began to take notice. In August 1897, the chamber took its first swipe at the bucketshops when it voted to prohibit members from "dealing in differences on the fluctuations in the market price of any commodity—without a bona fide purchase and sale of property for an actual delivery."[68] It soon became apparent, however, that the chamber would have to do more than make minor changes to its rules if it wanted to shut down the bucketshops. By 1900, chamber president C. M. Harrington was alarmed

MIKE—"Now, Pat, you know we've been getting knocked out lately in state politics; we must buy our way to the Legislature, then I will buy my way to the United States Senate, and if Cleveland is elected we can control the patronage once more and thus be the bosses of the Minnesota Democracy again."

"O. K." P. H. K.—"Yes, Mike, our money-bags will take us to the Legislature all right for we can buy up the necessary votes without much trouble; and then we must get you elected Senator, so that you can defeat the anti-option bill, and then do up the farmers on railroad legislation, so as to increase the value of our railroad stocks—and look out for Number One in other ways also; and after a while we will crack the whip over the State Democracy, just as we used to do."

Bucketshops were considered so unsavory that they sometimes served as props in political smear campaigns. This poster, from the late 1800s, depicts two St. Paul Democratic politicians—Patrick Kelly and Michael Doran—attached at the hip and standing outside a bucketshop. The implication is that both men, like the bucketshop in the background, are untrustworthy.

enough to call the threat a matter of "life or death":

One or the other must give way, and in the end it will be the bucket shops. In the last few years those concerns have obtained a wonderful foothold. They are a menace to industrial conditions, and annually divert millions of dollars from the farmers of this country. It is estimated that there are 25,000 bucket shops at present operating in the United States. There are a good many in Minneapolis. Legitimate trading centers like the Minneapolis Chamber of Commerce or the Chicago Board of Trade cannot exist along with these concerns. We must down them or they will down us. There is no alternative.[69]

Of all the bucketshop operators who pestered the chamber during the first few years of the 1900s, none was more annoying—or successful—than George J. Hammond. Hammond arrived in Minneapolis in the fall of 1900 after amassing a dubious record of achievement in Chicago. He had enjoyed a good deal of success there, acting as a financial adviser whose "inside advices" helped clients make "fortunes in wheat." By all accounts, "inside advices" was a gentlemanly way of saying "wire-tapping." In May 1898, he and a compatriot were caught tapping a wire while perched near the top of a telegraph pole in Terre Haute, Indiana. (The farmers who discovered and apprehended them suspected they were spies for the Spanish government, which, at the time, was at war with the United States.) Criminal charges against Hammond were eventually

**Bucketshops relentlessly targeted the Chicago Board of Trade.**

dropped on a technicality, but the fiasco in Terre Haute effectively ended his career in Chicago. He needed a new place to set up shop, one where people weren't familiar with his checkered resume. The place he chose was Minneapolis.[70]

Hammond opened an "independent brokerage house" called the Coe Commission Company, and before long he was taking in more money than any other bucketshop operator in Minneapolis. Hammond advertised heavily in several Twin Cities newspapers, and in one case, placed identical advertisements—disguised as real, two-column news articles—on the front pages of the *Minneapolis Tribune* and the *Minneapolis Times*. By 1902, the Coe Commission Company was operating branch offices in fifty cities throughout the Upper Midwest and as far north as Winnipeg and Brandon, Manitoba. Its headquarters, on the fifth floor of Minneapolis's Bank of Commerce Building, was an elegant office suite with its own, regularly updated quotations board. Hammond himself worked hard to project an image of considerable financial success, even under the most difficult circumstances. In the fall of 1902, when he appeared in court to be arraigned on grand larceny charges—charges that were later dropped—he made sure that everyone in the courtroom could see he

The Bank of Commerce Building in Minneapolis became headquarters for George Hammond's duplicitous Coe Commission Company.

was carrying what the *Minneapolis Times* called a "large roll" of cash:

Hammond appeared in court somewhat ill at ease, and when his case was called by the clerk, stepped to the desk and waived examination.

"Bail is fixed at $1,000," said the court.

"I believe in doing business on a cash basis," said Hammond, and he pulled out a roll of bills as large as a man's wrist.

On the outside of the roll there was a yellow $1,000 bill, which the broker "skinned" off and threw to the clerk.

"I would like a receipt," he said

to the clerk.

"The fact that you are at liberty is sufficient receipt," remarked Municipal Court Clerk Allen.

This seemed to satisfy Hammond, and he departed from the courtroom.[71]

Hammond came to personify what many Chamber of Commerce leaders considered the bucketshop "menace." In his annual address to members, President John Washburn called the bucketshop "a sore spot that must be removed by heroic measures" and promised that the

**John Washburn made the campaign against bucketshops his priority during his two years as president of the Chamber of Commerce (1900–1902).**

**The nephew of Cadwallader Washburn, from whom he learned the flour milling business, John Washburn worked his way up to president of the Washburn-Crosby Company in 1915. He held memberships on the Chicago Board of Trade, the New York Produce Exchange, the Winnipeg Grain Exchange, the Duluth Board of Trade, and the Kansas City Board of Trade. At home, he belonged to the Minneapolis Club, the Minikahda Club, the Lafayette Club, and the Minneapolis Civil and Commerce Association. His death in 1919 was caused by heart trouble brought on by overwork during World War I.**

board of directors was preparing to do just that.[72] He did not, however, reveal how much the board's concern had become a singular obsession with the "broker" from Chicago.

On the morning of January 18, 1903, when George Hammond and two assistants arrived at the Coe Commission Company headquarters in the Bank of Commerce Building, they were surprised to find two men apparently attempting to break into the office. The unwelcome visitors dropped what they were doing and ran, but only one managed to get away. Hammond and an assistant held the other man until the police arrived. The man who escaped was later caught and arrested at the nearby West Hotel. Once in police custody, the men revealed that their names were A. E. Tyler and C. S. Baldwin. A search of their belongings found tools commonly used by wire-tappers and four documents suggesting that they were employed by the Minneapolis Chamber of Commerce.[73]

At first, the chamber's directors denied any connection with Tyler and Baldwin. But when newspapers reported that the names of two top chamber officials—including its new president, James Marshall—were on the documents found in the men's possession, the truth was there for everyone to see. The chamber had in fact hired Tyler and

Baldwin to gather evidence proving that the Coe Commission Company was tapping telegraph wires to illegally obtain the chamber's proprietary market quotations. In an interview the following day with a *Minneapolis Tribune* reporter, President Marshall had no choice but to retract his denial:

"Did you not deny last night that you had any relations with Tyler whatever?"

"Yes, but I didn't know what the reporter was talking about. I didn't know that there had been an arrest or that there was any reason for talking about the private business of this chamber. Tyler was hired to do detective work. It is not unusual to hire a detective and then exploit him in newspaper interviews."

"The letters bearing your signature were written by you?"

"Yes, I wrote the letters. There is no further secret about the matter. We have been robbed of our continuous quotations. . . . Our quotations are just as valuable property as bales of dry goods are to a dry goods firm or any other merchandise to the merchant. If the man employed to find out who was robbing us has committed any overt act, he has done [so] without consent of those employing him."[74]

Marshall and the chair of the chamber's quotation committee, Gustav F. Ewe, had apparently engaged

Tyler and Baldwin with little or no input from their colleagues on the board, and some of their fellow directors were incensed. "I want to state emphatically," an irate George Rogers told the *Tribune,* "that I . . . did not know there was such a man as Tyler in the employ of the chamber, never heard of the negotiations that the letters indicate, and have been in total ignorance of the whole matter."[75] By that point, though, it didn't much matter what anyone at the chamber said; the entire organization had been tarred by the scandal. Even the usually sympathetic *Northwestern Miller* felt compelled to heap on the scorn. "[The chamber's] entire campaign against the bucket shops has been a series of mortifying fiascos," it proclaimed. "For its own sake and for that of its irreproachable members, who are in the overwhelming majority, it should either give over such futile and childish displays or go at the work in a manly, sincere and straightforward fashion."[76]

The chamber's members began resisting the board's broader efforts to fight the bucketshops. In May 1903, they narrowly rejected an amendment to the bylaws that would have strengthened the penalties against members who "make, execute, or give any orders for a trade or transaction in or upon any bucket shop or any so-called exchange." Sensing the member-

**Gustav Ewe, chair of the Chamber of Commerce's quotation committee. Many chamber members were angry that Ewe and President James Marshall had not consulted with other high-ranking chamber officials before approving the break-in at the Coe Commission Company offices.**

ship's waning interest in the bucket-shop fight, the directors sat back and waited to see what the courts would do.

In the spring of 1905, the U.S. Supreme Court issued a ruling that settled the bucketshop question once and for all. In a case involving the Chicago Board of Trade, the high court ruled that exchanges like those in Chicago and Minneapolis owned their quotations, and that they could legally restrain others from using them. In addition, the court dismissed arguments that speculation, as practiced in the futures markets, was nothing more than gambling. "Speculation of this kind is the self-adjustment of society to the probable," Justice Oliver Wendell Holmes wrote. "Its value is well known as a means of avoiding or mitigating catastrophes, equalizing prices and providing for periods of want."[77] The ruling was everything that the Chicago Board of Trade and the Minneapolis Chamber of Commerce could have hoped for. Not only was it a victory for the legitimate exchanges in their battle against the bucket-shops, it was also a "sweeping endorsement" of the way the exchanges did business.[78]

The Supreme Court decision dealt a lethal blow to the bucketshops, but it was not immediately fatal. Several bucketshops continued to operate in Minneapolis for at least another two years by routing pilfered quotations through a bogus commodity exchange in Superior, Wisconsin. They began shutting down in 1907 after the chamber successfully fought them in court.[79]

And what of George Hammond, the wire-tapping bucketshop king who played the victim so effectively in

GEO. C. BAGLEY

Little grains of number one
With a little rain and sun
Mean a lot of grains and, lo,
Bagley turns 'em into "dough."

George C. Bagley was one of Minneapolis's most successful independent elevator operators during the late 1800s and early 1900s. While this sketch indicates he was an employee of the Atlantic Elevator Company, he eventually started his own company, the George C. Bagley Elevator Company, with offices in the Minneapolis Chamber of Commerce Building.

the aftermath of the Tyler and Baldwin arrests? He did what most bucketshop operators eventually did: he went out of business, leaving thousands of "investors" in the lurch.

[Hammond's] big offices which but yesterday were the scene of activity, and where daily for several years many thousands of dollars have been lost or won in the bucketshop game, are today practically deserted. The long row of telegraph instruments and tickers are silent. Yesterday's stock quotations are still upon the big blackboards and are marked "Don't erase."

Outside there is an everchanging crowd of the curious, and those who are vitally interested in the failure. They read the sign pasted on the glass door that tells of the appointment of a receiver, exchange a few comments on the company's demise and then make room for others.[80]

Several years later, the Chamber of Commerce's George Rogers recalled the bucketshop fight in tones that sounded downright nostalgic. "The wire-tappers are the hardest men in the world to fight," he said with grudging admiration. "One wonders sometimes when he sees the bright fellows that are mixed up in it, if they couldn't make a better living using their talents honestly."[81]

## Futures Trading

Among the unintended consequences of the big exchanges' turn-of-the-century bucketshop battle was a significant shift in the trading of wheat futures. The Minneapolis Chamber of Commerce had introduced futures trading in the mid-1880s, but that side of the business had remained minuscule when compared to the cash wheat side. The Chicago Board of Trade was the center of the commodities futures universe, and even the chamber's biggest boosters doubted whether Minneapolis could ever seriously challenge Chicago's supremacy.

But in the summer of 1900, the Chicago Board of Trade—at the height of its war against the bucketshops—made several moves that opened the door to a new era of futures trading in Minneapolis. Among other things, it changed its rules to restrict trading times and raise commission rates—moves that encouraged traders to turn to other markets, like Minneapolis, where the rules were less restrictive.[82] By June, the volume of futures trading in Minneapolis was setting records almost daily, pushing up wheat prices more than twenty cents a bushel.[83] "The increase in the trading of futures has been phenomenal," crowed President Charles Harrington. "This portion of our business is capable of great development

and ought to be larger every crop for many years to come."[84]

While the intricacies of buying and selling futures seemed straightforward to the men in the trading pit, such activities remained incomprehensible to most people outside the industry. As futures trading increased and public misconceptions about it proliferated, the chamber began trying to explain the process in terms that even a novice could understand. One of its first, and more successful, attempts in this regard appeared in 1922. In an article titled "Future Trading, Hedging and Speculation in Grain Exchanges," the chamber began by acknowledging that "no feature of grain exchanges has met with so much adverse criticism as the buying and selling of grain for 'future' delivery." It then proceeded to explain how futures were traded and why they were beneficial.

"Futures," as the term is generally used in grain exchanges, are contracts for the purchase and sale of grain to be delivered during some future month. The great majority of future trades are made for delivery in one of four months, May, July, September or December. . . .

A purchase and sale of 5,000 bushels of Minneapolis May oats made in the Exchange Room of the Chamber of Commerce is a contract, in which the seller agrees to

deliver to the buyer, some time during the month of May next succeeding, 5,000 bushels of No. 2 white oats . . . at the price per bushel agreed upon. . . .

It is further understood between the buyer and the seller . . . that the delivery of this grain by the seller to the buyer shall be in the form of a warehouse receipt.[85]

The article then went on to present a hypothetical trade in which the seller was identified as "A" and the buyer was called "B." In this trade, "A" sold five thousand bushels of May oats to "B" at a price of seventy-five cents a bushel. "A" and "B" then both filed forms with the chamber's clearinghouse, detailing the transaction. "A" was now "short" five thousand bushels of May oats and "B" was now "long" the same amount. But this was not the end of the story. The article assumed that "B" was a speculator who hoped to profit from an advance in the market. Under this hypothetical scenario, the price of oats jumped one cent per bushel (to seventy-six cents), creating a paper profit for "B" of fifty dollars. "B" then sold his contracted oats to another trader, "C," for the new price of seventy-six cents a bushel. "B" pocketed his fifty-dollar profit and "C" became, in effect, the party responsible for accepting delivery of the oats originally sold by "A."

So that was how futures were bought and sold. How, then, did such futures trading benefit anyone other than the speculator who made his fifty-dollar profit?

Chamber officials realized this was a tricky question, and they addressed it by linking futures to the common, but often misunderstood, trading practice known as hedging. The article explained that hedging allowed the grain owner—"a farmer with wheat in his granary, a farmers' elevator company with wheat in the elevator, a terminal elevator with wheat in store, or a miller with wheat on hand"—to minimize the risks caused by fluctuations in grain prices. It illustrated the point with another hypothetical scenario.

In this case, an elevator operator bought five thousand bushels of wheat at three cents a bushel below the current, September cash price (freight charges were not included for simplicity's sake). If the elevator operator held onto that grain, he ran the risk that prices would drop and his three-cents-a-bushel profit would disappear. So what did he do? He hedged his grain on the futures market. He did so by selling five thousand bushels of wheat for December delivery. That was his hedge. Two months later, the elevator operator sold the grain on the cash market and bought back his futures contract.

ANNUAL

# Base Ball Game

FOR

## CHILDREN'S CHARITIES

SWIMMING POOL DONATED BY CHICAGO BOARD OF TRADE

### CHICAGO BOARD OF TRADE

vs.

### MINNEAPOLIS CHAMBER OF COMMERCE

THE WHITE SOX BALL PARK,
35TH STREET AND SHIELDS AVENUE

## SATURDAY, JULY 29TH, 1911

JOHN F. HIGGINS, PRINTER 80 376 WEST MONROE STREET

**America's pastime was part of the social fabric of the Chamber of Commerce as early as 1887, when the *Northwestern Miller* reported a game between the commission men and the millers. Despite uniforms made of flour sacks, the millers won the game 21–7. The rivalry between the Minneapolis Chamber of Commerce and the Chicago Board of Trade also spilled onto the ball field occasionally. In 1911, teams representing the two exchanges played a series of charity baseball games in Minneapolis and Chicago. At the end of the season, the Minneapolis team took home the championship trophy.**

This, the article explained, was the essence of hedging:

If in the meantime the price of wheat had advanced 5 cents per bushel, an apparent profit would be made in the sale of the cash wheat through the advance price. But, as is ordinarily the case, the future month (December in this case) would also have advanced 5 cents per bushel, and in the purchase of this hedge a loss would be made of 5 cents per bushel, which would exactly offset the gain in the sale of cash wheat of 5 cents per bushel, still leaving the original profit of 3 cents per bushel.

This 1922 attempt to explain futures trading in terms that everyone could understand may have been admirable, but it was only marginally successful. As time went by, the chamber kept trying, but the results were usually similar. Futures trading was, quite simply, a difficult concept for most people to fathom, and explaining it would remain one of the chamber's biggest public relations challenges for years to come.

## Fourth and Fourth

While the action in the futures pit was encouraging, it exacerbated the chamber's most vexing problem: its overcrowded building. Plans to build a new structure adjacent to the Northwestern Guaranty Loan Building had fallen apart the previous autumn, and little had been done

since to readdress the organization's desperate need for additional space. As the *Minneapolis Journal* noted, the increased activity on the floor of the exchange, spurred by the moves of the Chicago Board of Trade, was only making matters worse:

Chamber of Commerce men are roaring as loudly for a new building as they ever do in excited moments on the floor. The recent flurry in wheat has crowded the building, already overcrowded, to an exasperating degree, and it has been shove, push, crowd, jam, to get through the halls, move about on the "floor" or get about the building at all. The legitimate business of the chamber is inadequately cared for by the present structure, and when some little excitement like that in wheat during the past three weeks comes, with its crowds and strangers, there is no living in the building. The rooms are already overcrowded and now the halls are utilized to accommodate the crowds that overflow into the offices and on to the street. A new building is the crying need of the hour. More room, whether down town or up town, must be arranged for, and at once, if one of the greatest grain markets in the world is not to suffer material damage.[86]

By the end of June 1900, the situation had gotten so bad that the chamber's board of directors voted to rail off the entrance to the trading room's visitors gallery and admit only those spectators who obtained special tickets from the secretary's office.[87] The restrictions on visitors helped somewhat to alleviate the overcrowding, but the larger problem remained: the chamber still needed a new building.

After years of starts and stops, the chamber's leaders moved quickly to solve the association's overcrowding problem once and for all. They solicited new proposals from business leaders in and out of the chamber, and by the end of the summer had whittled the possibilities to two. The first plan, known as the "uptown proposition," called for the construction of a building at Fourth Street and Second Avenue South, about two blocks away from the chamber's current address.

Under this proposal, the chamber and its members would lease the new building from a group of Chicago investors and would then have to arrange separately to dispose of the old structure. The second plan called for construction of a building next to the current one, at the corner of Fourth Street and Fourth Avenue South. Under this proposal, the chamber would retain possession of the old building and update it so that it could provide additional office space.

Once again, the chamber's members aligned themselves in opposing camps. Those favoring the uptown proposal included prominent grain commission men such as James Marshall, George Daggett, W. T. Fraser, and F. R. Pettit, as well as many "younger members" and

**This postcard image of Minneapolis was made two years before the Chamber of Commerce added its East Building in 1909.**

**Banker Clinton Morrison was the son of Dorilus Morrison, a pioneer Minneapolis lumber man, railroad builder, flour miller, and the first mayor of Minneapolis.**

"members who now have offices uptown." Prominent among those supporting the "Fourth and Fourth" plan were a handful of powerful members whose financial interests would be hurt by a move uptown, including John Washburn (the *Minneapolis Journal* referred cryptically to "certain loans made by the Washburn estate"), financier Clinton Morrison, and, of course, William Eustis, who still owned the neighboring Corn Exchange and Flour Exchange Buildings. The big elevator operators, including Frank Peavey and the Cargills, couldn't seem to make up their minds which plan they preferred.[88] Under the

chamber's bylaws, the directors could have made the decision on their own, but the directors knew if they did, they'd be open to heavy criticism, no matter which plan they chose. Not surprisingly, they decided to put the matter to a vote.

At a special meeting on September 14, 1900, the chamber's members voted 232 to 162 in favor of the "Fourth and Fourth" plan. (Fifty-one voted to reject both proposals.) The results, while reflecting the majority's will, nonetheless generated only muted enthusiasm. Most members had hoped to move the chamber closer to the city's main business district, but many balked at the rental provisions included in the uptown proposal. For them, the "Fourth and Fourth" plan was the least objectionable of two bad choices. The final vote was, in the words of the *Minneapolis Tribune,* "a great disappointment to a large majority" of members.[89]

It did not take long, however, for anticipation to overtake the majority's disappointment. The plans for the chamber's new home, submitted by Minneapolis architects Frederick Kees and Serenus Colburn, impressed nearly everyone who laid eyes on them. The building was to be a nine-story structure of brick and terra cotta with a large trading room and plenty of office space. It would connect to the old building by a

**Clinton Morrison donated his father's ten-acre, sixteen-room homestead, called "Villa Rosa," to the Minneapolis Society of Fine Arts to make way for the construction of the Minneapolis Institute of Arts, which opened in 1915.**

fourth-floor walkway. If everything went as planned, it would open for business in about a year.

For a while, it looked like the project might actually stay on schedule. In October, the chamber officially purchased the land at the corner of Fourth and Fourth from Minneapolis's Security Bank (whose president, F. A. Chamberlain, was a longtime chamber member) for $50,000. Excavation and foundation work began almost immediately. A few months later, financing for the project was secured when four of the city's largest banks and a separate trust company agreed to underwrite a $400,000 bond issue.[90] By the spring of 1901, prospective tenants had applied to occupy 75 percent of the building's office space.[91]

But as work on the building proceeded, it became increasingly obvious that the project would take much longer to complete than first thought. Faced with an unanticipated demand for office space, the directors approved plans to add another floor, a decision that increased the price tag by $30,000 and required an additional bond issue. Delays in the delivery of construction materials, especially decorative marble, began to plague the project. And after more than a year of construction, the directors decided to add what President John Washburn called a "somewhat more elaborate finish and improvements," including better heating, lighting, and electrical fixtures. "There has been some concern among our members on the slow progress of the Chamber," Washburn acknowledged, but he asked for patience, reminding members that high-quality construction "requires time."[92]

In the end, the opening of the building turned out to be a gradual—and confusing—process. The first tenants began moving into their offices in late September 1902, initiating a procession that the *Minneapolis Journal* called "the greatest general

The new Chamber of Commerce Building at the corner of Fourth Street and Fourth Avenue South, circa 1908, was one of the first steel-frame structures in Minneapolis.

shifting about of office renters ever known at one time in the history of the city."[93] Unfortunately for them, the new exchange room still needed a lot of work, so traders with offices in the new building had to scurry back regularly to the old building to get their work done. Meanwhile, the old building was undergoing major renovations to improve the quality of its office spaces. Those who continued to work there squeezed through corridors teeming with carpenters, masons, and steamfitters, and, much to George Rogers's amazement, "endured all this annoyance with good nature and accepted it with philosophical composure, much to their credit."[94]

As the weeks went by, the building began taking on the highly polished sheen of a finished product. Newspapers noted that the Brooks Elevator Company, the F. H. Peavey Company, and the Washburn-Crosby Company had filled their office suites with "the finest office furniture ever seen in the northwest . . . and every stick of it is of mahogany."[95] In the exchange room, the new, octagonal trading pit was added to the floor, telephone lines were connected, blackboards were installed, and cash grain sample tables—too bulky for stairs or elevators—were hoisted in through the fourth-floor windows.[96]

On the morning of November 3, 1902, several hundred people—

members and visitors—crammed into the newly completed exchange room to witness what the *Minneapolis Journal* called "the beginning of an epoch in the grain trade."[97] The gong sounded, and two men—the chamber's outgoing president, John Washburn, and its incoming president, James Marshall—stepped into the recently completed trading pit.

Marshall turned to Washburn. "I'll buy five December!" he shouted.

"Taken at 71!" Washburn cried.

With that, dozens of traders moved into the pit, shouting bids and acceptances. The business of the new building at Fourth and Fourth was officially under way.[98]

Construction on the building continued through the winter, much to the members' dismay. Among the jobs that remained unfinished was the final installation of the building's heating system—a fact that "caused much trouble and annoyance . . . [and] to some extent interfered with business."[99] But by spring, the building was ready for its grand opening. Twenty years earlier, the chamber had hosted a similar gala to celebrate the completion of its first permanent home. That building had fallen out of favor more quickly than anyone had expected. This time, as the *Minneapolis*

*Journal* observed, expectations were even higher:

In planning the structure the officers of the chamber and the architects, Messrs. Kees and Colburn, determined to have a building which would not only be suitable but in every way permanent; for it was a part of the thought of the Chamber of Commerce men that this was to be the home of a permanent organization which would probably be doing business right here when the sons and grandsons of the present members have succeeded to membership. The occasion seemed to be one which called for excellence of construction, durability, solidity and permanence. . . . From foundation stone to roof everything was put in with the thought it must stay and not wear out.[100]

## The Equity Threat

The feud between the Chamber of Commerce and the region's farmers, which had broken into full boil back in the early 1890s, had settled to a gentle simmer by the time the organization moved into its new home. Many farmers still believed that the chamber was a monopolistic club that allowed "elevator combines" to fix prices at the farmers' expense, but the populist outrage that had fueled anti-chamber sentiments in the region's wheat-growing sections no longer held sway. The success of farmer-owned,

**The old Chamber of Commerce Building (center), with the new building visible to its right, circa 1905.**

**The new Chamber of Commerce Building was a popular subject for postcard publishers. This view of the building, taken in 1905, shows that the surrounding neighborhood was still partially residential.**

RIGHT: The Duluth Board of Trade operated from 1881 to 1967. As ever-increasing grain crops poured into Duluth in the late 1800s, the city became a prominent wheat market. This Duluth Board of Trade Building was erected at Third Avenue and First Street in Duluth in 1895.

BELOW: New Year's Eve on the Duluth trading floor, circa 1920s.

country co-op elevators had convinced many farmers that they were making progress in their efforts to control the price of the grain they produced. The result was a kind of unofficial truce that allowed the farmers and the chamber to go about their business without flinging 1890s-style insults at each other.

But that didn't mean all farmers were happy with the state of the grain trade. Ulcer-inducing price swings remained the norm, and fixed marketing and transportation charges continued to chafe. Even with the proliferation of local cooperative elevators, the farmers' grain still had to go through one of the big exchanges, usually the chamber or the Duluth Board of Trade. Sentiment was growing among the region's farmers that country co-op elevators, while nice, just weren't good enough. Terminal markets, not local markets, were the problem, they thought, and many farmers were coming to believe that something had to be done about them. In May 1908, a small group of reform-minded farmers met in Minneapolis to form an organization called the Equity Cooperative Exchange. Their goal was to create a new terminal grain market, "fed by a chain of local co-operative elevators," that would compete directly with the Minneapolis Chamber of Commerce.[101]

At first, the chamber's leaders took little notice of the upstart exchange founded in their shadow. There was no reason they should have; the Equity Cooperative Exchange posed no immediate threat. During its first four years, the ECE put on what one historian called "a feeble performance,"[102] recording sales of only 805 cars of grain—the great bulk of which had to be traded on the floor of the Chamber of Commerce. The ECE didn't even get around to incorporating itself until 1911. Its leaders were activists, not businessmen, and their lack of business savvy showed.[103]

But after a few years in business, the ECE made a change at the top that energized the organization— a personnel move that was, in the words of historian Theodore Saloutos, "tantamount to a declaration of war against the Minneapolis Chamber of Commerce." On August 1, 1912, a fiery grain merchant named George S. Loftus took over as the ECE's sales manager. Loftus was a committed populist who, over the years, had become firmly convinced that the organized grain trade was rigged to further enrich a handful of wealthy businessmen, including railroad barons, millers, and elevator operators. He sympathized with the farmers and spoke their language. He was a devastatingly effective speaker who rarely passed up a chance to pillory the institution that, in his mind, embodied the evil "grain combine"—

the Minneapolis Chamber of Commerce. Under his guidance, the ECE began making plans for an independent grain exchange to "serve as a sort of chamber of commerce for the farmers."[104]

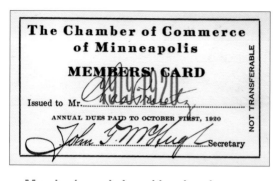

Member's card signed by chamber secretary John G. McHugh.

The leaders of the Minneapolis chamber had virtually ignored the ECE during its initial years of existence, but Loftus worried them. They were afraid that the ECE's new sales manager might actually succeed in using his position to reinvigorate the cooperative movement in the Upper Midwest and weaken the chamber by establishing a competing grain market. In the weeks following Loftus's arrival, the chamber's secretary, John G. McHugh, initiated what would turn out to be a lengthy campaign to undermine the ECE. The campaign began with what the U.S. Federal Trade Commission would later call "a system of espionage," in which McHugh urged like-minded businessmen to "keep an eye" on the ECE and inform him of any information that might be used against it. He spelled out his plans for monitoring the ECE in a letter dated August 23, 1912, to the president of the Commission Merchants' Association:

Since Loftus has taken over the management of the Equity it is probable that their operations will be pushed most aggressively and we believe the commission merchants,

thru their representatives, should keep our office closely advised regarding any information as to shipments to this Company—We believe the matter deserves the careful consideration of the Commission Merchants' Association.[105]

McHugh and his colleagues feared that the ECE would siphon business from the chamber, and they moved quickly to restrict the would-be exchange's access to grain. In October 1912, the chamber adopted a resolution known as "Circular 405" that, in effect, prohibited members from buying ECE grain. The resolution referred indirectly to the ECE as a nonmember institution that regularly disparaged the chamber with false accusations of corrupt business practices, and it directed chamber members to avoid doing business with all such institutions. "Circular 405" threatened to derail the ECE's plans to establish a competing exchange by assigning it pariah status among the city's most active grain traders. Nonetheless, in early 1913, the ECE went ahead with its plans and established the Independent Grain Exchange. The IGE was, in many ways, an exchange in name only, but it did have a few things going for it. Among other things, it shared offices with the ECE in the Corn Exchange Building across the street from the Chamber of Commerce, and it had the ability to store commissioned grain in a St. Paul elevator partially owned by George Loftus.[106] It was, despite its questionable prospects, a potential challenger to the chamber's pre-eminence in Minneapolis, and the chamber's leaders did not intend to let it fulfill that potential.

Shortly after the ECE established its new grain market, the Minnesota Senate and the Minnesota House of Representatives each appointed a committee to investigate how grain was traded in Minnesota and the Upper Midwest. The two committees were biased in the extreme. The Senate committee, chaired by Samuel D. Works, favored the Chamber of Commerce; Christopher M. Bendixen's House committee was partial to the ECE. Their hearings, held simultaneously during February and March, produced heated exchanges that served mainly to solidify existing opinions.

Petty bickering consistently overshadowed the serious discussions that occasionally broke out during the hearings. The *Duluth News Tribune* called the proceedings "a kettle of fish of uncertain antecedents" that the committees should "stop stirring, lest it become as noisome a compound as that tended by the three cronies in 'Macbeth.'"[107] The newspaper's account of the March 23 hearings featured a particularly colorful exchange between the House committee's chief counsel, James Manahan, and an attorney representing the Chamber of Commerce named C. R. Fowler:

"No self-respecting member of the chamber of commerce would [employ] you," returned Manahan.

"You're a liar," was Fowler's next blast.

"Rowdy," shouted Manahan. "It's by such terms that you get noticed in the newspapers; you can not attract attention any other way but by such language."

"Turncoat," shouted Fowler, hotter than ever.

Manahan laughed a scornful laugh and turned his back on the lawyer whose professional standing he had so pointedly attacked. [Committee member A. F.] Teigen of Chippewa had been shouting for the sergeant at arms to put out Fowler.

"Gentlemen, gentlemen," shouted Teigen, "for God's sake this sort of thing won't do."

"It won't get the committee

State Senator Samuel Works was an ally of the Chamber of Commerce. A Democrat born in 1862 in Steuben County, New York, Works engaged in lumbering, real estate, and loans in Mankato, Minnesota.

State Representative Christopher Bendixen supported the Equity Cooperative Exchange. Born in Denmark in 1858, Bendixen farmed in Redwood County, Minnesota.

Attorney James Manahan (holding hat) and Equity Cooperative Exchange leader George Loftus (in shirtsleeves) had frequent run-ins with representatives of the Minneapolis Chamber of Commerce.

anything," shouted [committee chairman] Bendixen, but Teigen continued to call for the sergeant at arms. Fowler then called Teigen the "most disorderly" member of the committee and Manahan protested such remarks. Bendixen turned upon Fowler and bade him cease. Former Judge [and Chamber of Commerce attorney David F.] Simpson took a hand and protested what he termed the "insults" of Manahan in relation to Fowler.

"But Fowler insulted Mr. Manahan," insisted Bendixen. The high old row could be heard for yards along the corridors and lawmakers, place holders, and the rag tag and bobtail of the capitol population came hiking from every direction.[108]

As expected, the final reports that emerged from the hearings reflected the unconcealed biases of the two committees. The pro-ECE House committee recommended,

among other things, that the state adopt stricter controls over the internal operations of the chamber—a recommendation that soon vanished in legislative quicksand. The pro-chamber Senate committee mainly refuted the charges made in the House report. The chamber and the ECE both emerged bloody from what amounted to a legislative split decision, but neither side was ready to walk away from the fight.

About a month after the legislative hearings ended, the chamber began soliciting $25 contributions from its members to help it avoid the kind of "expensive and trying experiences" that it had just endured at the capitol. With contributions in hand, the chamber's new "publicity committee" then set out "to remove misunderstandings with regard to the methods of the chamber of commerce" and to make its case against its pesky rival, the ECE.[109]

The hearings had actually given the chamber some powerful ammunition to use in its "campaign of education." At one point during testimony before the Senate committee, an attorney representing the chamber asked the IGE secretary, A. A. Trovaten, whether there really was a "trading room" at the IGE offices. "In a way there is, and in a way there isn't," Trovaten stammered. He admitted that the IGE had no trading pit and that nearly all the business conducted in its offices was done by George Loftus's grain firm.[110] These and other revelations exposed the IGE as a poor imitation of a legitimate grain exchange, and the chamber's publicity committee wasted no time in playing up the embarrassing truth to the ECE's distinct disadvantage.

The funds assigned to the chamber's publicity budget went primarily to two publications that, while nominally independent, relied heavily on the chamber's financial support. The first, the *National Grain Grower and Equity Farm News,* had started out as the "official organ" of the ECE, but switched allegiances after the chamber helped it climb out of a financial hole with an infusion of much-needed cash. The second, the *Cooperative Manager and Farmer,* was a monthly periodical, published in Minneapolis, that was heavily "under the influence" of the chamber.[111] Its editor, John H. Adams,

excelled at printing what the U.S. Federal Trade Commission later called "false, misleading, and unfair statements" about the ECE.[112] The Minneapolis Chamber of Commerce paid thousands of dollars to both the *National Grain Grower* and the *Cooperative Manager* to reprint and distribute articles that reflected well on the chamber and unfavorably on the ECE.[113]

In December 1914, the *Cooperative Manager* published and circulated what may have been its most brutally effective piece of pro-chamber propaganda. A few months earlier, the ECE had moved its headquarters from Minneapolis to St. Paul and replaced its original grain market,

"You bet I'm going to HANG ON to these as long as I Can Get Minnesota State Senate Reactionaries to make reports in My Favor"

Voted for the Combine:
SENATOR S. D. WORKS
SENATOR G. H. SULLIVAN    } 3
SENATOR VICTOR L. JOHNSON

Voted for the People:
SENATOR S. A. HANSON
SENATOR O. A. LENDE
REP. C. M. BENDIXEN
REP. MARTIN SCHWARTZ } 7
REP. A. F. TEIGEN
REP. FRANK HOPKINS
REP. D. P. O'NEIL

SEVEN FOR THE PEOPLE AND THREE FOR THE COMBINE

Supporters of the cooperative movement continued their attacks on the Chamber of Commerce once the legislative hearings were complete and the committees issued their reports. This cartoon suggested that "reactionaries" in the state senate were providing unfair advantages to the chamber.

the IGE, with a new one called the St. Paul Grain Exchange. The ECE's new St. Paul exchange was a more substantial operation than its failed predecessor (by early 1916, fifty-three buyers were purchasing grain in St. Paul),[114] but it still made an easy target for the chamber and its unofficial publishing arm, the *Cooperative Manager.* In an article titled "Equity Exchange Moves to St. Paul," editor John Adams dismissed St. Paul's meager milling and grain-storage capabilities, and mocked the ECE's new enterprise as "The St. Paul-Department-Store-Mail-Order-Grain-Exchange":

St. Paul business men may well pause and consider whether they are advancing their real interests in a permanent way, by assisting in the deception practiced upon the farmers through the operation of a pretended grain exchange. By giving any support to a pretended grain exchange, which, for seven years in Minneapolis, has deceived and wronged the farmers and farmers' elevators of the Northwest, the business men of St. Paul will surely bring discredit upon their city and this must affect unfavorably the great jobbing interests of St. Paul. The farmer, country merchant, banker, and newspaper man will surely point the finger of scorn at a city whose newspapers, department stores and retail merchants join hands in assisting a make-believe grain exchange and exploit and deceive the farmers and farmers' elevator companies.[115]

The pro-chamber *Cooperative Manager* called the Equity Cooperative Exchange's St. Paul operation (above) a "pretended grain exchange."

Even as the publicity committee chipped away at the ECE's fragile reputation, another group of chamber members tried to neutralize the threat of cooperative competition by employing a different tactic: the frivolous lawsuit. Beginning in the summer of 1914, several chamber supporters in Minnesota and elsewhere went to court in hopes of further weakening the ECE. In one case, the chamber paid all the legal expenses of three men—each of whom owned a single share of ECE stock—in a lawsuit alleging financial mismanagement by the ECE. That lawsuit led to another, brought by North Dakota's pro-chamber attorney general, seeking to have the ECE declared insolvent and bankrupt. In the end, the latter case was dismissed "on the ground that the [ECE] was not insolvent." But the legal jockeying was not over. In yet another case, the Chamber of Commerce paid an attorney named J. M. Witherow to represent two men in a breach-of-contract lawsuit against the ECE. In a letter to chamber member P. L. Howe, Witherow intimated that the merits of the case were secondary to its public relations value:

The publicity which we have been giving [the ECE] in the newspapers has had a very unfavorable effect upon them and is making many of the farmers suspicious of their actions. When I am able to make public the affidavit which I yesterday secured . . . and also the fact that they were securing accommodation notes from the farmers in large amounts which are being pledged to terminal banks, I think you will find the farmers will be very much more frightened.[116]

In all, the ECE wound up spending at least $20,000 to defend itself against lawsuits brought at the instigation of the Minneapolis Chamber of Commerce. An investigation by the Federal Trade Commission later determined that the

litigation was initiated "in bad faith with the purpose, intent and effect of hindering and obstructing the business of the [ECE]," and that the lawsuits had "injured greatly [the ECE's] credit and standing with the public generally and with shippers of grain."[117]

The chamber's efforts to discredit the ECE and its offshoot grain exchanges produced a predictable backlash, especially among rural folk who already suspected the grain trade was rigged against the farmers. Arthur C. Townley, leader of the insurgent Nonpartisan League, spoke for many growers when he expressed the hope that the Federal Trade Commission—acting on a complaint filed by the ECE—would uncover "all the rottenness of the Minneapolis Chamber of Commerce so the good people in the city will learn how hard working farmers have been gouged."[118] Support for the ECE continued to grow, and in 1918, the organization enjoyed its biggest year, with fifteen million bushels of wheat handled and twenty-one new elevators built in North Dakota alone.[119]

But anti-chamber sentiment among farmers was not enough to sustain the ECE in the long run. By the early 1920s, the organization's lack of business acumen was becoming increasingly obvious. Internal audits uncovered lax bookkeeping and poor

investments. ECE stockholders were irate, and it seemed that every ECE manager was at one time or another accused of being "a bandit, a gangster, a thief, a looter, a falsifier of records, an embezzler, a robber, or a porch climber."[120] In the final analysis, the ECE "was geared more for war against the Minneapolis Chamber of Commerce than for the adoption of sound business policies," wrote historian Theodore Saloutos. "It was far simpler to combine to resist the Chamber's attacks than to adopt the needed business policies."[121]

In 1924, the Federal Trade Commission finally issued a ruling in the complaint that the ECE had filed against the chamber several years earlier. The Federal Trade Commission found that the chamber had "engaged in a conspiracy . . . to annoy, embarrass and destroy the business of [the ECE] . . . [in order] to secure and maintain for it and its members a monopoly of the grain trade in Minneapolis," and it ordered the chamber to immediately cease all "unfair methods of competition."[122] But the ruling was, by that time, almost entirely moot. The ECE had gone into receivership the previous year. The Minneapolis Chamber of Commerce had already prevailed in its long struggle to suppress its rival. The competitive threat posed by the farmers' cooperative movement was over—for the time being.

## By the Numbers

On the day John Washburn had taken over as president of the Minneapolis Chamber of Commerce in 1900, he had predicted a great future for the organization. "There is no reason," he proclaimed, "why we should not be the largest and most influential commercial body in the country."[123] Washburn's prediction was grandiose, given the long track records and reputations of other institutions such as the Chicago Board of Trade and the New York Stock Exchange, but in the three decades that followed, his conviction that the chamber and the city were entering a new era of unprecedented commercial growth proved accurate.

On the cash grain side, the numbers were impressive. Wheat receipts, which in 1900 topped 83 million bushels, peaked at 142 million in 1915, and from then on rarely dipped below the 100 million mark. But if wheat's numbers were good, the numbers coming out of the small grain markets were stunning. As farmers in southern and western Minnesota diversified and wheat production concentrated more heavily in the Dakotas and Montana, the volume of small grains coming through Minneapolis multiplied several times over. Between 1900 and 1930 receipts of oats and flax increased by about two-thirds; corn doubled, barley quadrupled, and the

Harvesting oats in
Beltrami County,
Minnesota, circa 1910.

Flax harvesting near
Fargo, North Dakota,
circa 1910.

John W. Daniels established the Daniels Linseed Company in Minneapolis in 1902 after having been in the flax-crushing business in Ohio's Miami Valley. In 1923 the firm became Archer Daniels Midland. Daniels and his partner, George A. Archer, addressed each other as "Mr. Archer" and "Mr. Daniels," and worked facing each other at rolltop desks.

volume of rye passing through the city jumped nearly twentyfold.[124] The numbers undoubtedly would have been even more impressive had it not been for the postwar agricultural depression of the 1920s.

The increasing importance of small grains was evident in the rapid growth of several new member firms, including, most notably, the Daniels Linseed Company. Founded in 1902 by John Daniels, the company soon became Archer Daniels when George Archer joined it. Archer Daniels specialized in turning the seed of the flax plant—linseed—into oil. In its first decade, the company's production capacity tripled. It began expanding from Minne-apolis by opening operations in places like Buffalo, New York, and Edgewater, New Jersey. In 1923, it merged with Midland Linseed Products Company to form Archer Daniels Midland, the world's largest producer of linseed oil. In the decades that followed, ADM continued to expand under such leaders as Shreve Archer, Sam Mairs, and Dwayne Andreas. It moved its headquarters from Minneapolis to Decatur, Illinois, but it remained a major presence at the Minneapolis exchange. By the turn of the twenty-first century, it was one of the largest agricultural processors in the world and a leader in the ethanol industry, with more than twenty-five thousand employees.

Thanks to a merger with Midland Linseed Products Company, Archer Daniels Midland became the top producer of linseed oil in the world in 1923. Internationally, it remains one of the largest processors of soybeans, corn, wheat, and cocoa.

But the growth of the small grain market was just part of the story. The first three decades of the twentieth century also established the Chamber of Commerce as a major futures market, second in size only to the Chicago Board of Trade. Futures trading at the chamber had started slowly, but by 1900, when Chicago's war on the bucketshops unexpectedly boosted futures activity in Minneapolis, traders were beginning to predict great things. While the growth in futures trading was not as steady as some members assumed it would be, the trend was decidedly upward. In 1917, the amount of grain traded in the chamber's futures pits topped fourteen million bushels for the first time—almost all in wheat, the rest in oats. The following year, the chamber introduced futures trading in rye and barley. By the early 1920s, the number of chamber members dealing primarily in futures was approaching 10 percent.[125]

In many ways the chamber's success during this period mirrored that of the city in which it conducted its business. Minneapolis was now the nation's undisputed flour milling capital, and the success of the milling industry encouraged the development of a diversified economy. The city's banks, many of which had gained prominence by providing the millers with much-needed operating capital, helped make Minneapolis

George A. Archer, who also had been in the linseed oil business in Ohio, joined his friend John Daniels in the new Minneapolis venture. In 1905 the company name was changed to Archer Daniels Linseed Company.

Sam Mairs, born in Hastings, Minnesota, began work as a bookkeeper for Daniels and Archer in 1903 and worked his way to up to board chair of Archer Daniels Midland. In the early years, young Sam bicycled to work each day from St. Paul. He was devoted to Archer and Daniels and later recalled that working for them was like having two fathers.

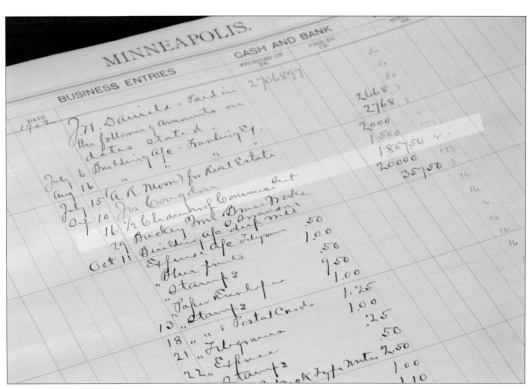

The fifth entry in the first Daniels Linseed Company ledger lists "1/2 Chamber of Commerce Seat" on September 16, 1902.

Shreve Archer served twenty-three years as president of ADM, from 1924 until 1947. Educated at St. Paul Academy and Yale, Archer was a third-generation lin-seed oil businessman. His grandfather, William Shreve Archer, was a pioneer in the field; his father, George Archer, was a founder of ADM.

"the financial center of the Northwest." A thriving packaging industry, the successor to the city's fading barrel-making trade, now produced millions of flour sacks every year.[126] Representatives of these and other associated businesses continued to appear on the chamber's membership roles.

As it turned out, the new building at Fourth and Fourth—while much larger than the old one—was not big enough to accommodate the chamber's growth spurt during these heady years. In 1909, the organization built a twelve-story annex (later known as the East Building), adjacent to the new

building, on Fourth Street. In 1928, the exchange razed the old structure at Fourth and Third and replaced it with a new one (later called the North Building)—seven stories tall and attached to the main building by two skyways on the fourth and fifth floors. As the 1930s approached, the chamber was conducting an incredible volume of business in a three-building complex that dwarfed nearly every other commercial enterprise in the city. The nation's stock and commodity markets were booming. The future "on 'change" had never looked brighter. But the chamber—along with the rest of the country—was in for a rude surprise.

A nocturnal view of the Minneapolis milling district on the icy Mississippi River.

# MORE THAN GRAIN
## Public Parks

**MINNEAPOLIS'S LONG-STANDING** reputation as a city of lakes and parks is due in no small part to the efforts of some of the city's most prominent grain men and millers, especially Charles Loring. A native New Englander, Loring arrived in Minneapolis in 1860 and quickly landed a job as manager of Dorilus Morrison's general store. From there Loring went on to establish himself as a successful merchant and flour miller. He was one of the founders of the Minneapolis Chamber of Commerce, a member of the Minneapolis City Council, and the first president of the city's Board of Park Commissioners. Loring believed that Minneapolis needed to preserve as many green spaces as possible, and he was instrumental in the development and expansion of the city's extensive park system. In his later years, he was often referred to as the "Father of the Minneapolis Parks."

But Loring actually was just one of many early Chamber of Commerce members who played active roles in the development of the city's park system. The extensive roster of grain men and millers who served on the Board of Park Commissioners included W. W. Eastman, Edmund J. Phelps, Frank G.

Peavey Fountain near Lake of the Isles, Minneapolis.

McMillan, William McMillan, William H. Bovey, B. B. Sheffield, A. C. Andrews, Arthur Fruen, Harold R. Ward, Harold Tearse, and Edward J. Grimes. Others made additional contributions that provided enjoyment to the people of Minneapolis for decades to come. William Hood Dunwoody donated much of the land surrounding Parade Stadium. Frank Peavey provided the funds for a fountain on Lake of the Isles Boulevard. And Frank T. Heffelfinger gave the city another fountain at Lyndale Park.

# TRADING PLACES

## *The Buildings*

From an architect's point of view, the Minneapolis Grain Exchange is a complex of three buildings spread across half a city block. The oldest structure—the Main Building, at the corner of Fourth Avenue and Fourth Street—was completed in 1903. The East Building, or Annex, was added six years later, in 1909. And the youngest of the trio—the North Building, at the corner of Fourth Avenue and Third Street—dates to 1928. All three are listed on the National Register of Historic Places. Yet despite their proximity and shared history, each structure is distinct with its own personality.

**The three-building Minneapolis Grain Exchange complex has graced the half-block lining the east side of Fourth Avenue between Third and Fourth streets since 1928. The North Building is visible to the left of the Main Building; the East Building is to the right of it.**

## The 1903 Main Building

The gray brick building that rose at the corner of Fourth and Fourth was a marvel of turn-of-the-century architecture. It was one of the first steel structures in Minneapolis. Before its construction, most of the city's big buildings—including the famous Guaranty Loan—were essentially piles of stone sitting on thick, heavy foundations. The Chamber of Commerce building was different. Its light, steel skeleton supported a ten-story masonry shell. It demonstrated the vertical advantages of steel-frame construction, and helped usher in the era of skyscrapers in Minneapolis.[127]

From the street, the building appeared to be a cube, but it was actually E-shaped. Its design, by architects Frederick Kees and Serenus Colburn, was difficult to describe. "It is not an 'adapted' or 'modified' anything," a reporter for the *Minneapolis Journal* observed upon the building's completion. "Messrs. Kees & Colburn give the style of the building no particular name."[128] But even if the architects refused to stylistically pigeonhole their new creation, their design was obviously "Sullivanesque." Louis Sullivan was one of the nation's most admired urban architects, and Kees and Colburn adopted many of his favorite stylistic techniques when designing the new Chamber of Commerce building.

The façades of Sullivan's buildings often recalled the three main elements of a classical column: base, shaft, and capital. The exterior of the Chamber of Commerce building reflected this Sullivan-inspired style. The first two floors of the façade served as the base. The top eight floors, connected visually

Frederick Kees (left) formed an architectural partnership with Serenus Colburn in 1899. The East Coast natives designed several significant buildings in the Twin Cities, including those for Brown and Bigelow printers, Advance Thresher-Emerson Newton Plow Company, and the Main Building of the Chamber of Commerce.

The Main Building's first two floors served as the "base" of its columnlike façade. Its vertical brick piers recall the shafts of classical columns.

Sullivanesque terra-cotta cartouches incorporate sheaves of wheat on the Main Building's first-level corner at Fourth Avenue and Fourth Street. The street names in bas relief are another decorative element.

by vertical brick piers, constituted the shaft. A boldly projecting cornice (removed during the 1930s) formed the capital.

But nowhere was the Chamber of Commerce building more obviously Sullivanesque than in its gray, terra-cotta ornamentation. The spandrels that separated the windows horizontally were masterworks of craftsmanship, featuring grain motifs such as wheat shafts and ears of corn. Additional stylized organic terra-cotta ornaments framed the doorways and topped the corners of the building.[129] "The ornamentation is very simple," the *Minneapolis Journal* noted. "It serves to relieve the plainness of the walls by the introduction of relief work

about the windows and doorways but the designs are so unobtrusive that they are not discernible at a great distance, but blend naturally with the general color effect."[130]

In a city awash in the "heavy classical drapery" of Victorian architecture, the Chamber of Commerce building seemed—despite its terra-cotta flourishes—remarkably understated.[131] Critics described the building as "plain" and "severely simple."[132] But, as the *Minneapolis Journal* observed, it was also a supreme example of form following function:

It should be remembered that the structure is designed as a home of that most prosaic of

**Terra-cotta capitals inspired by ancient Greek architecture grace the building's pilasters.**

**Terra-cotta panels of foliate, or organic, design decorate the areas between the upper floors.**

occupations, the buying and selling of bread-stuffs. Here the lighter styles of architecture would be out of place, and everything should suggest the substantial and solid character of the business housed. . . . Again, the superficial observer, who at first glance denominates the building as 'plain,' will find upon more careful study that its lines are beautiful, its proportions unassailable, its detail highly attractive—in fact that it is architecturally a constantly increasing pleasure. The more it is studied the more its dignity, fitness and congruity [impress] the intelligent critic.[133]

The gray-speckled Norman pressed brick that formed the exterior walls emphasized

the building's businesslike character and blended in well with the Chamber of Commerce's turn-of-the-century urban neighbors. "It should be called to mind that the chamber stands in the center of a great city and under the constant cloud of smoke issuing from the chimneys of the flour mills and other manufacturing establishments," the *Journal* reminded its readers. "The color of its walls is calculated to receive no injury but to be rather improved through the action of the elements."[134] Time would eventually prove the fallacy of that assessment.

The Fourth Avenue entrance opened into a commodious lobby with tiled floors and

Italian marble wainscoting. The first floor housed the office of the chamber's secretary and the boardroom. It also featured a post office, barbershop, newsstand, and cigar seller. An inconspicuous stairway led to the upper floors, but it was rarely used. To the right, a bank of five elevators, set within a curved wall, was in nearly constant use during business hours. "Only fast elevators are equal to the demands of the grain men," the *Journal* reported.[135]

While the building's exterior may have struck many as plain, its interior office spaces were often lavish. The companies that moved into the building upon its completion spared little expense on décor. "After being crowded for some years into small and rather unattractive quarters the members of the Chamber of Commerce have found it a pleasure to make their bright and sunny rooms in the new building as beautiful as possible," the *Journal* exclaimed.[136] The Washburn-Crosby Company (predecessor of General Mills), for example, occupied the entire second floor and boasted what may have been the most luxurious corporate headquarters in the city. Visitors stepped out of the elevator cabs onto a tiled mosaic floor incorporating a rendering of the company's Gold Medal brand. Directly in front of them stood a wall of white marble, glass, and decorative iron, behind which the company's department heads conducted business. The office of

The building's main entrance at the center of the Fourth Avenue façade.

Signal Lights

Blackboard

TRADING ROOM, CHAMBER OF COMMERCE, MINNEAPOLIS, MINN.

**TOP:** Architectural drawing of the Grain Exchange's trader room by architects Kees and Colburn, 1902.
**BOTTOM:** A postcard view of the completed and active trading floor, circa 1909.

President James Stroud Bell was a corporate sanctuary featuring mahogany furniture and matching woodwork.[137]

But nothing found in the corporate offices could compare with the magnificence of the building's centerpiece: the trading room. Located on the north end of the building's fourth floor, the trading room was an architectural homage to the grain trade. It measured 75-by-132 feet, and was more than twice as large as the exchange room in the old building. Its thirty-four-foot ceiling created a welcome sense of spaciousness, and its large windows let in the sunlight that

traders needed to best judge the quality of the grain they were buying and selling. The cash grain tables were clustered on the west side of the room. The wheat pit, pulpit, and quotation boards were on the far east end. A fifth-floor visitors gallery swept along the entire west side of the room, overlooking Fourth Avenue, and provided direct access between the new and old buildings via covered walkways connecting the fourth and fifth floors.

Determined that their new trading floor should be more than a cavernous open market, the chamber's directors hired one of

*Interior with Portrait of John Scott Bradstreet* by Steven A. Douglas Volk. A  much-admired furniture and art dealer, John Bradstreet was an arbiter of taste and style who oversaw the painting of the lunette murals for the trading room. Volk was the first director of the Minneapolis School of Art, which became the Minneapolis College of Art and Design.

the city's most respected interior decorators, John Bradstreet, to give the room the proper panáche. After consulting with a group of traders to determine which colors were most suitable for judging grain, Bradstreet and his team of painters bathed the exchange room in old ivory, pale gold, and contrasting patches of muted green. They stenciled representations of wheat, barley, and other grains onto ceiling panels and plastered beams. And they filled the lunettes of the seven gallery arches with murals of scenes from the history of milling. The four murals on the south end of the gallery depicted a German mill, an Icelandic mill, a Dutch windmill, and a camel-powered Egyptian mill. The three murals on the gallery's north side included renditions of two Native American women grinding wheat, an old English waterwheel mill, and the first mill at the Falls of St. Anthony. In a publication celebrating the completion of the new building, the chamber's directors extolled the trading room's aesthetic virtues. "It is both desirable and appropriate," they said, "that [the exchange room] should be a bright, beautiful place—not lacking in dignity but avoiding the somber and depressing

**Decorative metal plaques featuring stylized grain elevators and wheat fields adorn the Main Building's elevators, which were installed by the Otis Elevator Company of Chicago.**

effects too often found in places devoted wholly to commercial purposes."[138]

## The 1909 East Building

Built on a forty-foot parcel abutting the Main Building on Fourth Street, the twelve-story East Building of the Chamber of Commerce was, in some ways, a simple addition to the 1903 structure. The design, by the architectural firm Long, Lamoreaux, and Long, incorporated some of the Main Building's Sullivanesque features, especially the column-inspired base-shaft-capital motif. It also acknowledged many of the older building's horizontal lines. The East Building's windows, for example, aligned with those of its next-door neighbor, and the terra cotta separating the eleventh and twelfth floors recalled the Main Building's original cornice.

Still, even with its connections to the Main Building, the East Building stood on its own. Its two-story, terra-cotta "base" simulated hewn stone with receding joints— a formal treatment more Renaissance revival than Sullivanesque. The "shaft" portion of the façade was made of orange brick, which contrasted sharply with the lighter colors at street level. And the surfaces

The East Building, about a decade after its completion. Note on the right the exterior wall of the trading room's east side.

Chamber of Commerce Building, Minneapolis, Minn.

Fashionable strollers add ambience to this postcard view of the Chamber of Commerce with its new East Building addition at the right.

of its exterior walls were smooth and plain. Only inside did the lines between the East Building and the Main Building seem to blur. The hallways of the two structures connected seamlessly, making it difficult to determine where one building ended and the other began.[139]

## The 1928 North Building

Built on the site of the original 1884 Chamber of Commerce building at Fourth Avenue and Third Street, the North Building was remarkable mainly for the speed with which it was constructed. Demolition of the old building began during the first week of 1928. Construction began a month later. And tenants began moving into their offices in late July, just in time for the beginning of the 1928 crop-marketing season. The six-month construction period was widely reported to be "a new record of building in the northwest."[140]

The seven-story North Building was a workmanlike commercial structure, not nearly as architecturally ambitious as the two older Chamber of Commerce buildings. Designed by architect Edmund J. Prondzinski, the North Building appeared cubelike from the street. But it actually was L-shaped, with one wing extending 157 feet along Fourth Avenue and the other stretching 132 feet along Third Street. The design left room for a grass courtyard on the property's southeast corner. The North Building's first, second, and seventh floors were faced with limestone, while the exterior of the third, fourth, fifth, and sixth floors was made of tapestry brick. Covered walkways on the fourth and fifth floors connected the new North building to the Main Building.

## Additions and Renovations

Although the trading room in the Main Building was more than twice as large as the exchange room in the original 1884 Chamber of Commerce building, it was too small to accommodate the increase in trading activity that occurred during the first two decades of the twentieth century. Desperate for more space, the chamber's members finally voted in the summer of 1919 to expand the trading room, as well as the three floors of the building on which it rested.[141] The expansion project added approximately fifty feet to the east end of the trading floor and initiated a radical reconfiguration in which cash grain traders and futures traders essentially switched places. The

**The construction of the new North Building—on the site of the original 1884 Chamber of Commerce Building—was completed in six months. Chamber officials bragged that no commercial structure in the region had ever gone up so quickly.**

cash grain tables moved to the trading floor's expanded east end, where newly installed skylights provided even better light for judging grain. Two new futures pits were constructed on the west end of the floor, where the cash grain tables used to be. Western Union and the North American Telegraph Company moved their desks and equipment (including an elaborate vacuum-tube message system) to the center of the floor. And the chalkboards and telephone booths that previously had been located on the far east wall of the trading room shifted to the south wall—a move that resulted in the concealment of four of the room's seven distinctive lunette murals. The visitors gallery, which originally stretched along the entire west side of the room, was truncated so that only its northwest corner remained.[142]

The completion of the North Building in 1928 marked the beginning of a long period of architectural stagnation at the Chamber of Commerce. Financial hardships caused by

**The new 1928 seven-story North Building would itself be short on space within three decades.**

NORTH BUILDING MINNEAPOLIS GRAIN EXCHANGE   EDMUND J. PRONDZINSKI ARCHITECT

After decades of belt-tightening during the Great Depression and World War II, the Minneapolis Grain Exchange approved several midcentury improvements to the North Building. The greatest change came when three stories were added to make room for the Peavey Company's burgeoning business.

the Great Depression and World War II undoubtedly contributed to the lack of activity. But in the 1950s, the newly named Minneapolis Grain Exchange embarked on a series of building improvement projects. In 1955, three floors were added to the North Building to accommodate the Peavey Company's growing operations. That same year, the Grain Exchange installed a new central air-conditioning system and began buying all of its electricity from Northern States Power Company (instead of relying on its own generators in the Main Building's basement).[143] The trading room remained largely unchanged, although one of the two futures pits was removed.

The addition of the Main Building to the National Register of Historic Places in 1977 seemed to reinvigorate the exchange's appreciation of its buildings' historic and architectural significance. During the 1980s and 1990s, a series of exterior and interior improvements restored much of the

**Decades of soot and smog had turned the exterior of the Main Building nearly black. Acid washing would reveal the original glory of its gray façade.**

structures' fading grandeur. Acid washing removed decades of grime from the Main Building, revealing a façade that was actually gray, not black. The Main Building's lobby was expanded to create a more spacious and welcoming entrance. And the trading room was restored: walls and ceiling panels were repainted, floors were refinished, and murals—long covered with soot from gaslights and cigarettes—were cleaned. Some changes, such as the addition of an electronic quotation board in 1978 and a new futures pit (for sunflowers) in 1980, clashed with the exchange's newfound interest in historic preservation, but in the end, the restoration work was worth the effort. By 1995, all three buildings were listed on the National Register of Historic Places.

**Grain Exchange members spent several months in 1984 weaving in and out of scaffolding as workers restored the trading room to its former grandeur.**

**OPPOSITE PAGE:** Cash grain tables in silhouette. Because ringing phones couldn't be heard above the noise on the floor, lights were installed on each table to signal incoming calls.

**RIGHT:** The restoration of the main lobby's coffered ceiling proved to be an intricate and time-consuming job.

Construction of a new city parking ramp during the early 1990s afforded a rare east-side glimpse of the entire Minneapolis Grain Exchange complex.

# CHAPTER THREE

## 1930 — 1970
## Enduring Market Pressures

### Thursday, October 24, 1929

Sixteen-year-old Tony Owens was feeling pretty good about himself. He was but a senior in high school, yet had, over the previous two summers, already logged an impressive number of hours working for Logan and Bryan, a trading firm on the fourth floor of Minneapolis Chamber of Commerce's Main Building. He did whatever the company needed him to do. He monitored prices on the New York Stock Exchange and the Chicago Board of Trade. He kept the firm's boards up to date. And when orders came in, he ran the information over to the company's traders in the futures pit. He was a young kid in the thick of the action. What could be better?[144]

Despite his age, Owens already had absorbed important lessons at Logan and Bryan. He knew, for example, how important it was in the business world to project a professional image. As an up-and-comer with a bright future (including thirty years at the Pillsbury Company), he wanted to make sure he looked good. Good suit. Good hat. Good shoes. That's why, on this particular Thursday morning, he went out of his way to stop by the Standard Clothing Company at the corner of Sixth and Nicollet. He needed new footwear.

Owens walked out of Standard Clothing in a shiny pair of six-dollar wingtips and headed for the Chamber of Commerce, just a few blocks away. He planned to make an appearance in his new shoes, say hello to a few friends, and check on the market. He knew that trading had been volatile lately, but he certainly wasn't expecting the dire news he was about to hear.

**Tony Owens in 2005 at age ninety-two. Owens's career in the Minneapolis grain trade spanned nearly five decades. During the 1930s he worked with the grain commission firm Johnson, Case, and Hanson. He joined Pillsbury in 1946 and stayed with the company until his retirement nearly thirty years later. Owens also served as president of the Minneapolis Grain Exchange from 1971 to 1972.**

When Owens stepped out of the elevator and on to the fourth floor of the chamber, he could tell something was wrong. "Honestly," he recalled years later, "you never saw so many distraught people." Prices were free-falling on the New York Stock Exchange, and the stock tickers were finding it impossible to keep up with the frenzied trading volume. Investors were selling blind. Panic was setting in. And it wasn't just New York. As news from the stock market spread, other markets, including the Minneapolis Chamber of Commerce, succumbed to fear. With a quick look at the board,

Owens saw that wheat prices had already dropped twelve cents a bushel. It was, as the *Minneapolis Tribune* reported the next day, the chamber's "wildest morning since the war days":

The pit was a maelstrom of gesticulating traders during that flurry. Prices fell as much as four cents without a trade. Drops of two or three cents were common. The pace was too fast to execute stop losses and traders fell from two to three cents behind. Excitement and uproar of trading in the pit attracted dealers from the cash wheat floor

**Futures pit, 1933. Prices were low, but trading was often brisk during the worst years of the Great Depression.**

and hundreds of spectators filled the gallery as news of the break in the market was bruited about.[145]

Prices in the wheat pit rebounded toward the end of the trading session, and the rally continued into the next week. But the wheat market was an anomaly. Prices were rising in response to a new federal price support program that had just taken effect. The stock market—not the grain market—was the more accurate long-term economic indicator. "Black Thursday," which had taken so many stock traders by surprise, was followed a few days later by "Black Monday" (when prices on the New York Stock Exchange experienced a record loss of about 13 percent) and "Black Tuesday" (when the market dropped about 12 percent). Investors were now genuinely frightened. No one knew it yet, but the economic boom of the 1920s was over.

As the months passed and the stock market crash gave way to a broad-based economic depression, the grain trade and its allied industries followed suit. After receiving a record 126 million bushels of wheat in 1928, the Minneapolis market spiraled downward. Receipts dropped to 101 million bushels in 1929, and then remained below 100 million over the next decade. (The low point would come in 1934, when receipts failed to top forty-three million

bushels.) The trading of wheat futures, which reached record levels in 1929, suffered a similar decline.[146]

At the same time, the farmers who grew the grain on which the business of the Chamber of Commerce depended were becoming increasingly desperate. Between 1929 and 1932, the price of wheat in Minnesota plummeted from one dollar and twenty-one cents a bushel to forty-nine cents, while the price of a bushel of corn went from seventy-eight cents to twenty-one cents. As prices dropped, Minnesota farmers watched their incomes shrink by more than 75 percent.[147] Thousands lost their farms to foreclosure. In the years that followed, severe drought—especially in the Dakotas and far western Minnesota—would make matters worse.

**The years leading up to World War II were especially difficult for the farmers of the Upper Midwest. Prices collapsed after World War I and fell to historic lows during the Great Depression.**

Minneapolis's flour milling industry, facing a one-two punch of economic depression and new Great Lakes shipping rates that favored East Coast millers, fell on especially hard times. In 1930, Buffalo passed Minneapolis to become the nation's top flour-producing city. The following year, seven mills in the flour district surrounding St. Anthony Falls were demolished. The turbines from the old mills were refurbished for use in the generation of electricity.[148]

**General Mills' riverside milling complex. The company was created in 1928, when the Washburn-Crosby Company—under the leadership of president James Ford Bell—merged with several other regional millers. General Mills entered the packaged-foods business with the introduction of several products, including Wheaties and Kix breakfast cereals. After World War II, the company entered a period of rapid transformation. It began by expanding its packaged-food line with products such as Betty Crocker cake mixes. Then, in the 1960s, it closed more than half of its flour mills and moved into new lines of business, including toys, restaurants, and retail. In 2001, it acquired its longtime rival, the Pillsbury Company, to establish one of the world's largest food companies.**

The depression years of the 1930s and the three decades that followed would redefine Minneapolis's grain trade. Government intervention would help keep the market afloat during times of economic desperation, then serve as a drag on trading as the economy recovered. The cooperative movement, which had lost its momentum during the 1920s, would reassert itself during the Great Depression and ultimately shift the balance of power among grain traders. Even the Minneapolis Chamber of Commerce itself, which had operated under the same, venerable moniker for more than half a century, would rename itself. Change was afoot in the grain trade of the Upper Midwest, and met with varying degrees of unhappiness.

## Prelude to Crisis

The "Roaring Twenties," that swinging decade of short skirts, jazz music, and bathtub gin, had been anything but fun and carefree for the grain producers of the Upper Midwest. The high commodity prices of the World War I years had vanished in the face of large, post-war surpluses. Farmers kept hoping that they would soon start sharing in the prosperity that much of 1920s America was enjoying, but their hopes were continuously dashed. U.S. Senator Gerald P. Nye of North Dakota summarized the farmers' plight during a speech in the spring of 1929:

LEFT: *Mills on the Mississippi* by Erle Loran.
BELOW: *Tierney Mills* by Dewey Albinson.

The Eagle Roller Mill, owned by the Silverson family of New Ulm, was one of Minnesota's largest flour mills outside the Twin Cities. It was purchased in the early 1950s by International Milling Company, which later became International Multifoods.

The story of American agriculture during recent years is a story of extreme hardship, blasted dreams and hopes, beautifully maintained homesteads falling into decay, the growth of tenancy, foreclosures, bankruptcies, home abandonments, broken family ties, extreme worry and consequent paths leading to insane asylums and the creation of a population of wretchedness, hopelessness, and a distrustfulness where once there existed contentment and happy forward-looking spirit.[149]

By the late 1920s, farmers were looking for help wherever they could get it, and the best prospects for relief seemed to come from two places: the government and the moribund cooperative movement. The Republican administrations of Calvin Coolidge and Herbert Hoover were philosophically opposed to government intervention and preferred to let market forces iron out the problems facing the nation's agricultural economy. But by 1929, the situation on the nation's farms had gotten so bad that even Hoover was forced to admit that the federal government might have a role to play in stabilizing the markets. Likewise, the farmers' cooperative movement, which had stalled in the Midwest with the demise of the Equity Cooperative Exchange, had roused itself out of its slumber in response to the farmers' plight.

Almost from the beginning, the government's increased involvement in the grain trade intersected regularly with the reemergence of the cooperatives.

The federal government's first major effort to influence grain prices got under way in the spring of 1929, when Hoover signed the Agricultural Marketing Act into law. The legislation established the Federal Farm Board, an agency that loaned cooperative organizations millions of dollars in an effort to prop up sagging commodity prices. The Farm Board was popular among grain growers in the Upper Midwest, but officials at the Minneapolis Chamber of Commerce considered it a serious threat to the established grain trade. In an address to Minneapolis business leaders, the chamber's secretary and chief spokesman, John McHugh, called the Agricultural Marketing Act "the most socialistic piece of legislation ever enacted by Congress":

The far-reaching consequences of this act are hard to overestimate. For the moment the act threatens the existence of all those engaged in the distribution of all kinds of farm produce.

It is proposed that all of these individuals shall be driven out of business and their places taken by farmer-owned and operated agencies. A fund of $500,000,000 is provided to accomplish this result. The grain and produce dealers of this country are taxed among others, to supply this fund, the use of which is intended to bring about their elimination.[150]

McHugh claimed that the Farm Board's support of cooperative marketing would result in a government-run monopoly capable of dictating the price of wheat and other commodities. At the same time, he insisted that he and the Chamber of Commerce had "no quarrel whatever with the co-operative movement."

McHugh's claim that the chamber supported the concept of cooperative marketing struck the editors of the pro-coop newspaper, the *Farmers Union Herald,* as absurd. "Does not everybody know that the Minneapolis Chamber of Commerce, and Mr. McHugh in particular, have for years put every possible obstruction in the way of co-operatives?" they asked. The *Herald* reminded its readers of the chamber's long and successful fight to deny membership to the Equity Cooperative Exchange and tried to bolster its case against the chamber by using McHugh's own (reputed) words against him. "The Chamber of Commerce is against any kind of Co-operation that has anything to do with grain," the *Herald*'s editors wrote, "because, as Mr. McHugh once was alleged to have remarked,

'when the Co-ops come in at the front door of the Chamber of Commerce, the private commission men will go out the back door.'"

McHugh's concerns about a resurgent cooperative movement were well founded. Although the Equity Cooperative Exchange had essentially dissolved in the mid-1920s, its successor organization, the Farmers Union Terminal Association, was gathering strength. FUTA's general manager, M. W. ("Bill") Thatcher, was a determined organizer who rallied farmers with a consistent message of hope and defiance. "This is a fight," he told a group of North Dakota farmers in one of his typical crowd-pleasing speeches. "Hoofs and bushels are your bullets. Send

M. W. ("Bill") Thatcher, general manager of the Farmers Union Terminal Association and its successor organization, the Farmers Union Grain Terminal Association. Many grain traders admired Thatcher's skills as an organizer and orator while vehemently opposing his efforts to strengthen the cooperative movement at the expense of traditional grain merchants.

your hoofs and bushels to your own organization [the FUTA] and they will be bullets to fight for you. Give your hoofs and your bushels to your enemies [at the Minneapolis Chamber of Commerce] and they will come back to you in the form of bullets to blow your brains out."[151] Many farmers, buckling under persistently depressed crop prices, responded enthusiastically to Thatcher's fiery

**The Grain Exchange's early public relations efforts included an elaborate slide presentation explaining the grain trade in easy-to-follow terms.**

oratory. They were even more impressed when, in late 1929, Thatcher announced that the FUTA had secured more than a million dollars in loans from the Federal Farm Board.[152]

The FUTA and the Farm Board both posed potential threats to the established grain trade of the Upper Midwest, and the leaders of the Minneapolis Chamber of Commerce were determined to neutralize those threats if possible. When it became clear in early 1929 that Congress

intended to pass the Agricultural Marketing Act, the chamber's members agreed to assess themselves one hundred dollars a year to finance a special "educational campaign." In a letter summarizing the need for such a campaign, the chair of the chamber's public relations committee, C. B. Rogers, claimed that previous efforts to advance the chamber's interests had failed. The time had come, he wrote, for the chamber "to attack its problems offensively, rather than defensively":

The extremely technical character of the grain business and the difficulties of the average layman in understanding the complex workings of its machinery make it particularly susceptible to misrepresentation, and because the returns to the agricultural districts are so essentially the foundation of the degree of prosperity enjoyed, the producer is prone to attribute low prices to the marketing machinery which he does not understand, rather than to economic conditions, a situation with which the agitator readily avails himself. The Chamber of Commerce should make a definite effort to convince our agricultural communities, both farmers and business men, that the service rendered by the present established trade answers their requirements from every standpoint better and more cheaply than any other plan of marketing yet conceived.[153]

In the 1940s, the Grain Exchange published a guide to the grain trade called *Grain: From Farm to Market.* It featured a collection of exceptionally well-composed photographs taken at various stages in the grain marketing process.

TOP LEFT: "Off to the terminal market to compete with other grains from other points, it is important that grain be handled by experienced and able representatives."

TOP RIGHT: "To earn the farmer's business, country elevator operators must be expert in judging grains, accurate in testing and grading."

BOTTOM LEFT: "After purchase, car is moved to the terminal elevator, quickly unloaded, with the grain elevated and distributed to bins, according to grade and type."

BOTTOM RIGHT: "Official state sampler breaks the seal and opens car preparatory to sampling and inspection."

During the 1950s, the Grain Exchange beefed up its public relations efforts in an attempt to fend off criticism from farmers and other supporters of the increasingly powerful cooperative movement. One of its most creative efforts was a comic book called The *Story of Grain: From Farm to You.* The sixteen-page publication followed the adventures of a family of wheat growers—farmer Bob and his children, Jim, Bobby, and Betty—on a mission to decipher the impenetrable workings of the grain trade. After receiving a lesson in pricing from their kindly country elevator operator, Bob, Jim, Bobby, and Betty head to the big city for a date with Mr. Kaiser, the most knowledgeable commission man at the Minneapolis Grain Exchange.

WHAT IS A WEATHER MAP FOR, JIM?

ANY BUYER OR SELLER OF GRAIN IS INTERESTED IN THE RAINFALL AND TEMPERATURES IN OUR FARMING AREAS. DON'T FORGET THAT WHAT HAPPENS TO THE GROWING CROP IS A BIG SUPPLY AND DEMAND FACTOR.

It's not clear how many of the comic books were produced or where they were distributed, but the *Minneapolis Tribune* reported in April 1960 that the Minneapolis Grain Exchange handed out at least thirty thousand pieces of literature each year to educators and others.

HERE'S AN EXAMPLE THAT WILL HELP EXPLAIN HOW SUPPLY AND DEMAND FACTORS AS INTERPRETED BY ALL WHO BUY AND SELL GRAIN, ACTUALLY AFFECT PRICES.

AN IMPORTANT THING TO REMEMBER IS THAT THE GRAIN EXCHANGE HAS NOTHING TO DO WITH SETTING PRICES. PEOPLES' OPINIONS OF SUPPLY AND DEMAND ARE REFLECTED IN THE PRICES THEY PAY, WHICH PRICES ARE THEN MADE PUBLIC BY THE EXCHANGE.

PRICE

DOWN — UP

SUPPLY
RAINFALL
DROUGHT
FROST
HAIL
INSECT DAMAGE
STORAGE
ETC.

DEMAND
WAGES AND PAYROLLS
COSTS OF COMPETING FOODS
VALUE OF MONEY
TARIFFS AND QUOTAS
LIVESTOCK NUMBERS
ETC.

THE OPEN MARKET

WHO ARE ALL THOSE MEN IN THE PIT AND WHY ARE THEY WAVING THEIR ARMS AND SHOUTING?

THOSE ARE THE MEMBERS WHO ARE COMPETING WITH EACH OTHER IN THE BUYING AND SELLING OF GRAIN....

.... THE HAND SIGNALS INDICATE BIDS AND OFFERS. THE SHOUTING IS BECAUSE OF OUR "OPEN OUTCRY" RULE THAT ALL BIDS ARE PUBLICLY ANNOUNCED.

AND THOSE PEOPLE WRITING ON THE BLACKBOARDS ARE RECORDING PRICES OF SALES IN THE FUTURES MARKET, NOT ONLY THIS MARKET BUT ALSO PRICES RECEIVED ON THOSE TICKERS FROM OTHER MARKETS.

With the establishment of the "educational fund," the chamber began promoting its interests more actively through traditional avenues, such as newspapers and magazines. But it also put special emphasis on "direct contact"—sending speakers to farmers' meetings, agricultural schools, fairs, "or wherever farmers or business men get together to talk over their problems."[154] And as it was, farmers and businessmen had plenty of problems to talk about.

The Federal Farm Board, which John McHugh had predicted might destroy the established grain trade, turned out to be relatively toothless. As the months went by, the board struggled to cope with the nation's deepening economic crisis. In late 1930, the board authorized a subsidiary, the Grain Stabilization Corporation, to begin buying wheat futures in an effort to prop up prices. For a while, the GSC's buying program seemed to work. Prices for May wheat hovered above seventy-eight cents a bushel for several months, providing some much-needed encouragement for farmers and traders alike. But trouble was brewing. By the end of May, the GSC had accumulated more than 200 million bushels of surplus wheat and had virtually drained its coffers. With no money to spend and a huge surplus waiting to be disposed of, the GSC dropped out of the market. Prices plummeted. In a matter of

weeks, the contract for July wheat dropped to a record low of forty-eight cents. And that was just the beginning. By the summer of 1932, all wheat futures were trading below fifty cents for the first time in history. Hoover's agriculture policies had failed to stop the hemorrhaging on the farms and in the markets. The following November, Franklin D. Roosevelt was elected president in a landslide.[155]

## New Dealings

Word on the street was that the reliably Republican grain traders of the Minneapolis Chamber of Commerce had, in an act of defiance spurred by the policies of the Farm Board, abandoned Herbert Hoover and backed Franklin Roosevelt in the presidential election of 1932.[156] But if the chamber's members thought Roosevelt would curtail the federal government's involvement in the grain trade, they soon learned otherwise. In May 1933, Roosevelt signed into law the Agricultural Adjustment Act. Among other things, the AAA introduced a concept that would guide federal agricultural policies for years to come: parity.

The rationale behind the parity concept was simple: The prices that farmers received for their goods recently had fallen much faster than the prices for industrial and consumer goods; therefore, something had to be done to help farmers make up the difference. The numbers were, in fact, sobering. In the three-year period from August 1929 to August 1932, farm commodity prices dropped 65 percent while nonagricultural wholesale prices declined 24 percent.[157] With parity, the government instituted price supports to ensure that the ratio between farmers' incomes and expenditures would be similar to those experienced in the flush years leading to World War I. "It means," said FUTA's M. W. ("Bill") Thatcher, "[that] it will take [a farmer] no more bushels of wheat to buy his machinery, clothes, food, and other things he needs and uses than it took during the period 1909–1914, a five-year span which was a happy one for farmers."[158] Although the U.S. Supreme Court eventually ruled the AAA unconstitutional, the parity concept was rewritten into new legislation that guided U.S. agricultural policy for years to come.[159]

Government intervention in the grain trade continued to expand with the passage of the Commodity Exchange Act of 1936. The new law created the Commodity Exchange Commission, which had the power to enforce a series of new regulations on commodities futures trading.

Successful baseball teams sponsored by the Minneapolis Chamber of Commerce during the early decades of the twentieth century were a source of company pride. The 1937 Chamber of Commerce team won the city's Federal Division with a 7–3 record. From left: Joe Fudali, Gary Reme, Gale Freer, Jerry Katz, John Long, John O'Hara, George Dolz, Henry Coulombe, Robert Dunn, Lee Canterbury, Carroll Lund, and John Fudali.

Included in the regulations was a stipulation that prohibited market exchanges from excluding cooperatives from membership without a proper hearing. Cooperative organizations like the FUTA supported the measure. Grain exchanges, including the Minneapolis Chamber of Commerce, did not.

The cooperative movement received a further boost when the federal government's Farm Credit Administration approved a million-dollar loan to establish the Farmers Union Grain Terminal Association. The GTA was essentially the successor to FUTA, and Thatcher, FUTA's general manager, retained his position with the new organization. Under Thatcher's guidance, the GTA planned to handle "the marketing, manufacturing, selling, harvesting, drying, processing, grading, storing, handling or utilization of grain and grain products received from its members." The GTA began operating in June 1938. Eighteen months later it was the nation's largest grain marketing cooperative.[160]

Roosevelt's New Deal was transforming the grain trade. Price supports aimed at maintaining parity were overriding market forces. Regulations enforced by the Commodity Exchange Commission were restricting the futures markets. And government support for cooperative marketing organizations like the GTA was upsetting the long-established competitive balance on the trading floors in Minneapolis and elsewhere. Officials at the Minneapolis Chamber of Commerce monitored these developments with growing concern. As the 1930s gave way to the 1940s, chamber officials harked back to C. B. Rogers's advice of a decade earlier: that the chamber needed "to attack its problems offensively, rather than defensively." The time had come to combat what they considered serious threats to the future of the grain trade. They began to confront perceived threats—sometimes head on, but more often by relying on surrogates who supported the chamber.

This cartoon from the March 1940 edition of the *Farmers Union Herald* suggested that Congressman Oscar Youngdahl of Minnesota would fail in his efforts to discredit the GTA and its leader, M. W. ("Bill") Thatcher.

Cooperatives remained a major concern of the chamber, and they soon came under attack. In early 1940, U.S. Representative Oscar Youngdahl of Minnesota's Fifth Congressional District delivered a speech on the House floor in which he accused the GTA and its leader, Thatcher, of colluding with the Roosevelt administration to advance policies that actually hurt farmers. "I believe the time has come," Youngdahl proclaimed, "when the farmers themselves should put a stop to these self-styled representatives dashing into Washington, mixing a little medicine with the department heads, making a fleeting statement for the record, and then running back home to draw fancy salaries."[161]

Youngdahl did not claim to speak for the Chamber of Commerce, but his comments were widely considered reflective of the chamber's position. "It is a historic fact that whoever represents this [the Fifth] district, and of whatever party, also represents the Chamber of Commerce," the *Farmers Union Herald* proclaimed. "Naturally, any fostering of co-operatives by any governmental agency is, in the eyes of the Minneapolis Chamber of Commerce, bad. And what the Minneapolis Chamber of Commerce pronounces bad, likewise does its congressman."[162] Congressman Usher Burdick of North Dakota agreed with the *Herald*'s analysis. In his speech on

the House floor, Burdick claimed that Youngdahl's criticism of the GTA was just the latest salvo in the Chamber of Commerce's long campaign against the cooperatives:

The organized grain trade of Minneapolis is still at work. They see a chance to weaken the confidence of the farmers of the Northwest in the Farmers Union, and true to form they attack our leaders. This course is nothing new—they have been at it for 40 years. . . . Instead of weakening the farmers' movement, their attack upon its leaders will revive the same old fighting spirit that has held the Minneapolis Chamber of Commerce at bay for a quarter of a century— and more—it will revive the fight to mop up the whole nefarious business of grain gambling indulged in by the "grain trade." This fight will not end until the farmers of America have a just and open market, ridded of the rats that have gnawed holes in the farmers' grain bin for the last 50 years.[163]

Hostilities between the chamber and the cooperatives—largely dormant since the demise of the Equity Cooperative Exchange in the 1920s— were reawakening. But the cooperative movement was not the only potential threat demanding the chamber's attention. The trend toward greater government intervention in the grain trade was

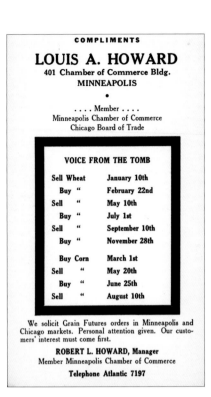

Louis A. Howard ran a successful futures brokerage business in Minneapolis for decades. Howard presented his clients with "Voice from the Tomb" cards, which became an early, and often accurate, predictor of market direction and seasonal tendencies in agricultural commodities.

Louis Howard, along with his son, Robert, are shown filling orders in the spring wheat pit in the late 1940s. Lou's son Adrian is also pictured. "Ade" became a successful independent "local," or pit trader, as well. Circled from left: Robert Howard, Ade Howard, and Louis Howard.

beginning to accelerate, and a new global war was responsible.

## War and Wheat

In the weeks and months that followed the United States' entry into World War II in December 1941, the federal government moved quickly to head off wartime inflation. It instituted price controls on a wide variety of goods and commodities, including grain. Most members of the Minneapolis Chamber of Commerce opposed price controls—even during wartime—and some of them (Cargill executives Ed Grimes and Julius Hendel were among the most prominent) lobbied the Roosevelt administration to let the

free market do its magic. They were unsuccessful.[164] When the newly created Office of Price Administration clamped down on wheat and flour prices in October 1942, Hendel composed an open letter expressing the frustration he shared with many of his trading colleagues:

The wheat marketing machinery in the United States is a product of many years of evolution, and is perfected to such a degree that the wheat price registered by it is extremely sensitive to influences extremely minute and widespread in nature.

Any attempt to establish a price ceiling, even temporary, by any

person or persons who are not conversant with, or expert in the workings of the grain marketing machinery might cause severe economic repercussions.[165]

Chamber officials were particularly worried that price ceilings on wheat would strangle futures trading by reducing fluctuations in the market. They figured if prices were capped at a certain level, traders would have little incentive to hedge. As it turned out, they were right. With price ceilings in place, futures trading at the Chamber of Commerce declined steadily throughout the war years. The linen-coated traders who populated the chamber's octagonal futures pit had little to do. The low point came in 1946, when wartime price ceilings were still in effect. Only thirty-two million bushels were traded for future delivery that year.[166]

Over on the other side of the trading floor, however, the market had never looked better. Bumper crops and wartime demand for foodstuffs coupled to push trading in the cash market to unheard-of levels. In 1943, three records were shattered in Minneapolis: wheat receipts topped 208 million bushels; barley receipts exceeded seventy-eight million; and flax receipts approached twenty-seven million. Two years later, corn and oats set records of their own.[167] Cash grain was king. Minneapolis headed into the postwar

**Futures pit, 1947. Government intervention in the grain markets helped keep trading volume low for more than two decades.**

**Cash grain tables, 1947. Trading on the cash grain side remained robust during the postwar years, even as trading on the futures side languished.**

years as the world's largest cash grain market and as the nation's foremost market of spring wheat, barley, rye, and flax.[168] While government price controls apparently had sent the futures market into a tailspin, they had done nothing to inhibit trading on the cash side.

Government intervention remained a top concern of Chamber of Commerce officials throughout the war years, but it was not the only potential threat keeping grain traders awake at night. The cooperative movement—specifically, the Grain Terminal Association—was continuing to gather strength. The GTA had started in 1938 with just thirty thousand dollars of operating capital. Now it was a multimillion-dollar concern. By the end of 1942, it was doing business with more than three hundred country elevators and was handling grain at eight terminal elevators throughout the Upper Midwest.[169] In May 1943, the GTA used some of its accumulated assets to purchase two of the Minneapolis grain trade's most venerable firms: the fifty-seven-year-old St. Anthony and Dakota Elevator Company and the thirty-five-year-old Brown Grain Company of Minneapolis. The acquisition of Brown was the big eye-opener. Brown owned several memberships in the Minneapolis Chamber of Commerce. Now those memberships belonged to the GTA. For the

first time, the chamber counted a cooperative among its members.

Minneapolis's grain men weren't quite sure what to make of the cooperative that was operating in their midst. The *Northwestern Miller* reported that the GTA had paid around $2.5 million for Brown, even though most of the company's traders already had defected with their clients to competing firms. Why, then, the *Miller* asked, were the GTA and Thatcher willing to pay such a "fancy price" for a crippled company? The chamber memberships were nice, but the GTA probably could have found other ways to force its way onto the Minneapolis trading floor. The grain traders at the chamber could come up with only one answer that made sense. Thatcher, they concluded, was determined to make the GTA "so large that the food boys in Washington will just have to listen to him."[170]

The GTA was growing quickly—too quickly, as far as many longtime traders were concerned. Leaders of the cooperative movement had made it clear for years that they wanted to reinvent the grain trade so that the "middlemen" at exchanges like the Minneapolis Chamber of Commerce were cut out of the process. If they succeeded, the chamber itself might cease to exist. The grain traders in Minneapolis did not intend to let that happen. The

GTA might now be a member of the Chamber of Commerce, but it was still the enemy.

As World War II came to a close, the chamber and its supporters initiated two separate but related efforts to undermine the GTA's effectiveness. One concentrated on the way the GTA conducted its business in the grain markets; the other challenged what many traders considered the federal government's preferential treatment of cooperatives. Both efforts would drag out into the postwar years. The *Northwestern Miller,* for one, believed that the attempts to rein in the GTA were necessary because the grain trade was facing a moment of decision:

The other day we asked a large terminal elevator operator what he proposed to do with his business if, with futures markets dried up and government agencies established in virtual control of grain marketing, it no longer could be operated save at ruinous loss. His reply was prompt— "quit." We then asked what would he and other terminal elevator operators do with their owned or leased elevators. His reply was equally prompt—"sell them or let their owners lease them to the co-ops."[171]

## The Battle Over Consignments

A new year's resolution put into effect by the Minneapolis Chamber of Commerce in 1948 was to change its name. The decision was made by the region's premier grain market largely because of the mail sent by mistake for years to the building at Fourth and Fourth. Most people outside the grain trade assumed that the chamber performed promotional functions for the city—duties that belonged to another organization, the Minneapolis Civic and Commerce Association. "Every day we receive a basket of mail from people wanting information on civic activities or commercial background," said the chamber's exasperated secretary, E. C. Hillweg. "We use a special messenger to carry letters to the proper office." By the fall of 1946, chamber members had had enough. They voted 268 to five to change the organization's name to the Minneapolis Grain Exchange. The switch took effect on January 1, 1948.[172]

Officials at the newly named Grain Exchange were hoping the new year would bring even more good news. A few months earlier, they had filed a lawsuit in U.S. District Court that, if successful, had the potential to destroy the GTA. At issue was the way that the GTA handled grain consigned to it by its members. The GTA, like many other cooperatives, sometimes purchased consigned grain when it believed prices were too low. It then tried to sell that grain

at a higher price in some distant market in hopes of passing along the profits to its members. The buying and selling of consigned grain was a well-established practice of cooperatives around the country, as well as one of their central functions.

The Minneapolis Grain Exchange, however, had rules prohibiting member firms from buying grain consigned to them. The lawsuit it filed in federal court sought to force the GTA to obey those rules. "This is not an attack on the Farmers Union Grain Terminal Association," insisted the Grain Exchange's lead attorney, Leavitt Barker. "It merely recognizes the fact that there is a difference of opinion regarding the right and propriety of exempting cooperatives from the provisions of the rule of the exchange which prohibits any member from serving both as principal and agent in the marketing of grain."[173]

Barker's claims that the Grain Exchange meant no harm to its "outstanding cooperative member" rang hollow. The effort to halt the GTA's practice of buying consigned grain had actually begun four years earlier, when five members of what was then the Minneapolis Chamber of Commerce filed a complaint against the GTA with the Minnesota Railroad and Warehouse Commission. The five men did not claim to represent the chamber, but they did, in the words of the *Willmar Tribune,* "speak as though their mission had the approval and support of many grain merchants operating on the Minneapolis grain exchange."[174] The case against the GTA eventually made its way to the Minnesota Supreme Court, which ultimately decided that the coop had done nothing wrong. With that ruling, it seemed the case was closed. But then the Grain Exchange jumped into the fray with its federal lawsuit. It was the first time that the exchange had openly taken a position in the case, insisting that it was just trying to settle the question "for the benefit both of the exchange and of the Farmers Union Grain Terminal Association." In a scathing editorial, the *St. Paul Pioneer Press* scoffed at the notion that the Grain Exchange was acting altruistically:

The true nature of this suit seems clear to us. Farmers and consumers should not be fooled by its look of innocence, nor by legal hairsplitting in descriptions of it. If this suit should bring forth a federal decision narrowly defining the functions of a grain co-op, then no consumer or producer cooperative in the land could feel safe from attack. And in these times of wild speculation and rocketing prices, the public could not feel safe from the monopolistic effects of such a decision. Instead of being lulled to sleep by words, this is a time for farmers and consumers to wake up, look realities in the face, and fight for rights that can be infringed or lost only with peril to agriculture and the public.[175]

On January 2, 1948, federal judge Gunnar Nordbye dismissed the lawsuit against the GTA. The Minneapolis grain trade's first wartime attempt to undermine the cooperative movement had failed. Now it would concentrate its efforts on a second strategy—one that, like the struggle over the GTA's handling of consigned grain, had its roots in the war years.

## Tax the Coops!

Few things irritated longtime grain traders more than the federal government's tax policies toward cooperatives. Cooperatives were not required to pay federal taxes on their net earnings, because, in theory, they did not retain those earnings for themselves. Instead, it was assumed that they distributed their "savings" to their members in the form of patronage dividends. Many established grain traders considered this reasoning specious. As they saw it, the cooperatives' earnings were not "savings" at all; they were profits, pure and simple. And if private grain companies had to pay taxes on their profits, cooperatives should have to pay too.

In 1942, a group of grain men, led by longtime Minneapolis Chamber of Commerce member Ben McCabe, formed the National Tax Equality Association. The NTEA's primary goal was to reduce or eliminate "the growing favoritism shown to co-operatives by the federal government in regard to subsidies, taxation and propaganda, the cost of which is borne largely by the private business concerns which must compete with the co-operatives."[176] In an article written for the *Northwestern Miller*, McCabe argued that "equality of taxation" was necessary to protect the American free enterprise system:

Paying their fair share of taxes will not hurt the co-operatives. Other businesses have paid taxes for years and years and they have still managed to grow in a modest way. Under good management the co-operatives can do exactly as well.

We are asking only that the co-operatives accept their responsibility to members of the American body politic that they pay their taxes and abide by the rules of free competition under which our country has grown great.[177]

The NTEA had no formal affiliation with the Minneapolis Chamber of Commerce, but there was little doubt that it enjoyed the support of many chamber members. A subsequent congressional investigation found that representatives of the Peavey Company, Cargill, the Russell-Miller Milling Company, and

As president of the National Tax Equality Association, Ben McCabe led the push to make cooperatives pay federal taxes on their net earnings.

Ben McCabe's McCabe Brothers Company—all member firms of the chamber—made financial contributions to the NTEA.[178] Supporters of the cooperative movement were convinced that the established grain trade in Minneapolis and other markets was behind the "tax fairness" movement. "The co-ops have recognized that the so-called 'tax the co-ops' campaign is a smoke screen for a broader and more bitter fight," the *Farmers Union Herald* reported. The outcome, it predicted, "would determine whether free enterprise could be shackled to preserve a prewar status quo, or whether co-ops will have the right to grow and expand in a free economy."[179]

For a while it appeared that the NTEA's campaign to force cooperatives to pay taxes on their earnings might succeed. In 1944, a new law took effect, requiring cooperatives to file annual financial statements with the federal government. Coops were worried. They feared that the new financial disclosure rules might lead to the imposition of taxes on their earnings, and the *Northwestern Miller* agreed that their concern "was not wholly unfounded."[180] Later that year, M. W. Thatcher warned GTA members that cooperatives still faced "tremendous opposition" and that "many difficult battles" lie ahead. He was right. In the years immediately following the war, the NTEA and its allies stepped up

their campaign. In late 1947, for example, a North Dakota group affiliated with the NTEA inundated the state with fifty-two thousand leaflets that raised questions about the legality of cooperative patronage dividends.[181]

But as time went by, the NTEA's campaign lost steam. Congress seemed to have little stomach for taxing cooperatives' earnings, as the NTEA proposed. When the Senate failed to include new taxes on cooperatives in its 1951 revenue bill, Ben McCabe, for one, was apoplectic. "Businessmen and taxpayers have been sold down the river by the political cowardice of a bare majority of the Senate Finance Committee," he said. The NTEA would never again come so close to victory.[182]

It was becoming increasingly clear that the efforts of the established grain trade to slow the growth of the cooperative movement were failing. In Minneapolis, the GTA continued to expand its reach. In 1950, it reported a net worth of about $20 million—a hefty sum for an organization that had started twelve years earlier with just thirty thousand dollars in operating capital. Clearly the GTA was not going away. The traders on the floor of the Minneapolis Grain Exchange would just have to get used to that fact. But they didn't have to be happy about it. When Bob McWhite of the

Peavey Company arranged to have GTA general manager M. W. Thatcher speak to a regular meeting of grain shippers, his colleagues at the chamber gave him "absolute hell." Why, they demanded, had he scheduled "a snake oil salesman" like Thatcher? McWhite felt vindicated when a standing-room-only crowd packed the ballroom of the Radisson Hotel to hear Thatcher speak. "You can say what you want about the guy," McWhite recalled years later, "but he was a showman. He more or less said, 'I'm here, boys, and I'm going to stay, so thanks for inviting me.'"[183]

## The Price of Supports

Minneapolis's grain traders had hoped that when the war was over, the federal government would go back to the way it used to do things and let the grain markets operate with little interference. But it didn't take long for them to see that they had been overly optimistic. Wartime price ceilings, for example, did not disappear. In the spring of 1946, with a hike in price ceilings only days away, the government ordered the Minneapolis Chamber of Commerce (it hadn't changed its name yet) and the grain markets in Chicago and Kansas City to essentially change the rules of futures trading. Under the government's plan, futures contracts completed before the new, higher ceilings went into effect could be traded at or

below the old, lower ceilings—no higher. Grain traders in all three cities were alarmed. As they saw it, compliance with the government's order would "destroy such futures markets for the time being and seriously threaten [their] possible future existence." In the end, the Chicago Board of Trade and Kansas City Board of Trade gave in to the government. The Minneapolis Chamber of Commerce, however, did not. In a statement announcing their decision to defy the government, the chamber's directors declared that they intended to "preserve the integrity of contracts and not regulate or allocate the profits or losses in any transaction."[184]

It was a gutsy move. One of the men who was in on the decision, A. G. Hessburg, recalled years later that all of the directors were aware that the government might respond to the chamber's defiance with "drastic action."[185] But no such action came. In its report on the entire affair, the Federal Trade Commission concluded that officials at the Minneapolis exchange had acted properly while their counterparts in Chicago and Kansas City had not:

The Minneapolis Chamber of Commerce deliberately chose to maintain the validity of its contracts so far as possible and to insist that its traders, both speculators and hedgers, cooperate and participate

Robert B. (Bob) McWhite began working as a grain inspector for the Occident Elevator Division of the Russell-Miller Milling Company in Minneapolis in July 1940. After serving as an army pilot during World War II, he returned home to become a trader for the Occident Terminal Division of Russell-Miller, which was bought out by Peavey in 1954. He ultimately oversaw all of Peavey's terminal operations and commodity trading in Minneapolis. Since retiring from Peavey in 1980, McWhite has operated as a private trader at the Grain Exchange under the McWhite Grain Company banner.

When in 1946 the Kansas City Board of Trade (right) and the Chicago Board of Trade complied with new federal price ceilings on futures trading, the Minneapolis Chamber of Commerce refused. The Federal Trade Commission stood by Minneapolis's position.

10th and Wyandotte
Board of Trade Building
1925-1966

in mutual settlements whereby the interests of both parties would be safeguarded so far as equitably possible under the circumstances over which neither the traders nor the Chamber of Commerce had control.[186]

The chamber was vindicated, but this early experience with postwar market meddling by the government was a sign of things to come. New Deal agricultural policies born during the Great Depression were now entrenched. It didn't matter that the war was over; price supports were a fact of the grain-marketing world. Grain traders in Minneapolis and elsewhere could only hope that government's interventionist ways wouldn't disrupt the market too much.

In the decade that followed the war, federal agricultural policy gyrated wildly, but price supports of some sort remained a constant feature. Under the 1949 Agriculture Act, the government maintained supports at a fixed level: 90 percent of parity. In 1954, it switched back to a system of flexible supports. Most grain traders in Minneapolis preferred the flexible system, but given the choice, they would have scrapped government subsidies altogether. Government-owned stocks of surplus grain were piling up under the price-support system. At the Minneapolis Grain Exchange, the effects were easy to see, especially in the futures pit. After peaking at 674 million bushels traded during World War II, the Minneapolis wheat futures market fell into a steep and prolonged decline that was halted only briefly by increased demand during the Korean War. By 1955, the wheat futures market in Minneapolis had shrunk to 357 million bushels, almost half its wartime size. "The causes for the decline in grain futures trading lie . . . chiefly in government price supports," explained John Cole, assistant vice president of Cargill's grain division. "Price supports become price protection—which is the role of the futures market."[187]

The rapid decline of the futures market was alarming. In March 1956, Grain Exchange president

Traders kept track of current prices by checking the black-boards that lined the trading room's south wall.

Women broke the gender barrier on the trading floor during the 1950s. Some took jobs as board markers. Others updated the weather maps, located adjacent to the cash grain tables on the east side of the room. Buyers and sellers depended on up-to-date weather reports to make informed trading decisions.

James Mullin went on record with his concerns. In a letter to the chair of a House agricultural subcommit-tee, Mullin warned that "creeping socialism" threatened the future of the nation's grain markets:

The grain market is at a crossroads. Either congress must remove some of the handicaps working against free, competitive marketing, or our grain exchange—and others like it—will be forced to shut down and let government take over the responsi-bility of grain marketing.

The issue is clear. Either we in this country believe in free enter-prise, or we believe in the statism practiced in some other countries. . . .

Ask any grain man what the effect of government grain trading has been on the free market system and you will find that many are in an actual state of crisis at this moment. With many, it is a case of having to drop out of the trade they have spent a lifetime serving—because of government competition.[188]

One government initiative that Minneapolis's grain traders did not object to was the "Food for Peace" program that Congress passed in July 1956. Public Law 480, as the program was popularly known, allowed the government to use sur-plus agricultural products, including grain, to further the country's for-eign policy goals. Much of the food that the United States exported under the program went to famine relief in Europe and Asia. Passed as a stopgap measure to reduce

**James Mullin (holding the Minneapolis Award from the Chamber of Commerce) was one of the Grain Exchange's most tireless advocates. As president of the exchange dur-ing the mid-1950s, he oversaw the organization's seventy-fifth-anniversary celebrations. "As a member of the Grain Exchange I feel we are fortu-nate to be located in Minne-apolis," he wrote. "As a Minneapolitan I am proud to be part of this great industry, which has been so clearly identified with the growth and prosperity of the city."**

**U.S. Senator Hubert Humphrey (left) chats with members at the Minneapolis Grain Exchange's seventy-fifth anniversary celebration in 1956.**

growing surpluses and stimulate depressed prices, PL 480 became a mainstay of American foreign policy. Even so, it couldn't keep up with mounting government stocks. Surpluses continued to pile up, and as activity in the Minneapolis futures pit diminished month after month, conversation among traders became increasingly morbid. Was the Grain Exchange headed for extinction? The debate over that question took on a new urgency.

## Cloudy Future

When viewed from the proper standpoint, the Minneapolis Grain Exchange looked healthier than ever. It was, after all, still the world's leading cash grain market.

**A huge storage bin at Port Cargill in Savage, Minnesota, was built to store grain during a time of large surpluses. Reputed to be the largest single bin in the world at the time, with a capacity of about six million bushels, it was emptied early in 1976 as the surplus dwindled.**

In 1955, for example, the men who gathered each day around the hefty grain tables on the east end of the trading floor bought and sold about 325 million bushels of grain—an average of more than a million bushels a day.[189] The general hubbub was impressive. "When you came off the elevator on the fourth floor . . . you could kind of tell whether [it was] an up or down day," barley trader Duane Fedje recalled. "The level of voices and noise that was going on in the Grain Exchange was humongous because it was just full of people."[190]

But that was the cash side. Over on the west end of the floor, futures trading in all grains continued to languish. In 1957, futures trading in the wheat pit dropped to a paltry 307 million bushels. That same year, the oats futures market—which had hit the 125 million bushel level during the Korean War—accounted for only 27 million bushels. The numbers were just as bad for rye and flax.[191]

A troubling fatalism began to settle over the exchange. Not even the continuing strength of the cash grain market could overcome the growing

**Ken McCoy, Cargill chief merchandiser, at cash grain table, circa 1954.**

**Atwood-Larson trader Tom Gardin surveys barley pans on August 4, 1958. Record barley receipts that day totaled more than three million bushels.**

pessimism fed by the troubles on the futures side. Many traders believed that if such trends kept up, the exchange might soon fade into history. "The fate of the Minneapolis grain market lies largely with the government," said Peavey vice president Ron Kennedy. "The entire grain industry now tends to carry minimum supplies of grain because of the risk of owning any more grain than actually needed. Any sudden change in government policy might change the situation overnight and ruin anyone who had too great a forward commitment." And it wasn't just the traders with the big companies who were worried. "The futures market is dying on the vine," confided an independent grain merchandiser who refused to let the *Minneapolis Star* print his name. "Things are not going to get any better for the little guy like me."[192]

The grain trade was, in fact, becoming increasingly inhospitable to the smaller concerns that had once formed the industry's backbone. In the 1940s, the membership roster of the Minneapolis exchange had included more than seventy-five grain commission companies. By the mid-1950s, that number of commission firms doing business on the exchange had dropped to fewer than twenty. Of those, only five did a pure commission business, acting exclusively as sales agents for grain owners. Consolidation was trans-

forming the entire industry. "Many years ago there were hundreds of small elevator companies," explained the Grain Exchange's executive vice president George Wilkins. "Today most of the line elevator stations are owned by six to ten companies. The same is true of the milling business, where hundreds of small country mills have discontinued operation."[193]

Grain traders in Minneapolis might not have fretted so much if the smaller companies had been gobbled up only by venerable member firms like Cargill and Peavey. What worried them most was the fact that their old cooperative nemesis, the Farmers Union Grain Terminal Association, was gobbling too.

In September 1958, the GTA made a move that many people in the business considered a potential death knell for the established grain trade: it purchased Ben McCabe's grain trading firm, the McCabe Company. McCabe and his colleagues in the National Tax Equality Association had fought long and hard to make the GTA and other cooperatives pay taxes on their earnings. Many of his friends at the Minneapolis Grain Exchange considered him something of a hero. But after sixteen years of fighting and only a few minor victories to show for his efforts, McCabe decided to surrender. "A co-operative has many advantages over private business," McCabe said in explaining the sale to his employees. "[The] ability of co-operatives to pay patronage dividends allows them to attract more business than their competitors . . .

Members of the Grain Exchange frequented several local watering holes, the swankiest of which was the Minneapolis Club with its "millers' table."

The Cavalier Room at the Minneapolis Athletic Club, circa 1950, was a choice spot for well-connected traders to eat, drink, and rub elbows.

to accumulate funds for working capital or plant improvement at a much faster rate."[194]

With its purchase of McCabe, the GTA increased its share of the combined Minneapolis and Duluth cash grain market from about 30 percent to more than 35 percent. Some traders worried that the GTA's growing dominance might signal the end of an era. "That does it," one long-time trader said after learning of the McCabe sale. "That means the end of the Grain Exchange." Others, including the GTA's M. W. Thatcher, disagreed with that gloomy assessment. "There will always be a need for a grain exchange in Minneapolis," he said. "And there certainly always will be a futures market."

Although most traders in Minneapolis considered Thatcher the enemy, many hoped he was right about the futures market. Robert Searles, president of the Grain Exchange's futures association, was among those who believed there was reason for optimism. He was convinced that the general public was losing patience with government policies that produced huge surpluses of grain:

We have charts to show that futures trading has declined in almost direct proportion to the increase in government-owned grain. When some limit eventually is placed on government accumulations of grain—and I don't think the taxpayers will wait much longer—the element of risk will tend to move out of government hands and back to the private trade. And when the private trade again faces a risk, they will return to use the futures market.[195]

Still, concerns about the Grain Exchange's prospects remained. In his introduction to a series of articles on the exchange in 1958, *Minneapolis Star* reporter Ralph Mason posed the question that many traders were asking themselves: "Is the 77-year-old Minneapolis Grain Exchange outliving its usefulness?" Mason's answer provided little comfort to those who feared for the exchange's future. "There is no doubt," he wrote, "but what the pendulum has swung against the musty old mistress of S. 4th St. and S. 4th Av."[196]

## Turbulent Times

Just as the traders at the Minneapolis Grain Exchange were getting used to cooperative muscle flexing and surplus-depressed futures trading, other changes began rocking the industry. In October 1963, during the height of the Cold War, President John F. Kennedy announced that he was temporarily lifting restrictions on exports to Communist countries so that the

New Symbol

U.S. WHEAT

*Minneapolis Tribune* cartoonist Scott Long saw the 1963 U.S.-Soviet wheat deals as a harbinger of peace at the height of the Cold War.

Soviet Union could purchase $250 million in American wheat. The announcement seemed to signal a major shift in the grain trade's status quo. Before, the Russians had been only minor players in the global grain markets. Now, after a poor crop and years of misguided agricultural policies, they were turning for help to the United States. In the months that followed Kennedy's announcement, Continental Grain Company and Cargill closed separate deals to sell the Soviets 1.5 million tons total of U.S. wheat. (The first talks with the Soviet trade delegation had been initiated by Minneapolis Grain Exchange member Burton Joseph of the I. S. Joseph Company, but

Joseph was eventually elbowed out by his bigger rivals.) The sales raised hopes that the Soviets would continue to buy American grain and, in the process, continue to draw down U.S. grain surpluses. But it didn't work out that way. The crop situation in the USSR improved and the Soviets left the U.S. market almost as quickly as they had arrived. It would be another eight years before they returned.

Among the other major changes affecting the Grain Exchange during this period was the rapidly accelerating decline of Minneapolis's flour-milling industry. The mills that had grown up around St. Anthony Falls had powered the city's remarkable growth during the late nineteenth century and early twentieth century. They also had helped generate the huge demand for wheat that gave birth to the region's robust grain market. But the glory days of Minneapolis flour milling were now part of a distant past. The city had relinquished its title as the nation's foremost flour producer back in 1930, to Buffalo, New York. Since then, its flour production had continued to shrink and its mills had continued to close. By 1959, Minneapolis was down to seven mills. When, in the early 1960s, the railroads instituted new rates that made it cheaper to ship wheat—but not flour—eastward, Minneapolis's remaining millers could tell the end was near.[197]

In the summer of 1965, one of the exchange's most venerable member firms, General Mills, closed its milling operations on the west side of the falls and moved its headquarters to suburban Golden Valley. The company's stately "A" mill had anchored Minneapolis's milling district for the better part of a century. Now it was a relic of the past, a victim of the flour industry's inability to reduce production and bring it in line with demand. The editors of the *Northwestern Miller,* like many in the grain trade, lamented the loss:

Flour and General Mills have been closely linked in Minneapolis for decades, and the company's milling complex near St. Anthony Falls has long been a landmark. Now, in a carefully-considered move to expunge excess capacity, the firm has decided to close the Flour City Mill, along with others across the U.S. Although the structure will continue to grace the skyline—or until disposition of it is made—the machinery will be silenced.[198]

General Mills' exodus from Minneapolis was just part of a disturbing shake-up taking place within the city's grain trade. Between 1960 and 1965, the Standard Milling Company shut down its "A" mill at the falls, the Peavey Company closed the old Russell-Miller mill in southeast Minneapolis, and dozens of terminal elevators in the area were either destroyed by fire, abandoned, or demolished. Hundreds of workers lost their jobs. The city's grain storage capacity declined by millions of bushels.[199] All of these developments caught the attention of the traders at the Minneapolis Grain Exchange. But other changes, much less visible to the general public, were threatening to cause even greater disruption on the trading floor.

For nearly one hundred years, grain had arrived in Minneapolis by train and departed Minneapolis by train. The farmers in the country and the grain traders in the city did not always appreciate the way the railroad companies did business, but they had little choice but to play along. Trains provided the only efficient way to transport grain to and from market. But in the 1950s, the transportation system that had ruled the grain trade for decades began evolving. The railroads, facing new financial pressures, began neglecting their less-traveled branch lines. As time went by, the farmers and elevator operators who lived in communities along those lines found it increasingly difficult to move out their grain. "You could hardly get any service from boxcars," recalled Ralph Bagley, whose firm operated a line of country elevators. "You'd maybe get one train a week and maybe you'd have some empty cars on that train to load, maybe you

wouldn't."[200] With the branch lines becoming less reliable, alternative forms of transportation were needed.

The most obvious alternative was the truck. In the years following World War II, the federal government had pumped millions of dollars into a new interstate highway system. Many rural routes laid out during previous decades had been paved. The improved roads that resulted from those efforts helped foster the development of commercial trucking. So now, for the first time, producers and elevator operators had another way to ship grain to the terminal markets. Trucks were not as efficient as trains, but they were often easier to secure. "We were forced to get trucks," Bagley recalled. "We were on the rail. We'd much rather load a car, but we couldn't get them."[201] The use of trucks increased steadily through the 1950s and 1960s until, by 1969, about half of the grain coming into Minneapolis was arriving by truck.[202]

As more and more trucks carried grain into Minneapolis, shippers began looking for new ways to send it out. In the past, when grain moved almost exclusively by rail, the system had depended heavily on transportation credits called transit privileges. If Cargill, for example, brought fifteen cars of wheat into Minneapolis, it then

Ralph Bagley, third-generation president of the Bagley Grain Company, also served as president of the Minneapolis Grain Exchange from 1965 to 1966.

**Al Donahoo worked at the Grain Exchange for thirty years, from 1954 to 1984. He was hired originally as the exchange's educational director. He rose through the ranks until he was named executive vice president in the late 1970s.**

received "transit" from the railroad that allowed it to send out fifteen cars. "Transit" was, in effect, a form of currency that kept grain moving. But as trucks began playing a larger role in the grain trade, the art of managing transit privileges became more complicated. A truckload of wheat coming into Minneapolis, for example, generated no transit privileges. If the owner of that wheat wanted to move it out by train, his company had to pay an additional charge. Most shippers wanted to avoid that additional charge, so it was in their best interest to find an alternative method of moving grain out of Minneapolis.

The alternative they settled on was the river barge. Minneapolis's location at the head of practicable navigation on the Mississippi and the steady improvement of the river's lock and dam system made barges the logical choice. During the 1950s and 1960s, a series of new grain terminals capable of loading barges began rising in the Twin Cities metro area along the Mississippi and Minnesota Rivers.[203] With these new facilities, grain could now move directly from farms or country elevators to river barges without being stored or cleaned.

In other words, grain coming into Minneapolis no longer had to make a stop at the Minneapolis Grain Exchange.

This was something new—and potentially demoralizing for the city's grain trade. The Minneapolis Chamber of Commerce had been founded back in 1881 on the assumption that grain sellers and grain buyers would always need a place where they could come together and do business. Now, with the growing success of commercial trucking and barge-loading grain terminals, Minneapolis's cash grain market didn't seem quite so essential. The amount of grain bypassing the trading floor was still relatively small, but Grain Exchange officials were concerned. "I'm sure they tried to resist, tried to make sure that everything did come through the Grain Exchange," said Al Donahoo, an executive at the exchange who would later serve as its executive vice president. "But that didn't work."[204]

## High Times

If the traders on the cash side were aware that trends in the business were working against them, they spent little time worrying about it. The camaraderie that had distinguished Minneapolis's cash grain trade since its inception still ran thick. Trader Shelley Walsh, for one, could hardly wait to hit the floor every day. "When I went to work in the morning, I never felt I was going to work," he recalled. "I was going down to enjoy myself. I looked forward to it."[205] For Duane Fedje of

River barges became an increasingly important component of the nation's grain marketing system during the 1950s and 1960s.

The barge *Cartasca,* owned by Cargill, gets loaded with oats in 1948 at the Minneapolis River Terminal.

"Gentleman" John McCaull was one of the exchange's most respected, well-liked traders. He operated McCaull-Lyman with his brother, Phillip.

Brooks Fields spent thirty-five years in the grain business, splitting his time between Pillsbury and Burdick/ConAgra. He is a past president of the National Grain Trade Council.

the Kurth Malting Company, it was the people he worked with who made the exchange such a special place. "They were all just wonderful people," Fedje said of his fellow barley traders. "I mean, they'd fight like cats and dogs and they'd actually probably get irritated with people on the floor once in a while, during the day, but when it was all over, we were all good friends."[206] Pillsbury grain merchandiser Brooks Fields felt the same way. "People would fight, bite, chew, scream, yell, do everything but cheat against each other," he said.[207]

Among the most respected members on the floor was "Gentleman" John McCaull of the merchandising firm McCaull-Lyman. McCaull was, in the words of fellow trader Bob McWhite, "sort of a dandy," a distinguished man with a fondness for expensive shoes. But McCaull did not let his refined manners get in the way of his work. McWhite remembered one day in particular when McCaull was facing down Cargill's cash wheat trader, a tough negotiator named Charles "Red" Swanson:

John was over, trying to negotiate him [Swanson] out of a few of his cars that his customers needed without paying a price that obviously was going to be too high. So Red was in a sour mood and was treating him pretty rough. And John said,

"Charles, I don't mind you shoving an umbrella up my rear end, but please don't try to open it." Red broke out laughing and threw the four cars that he wanted at John and said, "Take 'em and put your own price on 'em."[208]

The trading floor was, in many ways, an exclusive club comprising several hundred men who shared a common knowledge of an arcane business. And like most clubs, it had its own rituals. For a while, during the 1930s and 1940s, a group of veteran traders made a habit of initiating all new members. Rookies were herded into the futures pit, laid across a bench, and paddled. The practice ended suddenly in the late 1940s after the hazing section tried to initiate a World War II veteran named Ira Elsham. "He was one of the first of the real rebels," Brooks Fields recalled. "He turned around and said, 'The first guy that hits me, I'm going to knock right on his can.' And he was a big guy—played football at Carleton—and so that ended that."[209]

The end of hazing did not, however, mean the end of mischief-making. Among the most active practical jokers was a trader named Ned Brown. Brown was especially fond of targeting colleagues who spent their down time reading newspapers. When things got dull, he stalked the floor with a book of matches, setting fire to as many newspapers

No accounting for taste: winners of the trading floor's 1951 necktie and shirt contest.

as he could. "That was stupid," Fields recalled, "but it was typical."[210] Fortunately, there was little danger that Brown's small-scale arsons would ever get out of control. It seemed that a few traders were always on hand with a cup of water to help put out the flames—whether they knew it or not. Some carried the cups surreptitiously in the pockets of their trading coats in hopes of drenching an unsuspecting associate. Others were unwitting water carriers. Cargill's chief trader, Mike Laurel, remembered how a few self-styled comedians hooked paper cups to the collars of oblivious colleagues, then carefully filled the cups with water so that the targeted traders wouldn't notice what was happening. "It was just ridiculous," Laurel said.[211]

## The Duluth Board of Trade

In late 1960s, the Minneapolis Grain Exchange lost its closest competitor. The Duluth Board of Trade dated back to 1881, the same year that the then Minneapolis Chamber of Commerce was established. The Board of Trade was instrumental in Duluth's development as a major grain marketing and shipping center. In its first five years of existence, annual shipments of grain from the twin ports of Duluth, Minnesota, and Superior, Wisconsin, jumped from less than four million bushels to more than twenty-two million bushels. At the corner of Third

Avenue West and First Street, the Duluth exchange never seriously challenged Minneapolis's dominance of the Upper Midwest grain trade, but it was a power in its own right. Its membership rose to a peak of about 250 during the 1920s.

The Duluth Board of Trade's slow decline accelerated during the years after World War II. Some of the same developments that made life difficult for the Minneapolis Grain Exchange—among them, the switch to point-to-point rail shipments and the consolidation of large grain companies—proved fatal to the Duluth Exchange. "It was a great change," trader Frank Malnati recalled, "from a really bustling atmosphere to a slower pace." The Duluth Board of Trade's futures pit closed during the early 1960s. The exchange itself shut down in 1967.[212]

The Duluth Board of Trade, circa 1950.

A postcard view of the Peavey Elevator in Duluth.

Peavey Grain Elevator. Duluth, Minn.

## The Approaching Storm

As the 1960s came to a close, traders at the Minneapolis Grain Exchange were in generally good spirits, at least on the cash grain side. Activity at the cash grain tables remained robust, despite transportation changes that had made it possible to bypass the exchange altogether. Wheat receipts, for example, stayed above 120 million bushels a year for most of the 1960s, a record that compared favorably with that of the 1950s.[213] The numbers for corn, oats, barley, and rye were just as strong. The Minneapolis Grain Exchange remained the nation's busiest cash grain market, and exchange officials trumpeted that fact at every opportunity.

But all was not well at Fourth and Fourth. For one thing, trading in the futures pit remained pitifully lackluster. In the last half of the 1960s, the spring wheat futures market at the exchange averaged less than fifty-eight thousand contracts a year.[214] Government price supports were continuing to produce huge, market-stymieing surpluses, and few traders believed that the system would change any time soon. Beyond the ongoing weakness in futures trading, a new development in transportation technology was slowly, almost imperceptibly,

**Grain producers of the Upper Midwest gained a new route to international markets when the St. Lawrence Seaway opened in 1959. On May 3, the people of Duluth welcomed the merchant vessel *Ramon de Larringa,* the first upbound ship to arrive in the city via the seaway. The ship loaded grain at the Cargill and Peavey elevators before heading back to the Atlantic.**

**Lackluster trading in September 1965 continued to confound the men of the futures pit.**

beginning to chip away at the foundations of Minneapolis's cash grain market.

In 1963, the exchange's monthly newsletter, the *Minneapolis Grain Exchange News,* noted what appeared to be a major innovation in grain handling: the introduction of "hopper style" railcars. Unlike the old boxcars on which the grain trade had always depended, hopper cars were loaded from the top and emptied from the bottom, sort of like a bathtub. And they were big. They could hold about 50 percent more grain than standard boxcars. The newsletter reported that tests run by one large grain shipper found hopper cars—with their ease of use and increased capacity—could sig-

nificantly reduce the costs of loading and unloading grain:

At the conclusion of these tests and cost studies, this grain shipper remarked that the trough batch equipped hopper car is, for grain loading, far superior to boxcar usage. He went on to say that as to transport efficiency, cost per bushel per mile should be at least 30% more attractive.[215]

In the early 1960s, most traders in Minneapolis assumed that the hopper car would be a blessing—a technological advance that would deliver new efficiencies to the grain-handling business. Few suspected that hopper cars would soon threaten the exchange's very reason for being.

A blessing or a curse? Innovative hopper cars, introduced during the early 1960s, reduced the costs of loading and unloading grain and thus promised to revolutionize the grain marketing system.

# MORE THAN GRAIN
## Public Education

**IN 1956, UNIVERSITY OF MINNESOTA** president James Morrill claimed that the institution he represented owed its very existence to "an enormously effective pioneer of the milling world": John Sargent Pillsbury.

The university had started in 1851 as a preparatory school, but it soon fell on hard times. It closed during the Civil War, and might never have reopened had Pillsbury not devoted large amounts of time and money to it. "If man does not live by bread alone," Morrill wrote, "it is the duty which the man of imagination assigns himself to supply the needs of the citizen's mind as well as of his body. Having made a large contribution toward the availability of bread, Pillsbury

The University of Minnesota board of regents meets in President Northrop's office in January 1889. From left: Greenleaf Clark, William M. Liggett, Stephen Mahoney, Cyrus Northrop, Sidney M. Owen, John S. Pillsbury, Albert E. Rice, Ozora P. Stearns, Samuel R. Van Sant, unidentified man, and Thomas Wilson.

turned spontaneously to the task of broadening the availability of other requirements for solid civilization."[216]

Other men closely tied to the grain and milling industries also made significant contributions to the state's educational system over the years. General Mills founder James Ford Bell was a longtime regent and a driving force behind the development of the university's Museum of Natural History (renamed in his honor in 1966). His private book collection became the nucleus of the university's James Ford Bell Library. In later years, former Pillsbury executive (and former Minneapolis Grain Exchange president) Win Wallin demonstrated a similar devotion to higher education. In 1991, Wallin established a foundation that provides college scholarships to hundreds of needy Minneapolis high

school students. He also served on Carleton College's board of trustees and in several key advisory positions at the university.

**Pillsbury Hall at the University of Minnesota was built in 1889 in the Richardsonian Romanesque style using a variety of sandstones.**

**Students gather to study and chat on the stairs and bench of the John S. Pillsbury Memorial at the University of Minnesota.**

## CHAPTER FOUR

1970 — 2006

# Going Global

## Wednesday, August 2, 1972

It was like most afternoons at the Minneapolis Grain Exchange. When the closing bell sounded at 1:15, the hubbub died and people headed in all directions. The futures traders went back to their desks and offices to make sure everything was in order. A few set out for lunch and libations at Russell's Bar or the Little Wagon. The buyers and sellers on the cash grain side—those who were still around—sauntered off or lingered for a while at the big oak tables, laughing at each other's jokes. The clearinghouse staff got to work settling accounts. The board markers climbed down from their perches. In the members' room, just off the trading floor, a few men settled into leather chairs with cigarettes and newspapers. Front-page headlines sounded alarms about the record rainfall in west-central Minnesota and how the farmers in that part of the state needed emergency assistance. Inside, on the editorial pages, pundits criticized Democratic presidential candidate George McGovern for choosing Tom Eagleton as his running mate and then abandoning him when it was revealed he had been hospitalized three times for depression. This is what afternoons at the Grain Exchange were like: languid and drowsy, a welcome respite after 225 minutes of controlled chaos on the trading floor. No one at Fourth and Fourth on that lazy afternoon could have predicted that the grain markets in Minneapolis and elsewhere were about to turn upside down.

It's not clear where the rumors started. Maybe someone got a phone call from

a source with inside knowledge. Or maybe word just leaked from one of the big trading firms that kept offices at the Grain Exchange. But whatever the source, the word spread quickly through the building.

The Russians wanted more grain.

Four weeks earlier, the U.S. government had announced a historic trade agreement under which the Soviet Union promised to buy $750 million of American grain over three years. It was the kind of deal that could single-handedly drive prices in the futures pit to unheard-of levels. But in the weeks since the announcement, the markets had refused to take the bait. The Russians were being cagey. Numbers were being thrown around, but few traders seemed ready to believe that the final figures would actually be anything close to earth-shattering. Now, however, news was circulating through grain-trading circles that a Soviet bargaining team had just rushed back to Washington. The implications were clear: the Russians weren't finished buying. Something had happened that led them to return to the United States for more grain. This was big news. Maybe the Russians were planning to buy more than anyone had first dared to believe. The remaining traders at the Grain Exchange headed home for the night, eager to find out what the morning would bring.

During the previous four decades, the futures pit at the Grain Exchange had been a shadow of its former self. Government intervention in the grain trade had produced huge surpluses that robbed the market of volatility—the one factor on which the futures market most depended. Now, if the rumors were accurate, the Russians were getting ready to gobble up even more of that surplus grain than anyone had expected.

When the opening bell sounded Thursday morning, the excitement was palpable. The price of September wheat began rising. By the close of trading, it was up seven and a half cents a bushel. The Grain Exchange's executive secretary, Al Donahoo, couldn't quite fathom what had happened. "After the market closed Wednesday, the word was out that Russians wanted more wheat," he said. "That's the only reason I can think of for the flurry of activity or the price rise."[217] Donahoo did not realize it yet, but Minneapolis's long dormant futures market had just woken up, and the hungry Russians were largely responsible.

## The Russians Are Coming

Exports had been a factor in the Minneapolis grain trade since 1877, when Cadwallader Washburn sent his assistant, William Dunwoody, to England to establish a European market for Minnesota flour. But while the high-quality flour made by Minneapolis millers quickly grew in popularity overseas, the export market for grain produced in the city's trading region was slower to develop. The big grain-trading firms concentrated almost exclusively on the domestic market until the early

The futures market revives in August 1972 after years in the doldrums. All eyes are on the quotation boards as news of Russian grain purchases spreads.

On August 8, 1972, board markers struggle to keep up with a rapidly accelerating market one day after trading volume in the Minneapolis Grain Exchange wheat pit hit a six-year high.

Trader Clayton Moline writes a customer order during the Russian grain sale rebound.

1930s, when Cargill built a terminal at the new deep-water port in Albany, New York. In the years that followed, exports of U.S grain grew at a modest pace. Before World War II, the amount of grain that left the country seldom topped thirty million tons a year. Afterward, exports increased, especially to war-ravaged countries in Europe and Asia. But those shipments were often in the form of foreign aid, driven by a complex web of motives that included humanitarianism, cold war politics, and an overriding desire to dispose of surplus crops.[218]

The restricted flow of U.S grain exports seemed to burst open in 1963 and 1964, when Cargill and its com-

petitor, Continental Grain Company, agreed to sell American wheat to the Soviet Union. Grain traders crossed their fingers that more big grain deals would follow. But when Russian crops rebounded, the Soviets stopped buying U.S. grain. Memories of those earlier wheat deals were still fresh when the Russians returned to U.S. grain markets in 1972. American grain traders assumed that the food situation in the Soviet Union had to be desperate if Moscow was back in the market for U.S. grain. They had no idea how accurate their assumptions were.

In the eight years since the initial Russian grain purchases, the Soviet government had committed itself to

**One hundred forty-three miles from the Atlantic Ocean, New York's capital city of Albany became a seaport in June 1932 with the dredging of the upper reaches of the Hudson River.**

a new agricultural policy, one that sought to make sure that all Russians were well fed, or at least better fed. One of its main goals was to increase the amount of beef, pork, and poultry in the average Russian's diet. But cattle, hogs, and chickens needed to be fed. Between 1968 and 1971, the use of feed grains in Russia increased 40 percent and livestock herds grew accordingly. But there was no way that the Soviet Union—with its inefficient collective farms, foreign-aid obligations, and harsh weather—could grow enough grain to keep up with its long-term meat production goals. It needed to buy grain elsewhere, and no country had more grain to sell than the United States.[219]

The doors to America's granaries began opening to the Russians in the summer of 1971, when the administration of President Richard Nixon implemented two significant policy changes. The first change eliminated the requirement that exporters obtain licenses before making shipments to the Soviet Union. The second change abolished an earlier policy—instituted by the Kennedy-Johnson administration during the grain deals of 1963–1964— that required at least half of all grain sent to the Soviet Union be shipped on American vessels. Nixon and his national security adviser, Henry Kissinger, had embarked on a policy of détente—the creation of shared

economic and political linkages—in hopes of reducing superpower tensions. They believed that Russian grain purchases would establish yet another link between the two countries while simultaneously bringing smiles to the faces of America's farmers and grain traders.[220]

In the fall of that year, the two companies that had dealt with the Russians eight years earlier—Cargill and Continental—struck separate deals to ship the Soviets more than three million tons of feed grain. "Parties to this agreement, government and unions, deserve the gratitude of American agriculture for resolving this eight-year impasse on shipments of U.S. grains to Russia," wrote Cargill president Fred Seed. "Potential market[s] over the years appear to be substantial."[221] Assistant Agriculture Secretary Clarence Palmby agreed that the feed-grain deals constituted a sign of good things to come:

Taking a longer range view, we see this as the opening wedge in what could be an even larger volume of agricultural trade with Russia in future years. The U.S.S.R. is a desirable trading partner that can be of great value to us because it pays cash that contributes directly to our balance of payments. Its feed grain purchases are expected to expand as it strives to supply the demand of its people for more meat products. . . .

To call this transaction history-making is putting it mildly. . . . It is one of the most significant agricultural events of my public career.[222]

In fact, the feed-grain sales were small change compared to the deals yet to come. Over the next six months, Soviet agriculture officials choreographed a series of sometimes overlapping negotiations with representatives from the Nixon administration and executives from most of the world's largest grain-trading companies. In April 1972, U.S. Agriculture Secretary Earl Butz traveled to Moscow for a private meeting with Soviet leader Leonid Brezhnev. On his return, Butz revealed that the United States had offered the Russians a $500 million line of credit in exchange for a commitment to buy at least $750 million of American grain over the next three years. The Soviets had balked at the terms, especially the 6.5 percent interest rate on the credit line, but the offer remained on the table. In late June—just one day after Soviet agriculture officials issued what apparently was an alarming crop estimate—the Russians informed the Nixon administration that they had reconsidered and were ready to accept the American terms. A few days later, on July 8, Nixon and Butz held simultaneous news conferences to announce that the deal was done. "This is by all odds the greatest grain transaction in the history of the world," Butz declared. "And it certainly is the greatest for us."[223]

The commodities markets, including the Minneapolis Grain Exchange, were abuzz with the news. But activity in the futures pits was strangely muted. In the first few weeks after the announcement, prices rose only slightly. The fact was that traders still weren't sure what was going on. The U.S. and Soviet governments had made a deal, but the actual purchases were a matter for the Russians and the Cargills of the world to work out. Nobody on the Minneapolis trading floor could do anything but guess whether any purchases had been made or how big those purchases might be. At that time, "no one had even said in the press, or even hinted in markets, that the U.S.S.R. was going to buy any significant amount of wheat," recalled Mort Sosland, editor of the highly respected trade publication the *Southwestern Miller* (soon to become *Milling and Baking News*).

But in mid-July, Sosland began receiving phone calls from a man who spoke with a British accent. The man, who identified himself as "John Smith," claimed to be a reporter for the *Financial Times* of London, and he seemed to be privy to inside information about the

Russian negotiations. For some reason, he wanted to share his information with Sosland. In their first conversation on July 17, Mr. Smith told Sosland that he had "learned through an indiscretion on the part of a Russian official" that the Soviets had already purchased fifteen million tons of American grain, including five million tons of wheat. The numbers were staggering, much larger than most knowledgeable grain men thought possible. "I can't believe it," Sosland said.[224]

He and his staff at the *Southwestern Miller* tried to confirm the numbers Mr. Smith had provided, but they couldn't. With a little checking, the paper did determine that Mr. Smith did not work for the *Financial Times*. So who was he? Could he be trusted? Mr. Smith continued to call with news of bigger and bigger numbers, dropping hints that he enjoyed remarkable access to the inner workings of the grain negotiations. Yet Sosland continued to treat Mr. Smith's numbers with extreme caution.

Finally, in early August, Mr. Smith provided a tidbit of information that proved he was on the up and up. He told Sosland that a group of Russian buyers was heading to Minnesota to meet with representatives from Cargill. Now here was a piece of information that Sosland was confident he could either confirm or

refute. He called a trustworthy source in Minneapolis and asked him whether the Russians had arrived. "And he said, 'What? How did you know that?'" Sosland later recalled. "That really made me realize that, my God, this guy [Mr. Smith] was telling me the truth."[225] Sosland decided to run with Mr. Smith's numbers.

The news that began spreading through the Minneapolis Grain Exchange on August 2—that Russian grain buyers had just returned to Washington—was exactly the kind of information that traders were waiting for. Firm numbers were still elusive, but the fact that Soviet buyers were back in the United States seemed to confirm that the amount of grain changing hands was much larger than almost anyone had dreamed. Wheat prices began to rise. A few days later, the true scope of the Russian buying spree started to become clear. The *Southwestern Miller* reported that the Soviets had already bought about seven million metric tons of American wheat, and that they apparently planned to purchase an additional four million tons or so before they were done. These were hard numbers, and they were staggering. Only a few weeks earlier, even those few who had been willing to speculate were guessing that the Russians would buy, at most, about one million tons.

Mort Sosland, editor of the *Southwestern Miller* (later renamed *Milling and Baking News*), found himself at the center of the Russian grain sales story. His publication was among the most reliable sources of information during a time when rumors were fueling the Minneapolis market.

Contaminated

This Jerry Fearing cartoon, published in September 1972 by the *St. Paul Pioneer Press,* was accompanied by the one-word heading "Contaminated." While most traders at the Grain Exchange were glad that the Russian grain deals had reinvigorated the market, many farmers worried that they would see no benefits.

With the trade press finally reporting solid figures, the market responded with abandon, further fueling what was to become a historic run-up in prices. On August 7, more than six million bushels of wheat traded hands in Minneapolis—the highest daily volume in six years. Prices closed more than twenty-two cents over the previous week's highs.[226] As the month progressed, trading volume in the futures pit remained extremely high, at around six million bushels a day. Al Donahoo just smiled and shook his head. "Before all this Russian business started, it was running about a million bushels per day," he said.[227] At the same time, prices continued to rise. Most traders had never seen anything like it. "Nobody quite knows what's going on," one grain buyer admitted. "These are the experts," he

added, pointing to the trading floor, "and they're not sure either."[228]

Everyone on the exchange assumed that Minnesota-based Cargill was in the thick of the Russian grain deal, but hardly anyone, except a few privileged Cargill executives, actually knew what was going on. On August 11, the *Minneapolis Star* accurately reported that a Russian trade delegation had arrived in the Twin Cities to work out a deal with Cargill. The company had no comment.[229] A few days later, the *Star* reported that Cargill had agreed to sell the Russians about one million tons of wheat. Again, the company had no comment, at least initially. After thinking it over, Cargill executives decided they couldn't remain silent forever. On August 17, the company issued a statement dismissing the *Star* reports as rumors that "have no substance in fact." A spokesperson said the company had decided to break its silence "due to widespread public interest in the current sales of U.S. grains to the Soviet Union, and in order to help clarify public understanding of those transactions."[230]

Although few people realized it at the time, the Soviets were managing their grain purchases with the kind of finesse that would have made any capitalist proud. They purchased grain from six American and European trading firms—Cargill,

Continental, Dreyfus, Cook, Bunge, and Garnac—while managing to keep the details of each deal secret. As a result, no one but the Russians themselves had any idea how much grain they were actually buying. The Soviets' knack for secrecy helped keep prices in check until they finalized their purchases. When the numbers were finally tallied months later, they were difficult to comprehend. The Russians had purchased nearly twenty million metric tons of grain, more than half of it wheat. Cargill's share of the purchases accounted for about one-tenth of the total.[231]

As the details gradually emerged, criticism increased. Many people outside the grain trade, aware of the secrecy surrounding the deals, suspected that the big exporters such as Cargill had used inside information to generate huge profits at the expense of farmers and consumers.

**Cargill world headquarters in Wayzata occupy the former Rufus Rand mansion, "Still Pond," which president John H. MacMillan Jr. purchased for the company during World War II. Remote from the hubbub of the downtown Grain Exchange, where Cargill had previously officed, the secluded Rand property provided a think-tank type environment for the company's top officers. The idea had its genesis in France, where U.S. Army Captain John H. MacMillan Jr. had watched General John J. Pershing direct American field operations during World War I from a French chateau.**

**Duncan MacMillan was a fifth-line descendant of the Cargill family when he was admitted to the membership of the Minneapolis Grain Exchange in April 1954. "Dunc," as he was called on the trading floor, was introduced to the grain trade at age fifteen, when he spent his summer vacation at the exchange in Cargill's sampling room. The first family members to join the exchange had been William A. Stowell, followed by his son-in-law W. W. Cargill, both in the 1800s. John H. MacMillan, son-in-law of W. W. Cargill, stepped into the ranks in 1903, followed by his son John H. MacMillan Jr. (Duncan's father) in 1921.**

During a campaign stop in Duluth, Democratic presidential candidate George McGovern accused the Nixon administration of locking "the front door of its Agriculture Department to the American people and the American farmer and [giving] the giant grain companies the key to the back door."[232] Not surprisingly, McGovern's accusations did not sit well with executives at Cargill. In an uncommonly pointed press release, the publicity-shy company called the allegations "unfounded, uninformed in many cases, patently absurd and, overall, extremely damaging to the open competitive U.S. marketing system which serves every element of the agricultural community so well."[233]

As for editor Mort Sosland, he never did find out who Mr. Smith was, but he came to believe that his shadowy source with the British accent was probably Russian. "He said he enjoyed talking with us," Sosland later recalled, "and we replied in kind. In fact, our last words to him were, 'Don't get hit by a truck.' That was a sincere wish for someone who is in a hazardous occupation and has unusually good sources of information. He was a real joy to visit with, spy or not."[234]

## New Realities

The effect of the Soviet purchases on the Minneapolis market was profound. The amount of grain shipped to elevators in the Twin Cities and Duluth-Superior jumped dramatically. Railroads found it increasingly difficult to keep up with demand, prompting *Business Week* to predict a freight-car shortage of "monumental proportions."[235] Barge lines were stretched to the limit too, as the navigation season ended with a record two hundred million bushels of grain moving out by river from the Twin Cities area.[236] By mid-September, wheat futures were trading at their highest level in nearly ten years on the Minneapolis Grain Exchange, and were frequently topping out at their daily rally limit of ten cents a bushel.[237]

But the implications of the Russian grain deals stretched far beyond Minneapolis. Increasing grain prices combined with other factors, including the OPEC oil embargo, to drive up the cost of food. In 1973 alone, consumer food prices jumped 20 percent despite controls imposed by President Nixon. Between 1971 and 1975, the global grain trade increased almost 50 percent, with the United States accounting for most of that growth. And surpluses, long the bane of the grain trade, were vanishing. In the summer of 1972, when the Russians were bargaining for their grain, American wheat stocks had totaled more than twenty-three million tons. The following year, they were down to just under seven million tons. The Russian

In 1973, the year following the announcement of the Soviet grain sales, trading would occasionally grind to a halt in the Minneapolis wheat pit when the market was "locked limit-up"—the maximum daily upward price movement.

buying spree was not the only factor behind these changes (demand for grain was increasing due to global dietary changes and falling poverty rates), but, as journalist Dan Morgan pointed out in *Merchants of Grain,* it certainly accelerated the globalization of the grain trade:

Prices of all grains rapidly rose above the government support price, placing the markets firmly in the hands of the commercial grain trade. Now the American price—the price shouted out at the trading pits of the Chicago Board of Trade [and the Minneapolis Grain Exchange]—was the price for the whole world. On the electronic board that records prices and price trends, a line across various commodities in various deliveries read like this: UP . . . UP . . . UP . . . UP . . . UP . . . UP . . . UP . . . UP . . . UP . . . UP. There was no longer any need to bolster American farm prices. The days of soggy world wheat markets were over. U.S. food commanded top dollar, and the customers included every nation in the world.[238]

As surpluses dried up and government price supports became less of a factor in the grain trade, the exchanges reasserted themselves. In Minneapolis, the volume of futures trading increased steadily through the 1970s. Wheat prices, which had hovered below two dollars a bushel in the years before the Russian grain deals, never again dropped below the two-dollar

As trading volume increased, a long-dormant sense of excitement returned to the Grain Exchange's futures pit.

**Leo Odden has been cutting hair in his one-chair barbershop in the Grain Exchange for thirty-five years, and at age sixty-nine, he doesn't plan to stop now.**

threshold. These were high times in the futures pit. The free market, not the government, was in control—at least most of the time.

At times it seemed like everyone in the Grain Exchange building was caught up in the excitement over the Russian grain deals, even the barber. Leo Odden had recently moved his hair-cutting business into the old barbershop off the building's main entrance. His clientele included many of the traders who were helping the futures market set volume records, and they liked to talk. Odden had been warned when he first arrived at the Grain Exchange to steer clear of the commodities market. "You'll just get your fingers burned," he said he was told. But as he later admitted,

some of the traders who came in for haircuts were hard to ignore:

I remember, it was about '73. That was about the time the Russian deal came in. And a guy informed me, he says, "Soybeans are going to go up twenty cents." He told me about a certain broker, and I go to him and buy at three forty-three. And the next day, the guy comes by and he says, "Oh, you can make three hundred dollars if you sell today." One day, I says, "That's good, but I heard it's going to go up twenty cents." So I don't sell. But then two days later [the price] went down to three thirty-nine and a half, and he sells me out. Now I have a loss. He didn't suppose I was a sophisticated enough investor. I could've made a margin call. But he just sold me out. Probably wanted to get rid of me because I wasn't a big enough potato. One contract, you know?

Never again did Leo the barber act on a tip from a grain-trading customer. "All these years," he said with a smile, "and I haven't learned to get rich yet."[239]

Every once in a while, the government reminded the grain markets that it was still capable of tinkering with the law of supply and demand. In January 1980, traders in Minneapolis and elsewhere reacted with dismay when President Jimmy Carter announced he was imposing a grain embargo on the Soviet Union. The Soviets had recently invaded Afghanistan, and Carter— convinced that the 1970s grain deals had given the United States immense leverage over the USSR— decided to try to force the Russians to withdraw troops by cutting off their access to U.S. grain. Officials in the Carter administration realized that the announcement might trigger a wave of panic selling in the nation's grain exchanges, so the Commodities Futures Trading Commission voted in an emergency session to suspend futures trading in four commodities markets, including the Minneapolis Grain Exchange.

When the Minneapolis market opened on the Monday following

Carter's announcement, the futures pit was empty. Traders strolled aimlessly around the floor, coalescing in small groups to discuss—in colorful terms—what was going on. "This has never happened to us before," one trader lamented. "We can't cancel futures contracts. That's never been heard of in the grain trade, so we really don't know what to do." The inactivity in the futures pit also created confusion on the other side of the trading floor, at the cash grain tables. Most cash grain traders were unwilling to buy or sell without futures prices to guide them. "Everyone is still so terribly confused that it's impossible to make any intelligent decisions about what the government is doing," said another trader.[240]

When trading resumed two days later, the futures pit descended into near chaos. At the sound of the opening bell, the throng of nervous traders surged forward, displaying even more urgency than normal. Arms waved, shoulders collided, faces turned scarlet in frustration. *Minneapolis Tribune* reporter Dennis McGrath could hardly believe what he was seeing:

One trader in a blue smock was hit in the head by an errant elbow and his eyeglasses fell off. As he bent over to pick them up, it looked as if he was going down for good. Then the entire pack suddenly leaned dangerously to the left, and it appeared

The Minneapolis Grain Exchange trading pit was empty following President Jimmy Carter's 1980 announcement of the Soviet grain embargo. The Commodities Futures Trading Commission ordered the Grain Exchange and other commodities markets to suspend futures trading so as to prevent potential panic selling.

Trading resumed after a two-day suspension prompted by the Soviet grain embargo. After a couple of minutes of frenzied activity, most contracts were "locked limit-down"—the maximum daily downward price movement.

that they all would tumble into the pit. The trader regained his footing. In the next moment, the pack swayed back the other way. And back the other way again.

And on it went for about 100 maddening seconds until every-body realized that everybody else wanted to sell but that nobody wanted to buy.[241]

When the out-of-breath traders looked up at the electronic quotation board, they saw green "D20s" under all but one of the contract months for Minneapolis wheat. (December wheat was the exception.) D20 meant that the price of each of those contracts had already dropped twenty cents, the most it could fall in one day under the law. After two minutes of screaming and pushing in the pit, almost all futures trading was suspended for the day. "This is about what everybody expected," said the exchange's president, John Case. "It's also about the same thing that would have happened Monday if the market had been opened."[242]

In the two weeks that followed the imposition of the embargo, the price of spring wheat futures at the Grain Exchange dropped fifty-five cents a bushel, from $4.35 to $3.80. The members of the exchange's board of directors worried about the long-term implications of the embargo, and they asked Case to send a letter to President Carter outlining their concerns. In his letter, Case reminded Carter that American wheat exports had increased 91 percent during the 1970s, and he expressed the opinion that "only the private grain trade in the United States could have produced such dramatic results." The members of the Grain Exchange were gravely concerned, he wrote, that the federal government was tampering with the free market:

Recent action by the United States Government ordering an embargo on certain grain shipments to the Soviet Union . . . and the subsequent actions by the Government made in response to the embargo, including the suspension of futures trading in certain grains for two days, are viewed with great alarm by the Minneapolis Grain Exchange. These actions created considerable chaos for American agriculture and are feared by some to be the opening prelude to the nationalization of the grain export industry. If these fears are realized, the embargo and the subsequent Government actions taken are the beginning of a great tragedy for the United States.[243]

As it turned out, such fears were unwarranted. Within weeks, the markets rebounded. That autumn, spring wheat futures approached the five-dollar mark. In April 1981, the nation's newly elected president, Ronald Reagan, lifted the grain embargo. The free market was back in business.

Trading in the Grain Exchange's futures pit remained fairly steady, if unspectacular, for most of the 1980s. These were the years of what became widely known as the farm crisis. A variety of factors, including overproduction and increased foreign competition, played havoc with the nation's agricultural sector. Thousands of farmers, buffeted by falling crop

Duane Stich (left), executive vice president of the Bunge Corporation and president of the Minneapolis Grain Exchange (1977–1978), chats with John Case, his Grain Exchange successor (1979–1980) and president of Kellogg.

Ted Metz (left), of the Bunge corporation, and Ron Olson, vice president of grain operations for General Mills and past chair of the Minneapolis Grain Exchange (1984–1986).

prices and heavy debt, went bankrupt. At the same time, the nation's agricultural commodities markets also were feeling the pinch. The annual volume of futures trading in Minneapolis remained heavy by historical standards—usually well above three hundred thousand contracts traded—but the spectacular rate of growth that had become commonplace during the 1970s leveled off.

By the early 1990s, business was once again picking up. In 1991, the exchange posted a 31 percent increase in futures and options trading, making it the fastest growing futures market in the country.[244] Big-volume freelance speculators were entering the market, making it easier for the big grain and milling companies to protect themselves from price fluctuations. "Now they [the big companies] can come in and get their hedge without anyone knowing they are in the market," observed the exchange's president, Jim Lindau. "Our liquidity has grown dramatically. The more volume we trade, the easier it is. You don't have someone, on one trade, bringing the market down." As trading volume increased, the price of membership soared. By October 1992, exchange memberships were going for more than $11,000, more than double their 1985 value.[245] "Money-making opportunities are so dramatic in Minneapolis that people, especially locals, are flocking

The volume of futures trading began increasing again during the early 1990s, thanks in large part to the arrival of more large-volume freelance speculators. With speculators assuming a greater share of the market's risk, big grain and milling companies found it easier to hedge.

to Minneapolis," said trader Helen Pound. "The pit population is six times what it used to be. We have the ability to trade a lot more paper than what we're doing."[246]

In 1993, the number of wheat futures contracts traded in Minneapolis topped 750,000 for the first time. Five years later, volume passed the one million mark. As the Grain Exchange entered the twenty-first century, it seemed as though the futures market was breaking records every few months. The annual volume for 2004—nearly 1.4 million futures contracts traded—was more than twenty times larger than the volume recorded in 1971, the year before the Russian grain deals.

## Low on Cash

As the futures market at the Grain Exchange soared, the cash grain market headed in the opposite direction. To be sure, Minneapolis remained the country's largest cash grain market, with wheat receipts reliably topping 100 million bushels a year. But troubling changes were afoot. Most of the Grain Exchange's members still spent a majority of their time trading in the cash market, but they had less grain to trade. The statistics tracking receipts told only part of the story. While plenty of grain was still arriving in Minneapolis, less and less of it was being bought and sold on the floor of the Grain Exchange. Fewer traders gathered around the cash grain tables, and those who did found fewer grain pans over which to haggle. In the old days, so much grain had spilled onto the floor every day that it took two janitors the better part of the afternoon to clean it all up. Now when the trading was over, the floor was nearly pristine.[247] The sun still shone bright through the tall windows on the trading floor's east side, but the mood was slowly darkening.

While plenty of competing theories made the rounds about what was happening to the cash grain market, most traders agreed that the drop-off in activity on the east end of the floor was due largely to changes in the transportation of grain. Trucks and barges continued to divert grain from the exchange, just as they had during the 1950s and 1960s. And now another transportation phenomenon was disrupting the cash grain market in ways that few people had anticipated.

The rail freight system on which the grain trade had always depended was undergoing a major transformation. Hopper cars, introduced during the early 1960s, were catching on quickly. They held more grain and were much easier to load and unload than the old, leaky boxcars they replaced. As shippers and processors improved their facilities to accommodate the new cars,

By the 1980s, trading at the cash grain tables was beginning to slow considerably.

Despite reductions in the amount of grain actually coming through the Grain Exchange, sellers still brought their grain pans to the tables and buyers continued to show up to get a close look at what was being offered for sale.

another innovation—the unit train—appeared on the scene. Unit trains consisting of dozens of hopper cars could carry huge amounts of grain much more efficiently than boxcar trains could. They were especially efficient when they traveled point-to-point—from the country directly to the processor or the exporter—without making stops or switches in between. "With that fifty or seventy-five car unit, you've got one bill of lading, one waybill, one freight bill, one destination, and one

Huge unit train being assembled from Illinois Central cars outside Gibson City, Illinois, in 1968.

A sign of the times: This grain pan contained a sample drawn from a new type of railway car: the hopper car. The growing popularity of hoppers was one of the main factors in the gradual shrinking of Minneapolis's cash grain market.

turn-around," explained longtime trader Shelley Walsh. "It's considerably easier than the idea of shipping one or two cars at a time or one truck at a time."[248] The railroads were eager to encourage this new, more efficient hauling method, and they began offering lower rates to

shippers that were willing to move their grain point-to-point.

The advent of point-to-point shipping had huge implications for the Grain Exchange. In years past, almost all the grain produced in Minnesota, the Dakotas, and Montana had gone through Minneapolis in one way or another. Samples from nearly every boxcar of the region's grain eventually appeared on the exchange's cash grain tables, even if the grain itself went elsewhere. Now, though, the railroads were encouraging some of the Grain Exchange's biggest member firms to ship their grain directly. And if Cargill, for instance, wanted to take advantage of the railroads' point-to-point rates, it had to buy its grain in the country, where it was produced, not in Minneapolis.

Not surprisingly, that's exactly what Cargill and the other big grain firms started doing. They opened offices in small towns and began buying grain directly from country elevators. Suddenly, many of the Minneapolis commission firms that represented those elevators were losing business. Shelley Walsh was among the traders who noticed the shift:

There were some twenty to twenty-two commission firms that represented country elevators [at the Minneapolis Grain Exchange]. In many cases they, the commission firms, financed the country elevators and they shipped all their grain to them. But later on as the information age became more prevalent, where the grain elevators were more informed as [to] what the prices might be . . . they would sell direct, rather than shipping it to the market, to have it sold on a commission basis.[249]

As point-to-point shipping siphoned grain from Minneapolis, other factors came into play. For example, more and more grain was being purchased on a "to-arrive" basis. Buyers sent bids to country dealers, offering to purchase a certain amount of grain at a certain price for

delivery on a certain date. If the dealer accepted, the grain counted as "to-arrive." "Most everything is sold to-arrive today," trader Ralph Bagley observed. "[Before,] we used to wait for the grain to arrive at an inspection point, Aberdeen or Grand Forks or one of those places, [to] be sampled out there. We'd get the sample overnight and display it on the trading floor and sell it. But it would be actual cash grain. . . . Now most of the grain is bought out in the country, is sold the same day

Shelley Walsh (left) and his father, Matt Walsh, incorporated the Walsh Grain Company in 1948. Matt was an experienced grain man who had worked with Archer Daniels Midland. Shelley began his career with the Mullin-Dillon Company following four years of service with the U.S. Air Force during World War II. Walsh Grain operated as a merchandising company, buying grain on the trading floor of the Minneapolis Grain Exchange and selling it to feed dealers, oat millers, distillers, and retailers in other markets. Later the company acquired storage facilities that enabled it to better serve its customers. Matt Walsh retired at age ninety-two in 1985. Shelley Walsh took "early" retirement at age seventy-eight in 1996.

Fritz Corrigan, the first non-family president of the Peavey Company, from 1965 to 1977. He was president of the Grain Exchange from 1967 to 1968.

with a guaranteed grade or an approximation grade subject to adjustment."[250] Although "to-arrive" sales counted as receipts on the Grain Exchange's ledgers, the grain itself was never bought or sold on the trading floor.

The industry-wide trend toward consolidation also contributed to the decline in activity at the cash grain tables. The McCabe Company's decision to sell out to the Farmers Union Grain Terminal Association during the 1950s had signaled bigger things to come. In 1983, the GTA merged with North Pacific Grain Growers to become Harvest States Cooperatives. Fifteen years later, Harvest States merged with

another major cooperative, Cenex, to create Cenex Harvest States, a Fortune 500 company with diversified interests in the energy, grains, and foods sectors. CHS's owners included farmers, ranchers, and cooperatives over most of the western half of the United States, as well as thousands of preferred stockholders.

But mergers within the cooperative movement were just part of the story. In 1976, the Swiss agribusiness concern, the Sandoz Corporation, acquired Minnesota's Northrup King. In 1999, archrivals Cargill and Continental combined their operations. And in a series of moves that significantly reduced the number of member firms at the

James Mullin (left) and Ed Mullin, celebrating James's birthday on the trading floor in 1987. The men were not related, yet they were fondly known as the "Mullin brothers" at the Grain Exchange. Ed was cofounder of Mullin-Dillon, from which he retired at the age of ninety, while James was manager of the Dreyfus Corporation and legendary for his knowledge of the grain business.

Grain Exchange, ConAgra of Omaha, Nebraska, embarked on an aggressive acquisition campaign. In 1977, the company made its first foray into the grain merchandising business by purchasing the McMillan Company (formerly Osborne McMillan), a four-generation grain firm with elevator operations throughout the Upper Midwest. It followed that purchase with the acquisitions of several other longtime member firms, including Burdick Grain, Atwood-Larson, and, in 1982, the Peavey Company. In the years that followed, ConAgra established itself as one of the world's leading diversified food companies, with a roster of well-known brand-name products, including Egg Beaters, Slim Jim, and Butterball turkey.

These and other consolidations significantly reduced the number of buyers and sellers on the floor. In 1960, the Grain Exchange had listed 167 firms and corporations on its membership rolls. But as the years went by and the consolidation trend accelerated, that number steadily declined. By 2000, the number of firms and corporations on the exchange's membership list was down to forty-one, less than a quarter of the number listed forty years earlier.

Advancements in communications technology also played a significant role in the cash grain market's slide. The Grain Exchange's imposing assembly of cash grain tables had always been a marketplace in the truest sense of the word. Grain was traded there, certainly, but so was information. The cash grain market was a kind of gentlemen's bazaar where buyers and sellers absorbed news, information, and rumor as they haggled over prices. During the exchange's first few decades, traders had depended almost exclusively on in-house telegraph companies—usually Western Union—to provide timely market data. Later, with the advent of the telephone, trading firms arranged to have lines connected directly to their trading tables. Noise on the floor made it nearly impossible to hear a phone ringing, so lights were installed on each table to signal incoming calls. Weather reports were updated regularly. Bids and offers were sent by telex machine. The exchange's cash grain market was a beehive of information, filled with expensive communications equipment benefiting every member firm. But as communications technology became less cumbersome and more affordable, the cash grain tables lost some of their luster. With information now readily available from multiple sources, traders had fewer reasons to visit the floor.

All of these changes—the development of communications technology, the consolidation of trading companies, the growing dependence on

A fourth-generation grain man, Truxtun ("Truck") Morrison grew up at "Highcroft," his great-grandfather Frank H. Peavey's home in Wayzata (see page 46). Following the merger of the Peavey Company with ConAgra in 1982, Morrison was named president of ConAgra Trading Companies and later became chair of ConAgra International.

**John Duncan McMillan, president of Minneapolis's Osborn-McMillan Elevator Company, served as president of the Chamber of Commerce from 1907 to 1908. The Osborn-McMillan Company owned the giant Shoreham elevator in Minneapolis; maintained a chain of well-equipped country elevators along the lines of the Great Northern and the Minneapolis, St. Paul, and Sault Ste. Marie Railroads; and had large holdings in the wheat-producing regions of the Canadian Northwest. McMillan's son, Howard I. McMillan, succeeded him as president of Osborn-McMillan and was president of the Minneapolis Grain Exchange from 1956 to 1957. In 1968, Howard I. McMillan Jr., a third-generation granger, founded the McMillan Company, a terminal elevator company that was acquired in 1978 by ConAgra.**

"to-arrive" sales, the dominance of point-to-point unit train shipping, the advent of direct buying by Cargill and other big grain companies—combined to transform the culture of Minneapolis's venerable cash grain market. By the early 1980s, many longtime traders hardly recognized the place where they had always come to do business and make a living.

As the Minneapolis Grain Exchange entered the twenty-first century, it remained the biggest cash grain market in the country, but its promotional materials rarely mentioned that distinction. The fact was the east side of the trading floor was usually empty now. The old tables—all twenty-three of them—were still there, dominating the scene like a herd of grazing, six-legged cattle, but they rarely attracted anyone other than an occasional straggler from the futures side. Most mornings, a dozen or so buyers and sellers gathered at the tables to trade a few cars of grain, but they usually finished their business in fifteen minutes. Much of the grain coming through the exchange now was displayed in the sample rooms of member firms and was traded off the floor by phone or fax. Those who remembered how busy the cash grain market used to be didn't appreciate the change. "To me, it was a lot easier to trade eye to eye with a buyer," durum trader Howard Smith observed. "You

don't see the person anymore. It's a lot harder to feel the camaraderie and the friendship."[251]

## New Contracts

By early 1980, the powers that be at the Grain Exchange figured the time had come to add a new futures contract to the mix. Granted, the futures pit's two most recent additions—pork bellies in 1971 and durum in 1973—had failed miserably due to lack of interest, but the timing seemed right this time. On the one hand, 1979 had been a record year in the trading of hard red spring wheat futures; with wheat doing so well, surely other commodities could catch the wave. On the other hand, trading on the cash grain side was dwindling, and the chances of recovery there looked slim; an additional futures contract could help the exchange offset whatever losses it might suffer at the cash grain tables. But which commodity offered the best chance of success? After several months of study, officials at the exchange came up with what they believed was the perfect answer: sunflower seeds.

By most measures, it appeared that sunflowers were indeed on the verge of becoming a major cash crop. Farmers in the region had begun planting sunflowers in the late 1960s. Lack of demand from domestic processors initially had kept production down, but by the mid-1970s, several companies were beginning to produce sunflower-based consumer products such as Promise margarine and Puritan cooking oil. Demand took off and farmers took notice. Between 1977 and 1979, sunflower seed production in Minnesota alone increased sevenfold.[252] With the number of acres planted in sunflowers increasing rapidly, a sunflower futures market suddenly looked feasible. "Until 1979 we ran out of the crop before the end of the year," said Grain Exchange president Ralph Hayenga, who was also senior vice president of oilseed processor Honeymead. "Everything was sold the year it was grown." Now the crop was large enough to produce a carryover from one year to the next, he said. That carryover produced price uncertainty, one of the necessary ingredients for a successful futures market.[253]

The Grain Exchange's previous experiments with new futures contracts had taken place in the same octagonal trading pit where, for years, wheat futures had been bought and sold. This time, though, officials at the exchange wanted to do something that signaled their confidence in the long-term viability of their newest product. With that goal in mind, they approved the construction of a new pit, adjacent to the old one, made especially for the trading of sunflower futures. In a nod to wheat's long-established

dominance in Minneapolis, the sunflower pit was smaller, shallower, and had two fewer sides (it was hexagonal) than the wheat pit.

On the morning of May 6, 1980, Al Donahoo, the exchange's executive vice president, stood on the steps of the sunflower pit, rolling a cigar between his thumb and forefinger. In the words of *Minneapolis Tribune* staff writer Dennis McGrath, "he looked very much like an expectant father." When the opening bell sounded at 9:30, the pit erupted in pandemonium, as about two dozen traders frantically screamed and gesticulated at each other. The first contract for one hundred thousand pounds of sunflower seeds traded

Incoming Grain Exchange president Win Wallin (left), president of Pillsbury, accepts an apple from Grain Exchange outgoing exchange president Ralph Hayenga of Honeymead on Apple Day 1981. Apple Day is a long-standing tradition at the Grain Exchange, held annually in mid-October to coincide with the announcement of the new slate of directors for the upcoming year.

**The first day of trading in the new sunflower pit—May 6, 1980—was one of the biggest events in the Minneapolis Grain Exchange's recent history. Newspaper, radio, and television reporters joined hundreds of spectators on the floor and in the visitors gallery.**

at $9.10. Fifteen minutes later, prices were up as much as seventeen cents a hundredweight. By eleven o'clock, all contract months were trading actively and the price of the July contract had jumped fifty cents, the maximum allowable by law. In all, 177 sunflower contracts were traded that first day. Donahoo retired to the traders' dining room with a cup of coffee, a half-smoked cigar, and a smile on his face. "I'm quite pleased," he said. "I don't know what would be a good volume of trade, but it seems to be quite substantial. Some people were saying if we traded fifty contracts it would be a good day."[254]

For a while, it appeared that the first day of trading might be the busiest the market would ever see. By July, only half a dozen sunflower-only traders—newcomers attracted by reduced-price trading permits—were showing up regularly on the floor. Established traders, especially those representing the big grain companies, stayed away. The sunflower futures market was proving too small and unstable to absorb the kind of large deals the big firms liked to swing. "One day we sold forty-two [sunflower] contracts in the pit and it sent the price down the limit," one trader said. "Now if we stand in there, nobody will bid or offer."[255]

Then, the following month, things began looking up. Minneapolis's sunflower market set volume records in August (435 contracts, or 43,500,000 pounds of seeds, traded), and then again in October (487 contracts traded).[256] It appeared that sunflowers might actually usher in a new, even brighter future on the exchange. The value of exchange memberships began rising. In November, a membership sold for a record $23,000. The following month, another sold for $25,000.[257] Some optimists began wondering aloud whether the Grain Exchange might soon challenge the dominance of the Chicago Board of Trade.

It wasn't long before reality set in. Action in the sunflower pit began falling off again. Representatives for the grain companies blamed speculators for abandoning sunflowers and other commodities in favor of hot-selling financial instruments, such as Treasury bills and foreign currencies. Speculators pointed fingers at the grain firms for failing to support the contract. Still others singled out growers for cutting production after the record year of 1979.

By the summer of 1982, Minneapolis's sunflower futures market was essentially dead. The sunflower trading pit was little more than a shortcut for traders on their way to the wheat pit. The space on the electronic trading board, beneath the heading "SUNFLOWER," dis-

played random messages ("Traders smocks for sale on the east end of the trading floor"), not prices. In his unofficial postmortem, the exchange's staff economist, Don Nelson, declared that the sunflower futures market was probably doomed from the start. "I think the exchange made a mistake in choosing the commodity itself," he said.[258]

The failure of the sunflower futures market did not, however, deter exchange officials in their quest to expand the organization's roster of futures contracts. In the years that followed, they introduced seven new contracts, most of which lasted no more than three or four years. Two of the contracts—oats (introduced in 1988) and durum (1998)—were based on grains that had been traded for decades at the exchange's cash tables. But the others left many people scratching their heads. White wheat (1984) was grown in the Pacific Northwest, far from Minneapolis's traditional growing region. High-fructose corn syrup (1987) was a processed commodity. Electricity (1998) seemed out of place for a market that specialized in grain. And then there was shrimp.

When the exchange introduced shrimp futures in 1993, many observers wondered how a landlocked market like Minneapolis could hope to attract traders in

Winston R. ("Win") Wallin became a member of the Minneapolis Grain Exchange in the early 1950s as a wheat buyer for the Pillsbury Company. Later, while president of Pillsbury (1977–1985), he also became president of the Minneapolis Grain Exchange, in 1981–1982. Wallin was keenly interested in the heritage of the Grain Exchange buildings, which were designated for historic preservation during his tenure. He went on to become the chair and CEO of Medtronic, headquartered in Minneapolis.

The shrimp contract, introduced in 1993, never met the expectations of its proponents. It was phased out less than a decade later.

crustaceans. Exchange officials responded that several big food companies in the area, including General Mills (Red Lobster) and International Multifoods (Boston Sea Party), were huge buyers of shrimp. As it turned out, most of those companies showed little or no interest. To some longtime members, including John Dill, the decision to expand into seafood was incomprehensible. "The board needed to be hit on the head with a two-by-four [for that one]," Dill said.[259]

The fact was that the Grain Exchange faced long odds in its attempts to expand its futures offerings. Most new commodities contracts—about 75 percent—failed within a few years of their inception.

Even Jim Lindau, who, as president of the exchange in 1993, oversaw the launching of the shrimp contract, conceded that nearly every new futures contract faced the same chicken-or-the-egg conundrum. "You can't get liquidity until you get traders and you can't get traders until you get liquidity," he said.[260] Not only that, many of the more established traders balked at learning the ins and outs of new commodities. "Quite frankly I wasn't interested in going 'back to school,'" said longtime trader Pete Ritten. "When all this stuff started to come, it was time for me to say thanks, but no thanks. I knew the grain business, but I didn't think I knew anything particularly about, oh, gasoline futures or what have you."[261]

## Modern Days

Many of the changes that occurred at the Grain Exchange during the last three decades of the twentieth century—the explosion of trading in the futures pit, the decline of the cash grain market, the introduction of new futures contracts—were the result of developments in agriculture, transportation, and the broader grain trade. But a few of the most visible changes on the floor were triggered by cultural upheavals in the non-grain-trading world. The 1960s had shaken the foundations of American society, and few institutions—not even the Minneapolis Grain Exchange—were able to ignore what was going on, particularly with gender issues.

Like most business enterprises of the time, the chamber had no women members. In fact, for many years, the rules had stated explicitly that only men could be members of the exchange. Once, back in the summer of 1901, a prospective grain trader identified in the newspapers as Mrs. S. M. Passmore had applied for membership. (This woman was possibly Sarah Passmore, the widow of grain dealer Reginald Passmore, former president of the Anchor Grain Company.) In deciding to reject her application, the directors set themselves up as easy targets for Ida Husted Harper, a well-known women's rights columnist for the *New York Sun:*

The Minneapolis Chamber of Commerce may pass just as many resolutions as those eight men who rejected Mrs. Passmore choose to vote for, but they can no more prevent women from eventually becoming members than they can check water from flowing over their falls or stop up the source of the Mississippi.[262]

The *Minneapolis Journal* agreed with Harper, noting that the directors' concern for precedent was "merely a honeyed way of concealing inherited prejudice against women in business, a species of moth-eaten conservatism." But the

exchange remained female-free. In the spring of 1966, however, Grain Exchange members were asked to vote on an amendment to its membership rules that would remove all references to gender:

Any person of legal age, whose character, credit and reputation for fair dealing are such as to satisfy the Association Membership Committee, the Directors' Membership Committee, and the Board of Directors, that the applicant will be a suitable person to entrust with the privileges and responsibilities of membership, and only such persons, shall be eligible to membership in this Association.[263]

The records of the Grain Exchange give no clue as to why the association decided, at that moment in its history, to consider what previous generations of grain traders would have considered a radical revision of its membership requirements. But this was 1966, and the women's rights movement was just beginning to gather steam. The membership's vote wasn't even close. The proposed amendment allowing women to become members passed by a vote of 190 to zero.

Those who expected the change in the rules to immediately transform what had, for the better part of a century, been a bastion of male-only commerce were to be disappointed.

John G. Dill Jr. served from 1983 to 1984 as board chair of the Minneapolis Grain Exchange, where three generations of his family have been members. In 1889 his great-uncle, Robert E. Jones, incorporated a country elevator company, also known as R. E. Jones, in Wabasha, Minnesota. It operated elevators from eastern Wisconsin to southwestern Minnesota. The name changed in 1934 to the J. G. Dill Company. John Dill ran the grain, feed, fertilizer, and farming operation until 2003.

**Marcia Hill of Cargill was one of the first women to break the gender barrier on the Minneapolis Grain Exchange's cash grain side.**

In the five years that followed the vote, not one woman was elected to membership in the exchange. About the only women seen on the floor were the chalk-wielding board markers who kept the exchange's huge quotations blackboard up to date. The real gender-barrier break-throughs didn't come until 1971, when Jeanette Hanson, a business-woman from Fergus Falls, Minne-sota, became the Grain Exchange's first woman member.[264]

Hanson was the wife of another Grain Exchange trader, Allen Hanson, and she intended to join her husband in the futures pit. The exchange was on the verge of launching its new pork bellies contract, and she wanted to get in on the action.[265] Unfortunately for her and other like-minded traders, the pork bellies contract lasted only about a year. Hanson's time in the pit was limited.

Still, as the decade wore on, more and more women made their way to the floor. Unlike Hanson, most of them started on the cash grain side. Marcia Hill, a trader for Cargill, was among the first. She was the only woman on the floor when she started in September 1973. "The men react-ed favorably," she recalled. "For the most part they were friendly, open and cooperative. I think I got more help because I was a woman." Two months later, Hill was joined at the cash grain tables by Sue Blank, a trad-er with the Benson-Quinn Company. "Everyone was just great," Blank said, looking back on the experience. "I feel like I've been treated as an equal in all respects. I've never felt that anyone tried to take advantage of me or showed me any favoritism because I was a woman."[266]

For whatever reason, few women ever built enduring careers in the exchange's futures pit. Helen Pound was the most notable exception. Pound had risen through the ranks as a cash grain trader at Pillsbury. In 1983, she moved to the other side of the floor in hopes of making more money as an independent trader in the high-flying futures market.

**Few women who worked at the Grain Exchange were as persistent as Helen Pound (foreground, facing camera). After getting her start as a cash grain trader for Pillsbury, she built a successful career as an independent trader on the futures side.**

Looking back on her career, Pound recalled with a smile that some of her male colleagues assumed she "didn't have a clue," but she insisted that their low expectations often played to her advantage:

You can't always control the way society looks at you for whatever reason, and you just do the best you can. . . . I can tell you one of my real advantages—and I kind of think that this is a woman's advantage, but I don't know—is that I can kind of sense the emotion of the pit pretty well. I've had some men in the pit tell me that they wished they could be totally unemotional about their decision-making, and they think that would be an advantage to them. They go to great lengths to not pay attention to the emotion of the pit. And I think a lot of what goes on is reasonable and rational and analytical, and a lot of the decisions that go on have to do with the emotion of things. People get carried away with exuberance or they panic on things. And it's kind of good to know whether you're in an environment where you're panicking or people around you are panicking. To assume that no one has emotion is not, in my book, realistic.[267]

Even as women were joining the men on the trading floor, other changes were occurring that reflected cultural transformations taking place outside the walls at Fourth and Fourth. In the mid-1980s, the exchange room committee—the group in charge of regulating daily life on the trading floor—tackled two issues inspired by the changing mores of the time: smoking and the dress code.

Cigarettes, cigars, and even chewing tobacco had long been considered standard-issue accessories among many traders on the floor. For years, the futures pit resembled a giant, octagonal ashtray, its hardwood floor spotted with thousands of tiny cigarette burns. But by the mid-1970s, smoking was losing its cachet among exchange members and the general public. In 1975, the Minnesota Clean Indoor Air Act established the state as a pioneer in what some people called the "tobacco control movement." The new law restricted smoking in public places, including workplaces, to designated areas. The Grain Exchange was, by the law's definition, a public place, and it had to be brought into compliance.

At first, the Grain Exchange responded to the law by designating certain places on the trading floor as smoking sections. On the cash grain side, for example, traders were allowed to smoke only in front of the weather maps. But in 1985, a complaint from a nonsmoking member prompted the exchange to contemplate revisions to its policies. After

considering several options, including the construction of a "greenhouse" for smokers ("a 'zoo cage' exhibiting idle persons tied to their coercive habit would present an unfavorable and unconstructive image of our business for visitors"), smoking was banned on the trading floor altogether. Durum trader Howard Smith was a smoker and a member of the board of directors. He opposed the smoking ban, but he knew he was fighting a losing battle. "Finally I said, 'Listen, I'm tired of beating my head on the wall. Eliminate smoking on the floor.'"[268] Smith and his fellow smokers took their cigarettes outside, capitulating to what the exchange room committee called "the trend of the times."[269]

Another trend of the times was the growing acceptance of more casual forms of attire. For most of the Grain Exchange's history, members had adhered to an unwritten code of conduct regulating what should and should not be worn on the trading floor. In earlier years, many, if not most, traders wore suits, ties, and hats. As time went on and fashions changed, the hats disappeared, but the jackets and ties remained. It was not until 1978 that the exchange's rules and regulations were amended to include a section on "decorum and dress." The new rules included few specifics beyond the stipulation that members wear "conventional busi-

nesslike attire and footwear" and that their clothes be "clean and presentable." The main exception was a requirement that men wear sports jackets, grain jackets, or business suits during winter months.[270]

But the codifying of the dress code seemed to bring out the sartorial rebel in some members. Traders began showing up on the floor in jeans, corduroys, and golf shirts, prompting at least one disgusted member to complain about "a dress code which permits floor traders to dress like ranch hands."[271] In 1991, the exchange room committee adopted new rules prohibiting jeans and requiring dress shirts and ties (either necktie or bowtie). But times were changing. Outside the exchange, many employers were actually encouraging their workers to dress more casually. As the Grain Exchange approached its 125th year, many floor traders were operating on the fringes of the dress code, decked out in loudly patterned trading jackets, knit shirts, bolo ties, and athletic shoes.

## Good Information

For nearly a century, the traders at the Minneapolis Grain Exchange had acquired the up-to-the-moment price information they needed by looking up at an elongated blackboard mounted well above the trading floor. The board listed not only the prices generated in Minneapolis, but those from Chicago and Kansas City as well. Fast-moving board markers armed with chalk and erasers kept the numbers up to date. During the busiest stretches, the markers hardly had time to catch their breath. It was a nerve-wracking job. Make a mistake, and the traders on the floor could lose a lot of money. At one time, the board markers all had been men, but by the 1950s, women had taken over. For many of them, board marking was a perfect part-time job, from 9:00 a.m. to 2:00 p.m.—five hours at work and back home by the time the kids returned from school. And despite the pressure, they had the satisfaction of knowing they were essential to the smooth operation of one of America's great commodities markets. They were the keepers of a long tradition, a link to a glorious past.[272] But in 1978, they became obsolete.

Electronic quotation boards were all the rage by then. They were fast. They were easy to read. And they announced to everyone who laid eyes on them that the future had arrived. All the other major exchanges in the country had traded in their blackboards for electronic replacements. The Minneapolis Grain Exchange was the last holdout. But in the summer of 1978, it finally made the leap.

The Grain Exchange's new electronic board—seventy-five feet long and sixteen feet high—represented a commitment to the future. It was capable of changing sixty numbers per second, an almost inconceivable speed when compared to the performance of even the fastest board

Even with the addition of a formal dress code, the trading floor became an increasingly colorful place.

markers. "From the standpoint of looks, speed, accuracy, the whole operation, it's just going to improve this grain exchange," marveled Jerome Katz of the Bunge Corporation. But the switch to electronics also signaled a break with the past. Board markers had been helping Minneapolis traders keep tabs on the market for nearly a century. Now they were being replaced by machines. "These guys are going to miss good human labor when they get computers that break down all the time," said board marker Mary Proell. "I don't like to see things torn down; there's a lot of history in this building."

In many ways, the Grain Exchange was a throwback to a time when Minneapolis was little more than a village with high expectations and the grain trade of the Upper Midwest was just beginning to blossom. Trades were still consummated with handshakes. Buyers still judged the quality of grain with eyes and nose. But the blackboard above the trading floor had been an integral part of the Grain Exchange since before anyone could remember, and now it was gone. Everyone on the floor seemed to appreciate the significance of what was happening. "There may be historical value [in the chalkboard system], but the

**Board markers equipped with chalk and erasers worked virtually nonstop during trading hours. The women who updated the boards were expected to write quickly, accurately, and legibly.**

business is changing," said Archer Daniels Midland trader Larry Lund. "More information is desired, and the quicker the better." Longtime trader John McCaull was a little more melancholy. "I guess you can't stop progress," he said. "If you still wanted to drive a horse and buggy, you wouldn't get very far."

In the spring of 1980, as the organization approached its one-hundredth anniversary, the board launched a new initiative aimed at propelling the exchange successfully into its second century. With the help of a consulting firm, the newly formed long-range planning committee surveyed the exchange's members. Presented with four possible scenarios for the Grain Exchange's future, members were asked to choose the one they deemed most desirable. Most of the respondents chose what was called the "agribusiness futures scenario"— a kind of crystal-ball vision that assumed great success for the recently launched sunflower contract:

The Minneapolis Grain Exchange will dramatically shift its emphasis from being the largest cash grain market to becoming a dynamic agribusiness futures trading center. The trend is already starting with the approval of the Sunflower contract. This will attract aggressive new members who, in turn, will attract new speculators and speculative activity to the markets.[273]

Jerry Johanning makes a bid in front of the Grain Exchange's new electronic quotation boards. The boards catapulted the trading room from the black-and-white era to the color era.

In 1891, the Grain Exchange was the first clearinghouse to become the buyer to every seller and vice versa at the end of each trading day. By the early 1980s, clearinghouse operations were fully computerized.

But while most members hoped to see the "agribusiness futures scenario" come to fruition, few believed it would. Instead, most of the respondents placed their bets on the "dwindling Minneapolis market

scenario," in which cash grain would continue to bypass Minneapolis and the Chicago Board of Trade would continue to dominate the grain futures trade. Even so, the exchange's directors still felt "very strongly that the Minneapolis Grain Exchange long-term strategy should be based on [the agribusiness futures] scenario," and they continued to pursue that strategy. They were not, however, blind to the challenges ahead. As the survey's final summary acknowledged, "the success, or lack of success, of the sunflower program will dictate whether this scenario could work."[274]

In the end, of course, the sunflower contract did not succeed. Nor did any of the other futures contracts added over the next two decades. About the only lasting change resulting from the long-term planning process was the switch to a full-time, paid president. Over the years, the presidency of the Grain Exchange had developed into something of a ceremonial post, a rotating position filled annually by an exchange member who had served as the previous year's vice president. But the survey found that many members believed the exchange needed stronger leadership. As a result, the board of directors approved plans "to hire a prominent member of the Agribusiness, or related business community, to become a full-time paid President."[275]

The man who ultimately landed the job, Paul Tattersall, did not quite fit that original job description. Instead, he had a background in communications and computer technology. Tattersall was a former senior vice president of the Minneapolis Star and Tribune Company, and had held technology-related management positions with the *Washington Post* and IBM. In the two years since the board had begun considering the hiring of a full-time president, sentiment had grown that the Grain Exchange should begin looking for ways to navigate "the communications and electronics revolutions that will probably change the way commodities are traded." Tattersall seemed the perfect man for the job. "I think trading has become more and more computerized," he said when his hiring was announced. "I think it will also become more national and international. The rapid communication of information is becoming more important. I think that's a fact. It's already happening."[276]

## Computer Age

Although few people at the Grain Exchange realized it at the time, Tattersall immersed himself in the possibilities of what would become known as electronic trading. By 1985, he and several outside consultants had drawn up a business plan for a "computerized futures trading market" called the Automatic Futures Exchange. As he envisioned it, AFEX would be a wholly owned subsidiary of the Minneapolis Grain Exchange. It would initially offer contracts not in grain, but in financial instruments such as T-bonds, T-bills, and foreign currencies. Tattersall was convinced that advancements in technology would soon transform the industry:

In the current environment for futures trading with volume growing rapidly, with new products constantly being introduced, with growing sophistication on the part of participants including the increasing use of computer based technical systems to make bids or offer decisions, and with growing concern on the part of the public for assurances that futures trades are executed by the rules, the AFEX exchange will represent a vital step forward from traditional order filling methodologies.[277]

Whatever the merits of Tattersall's business plan, the idea went nowhere. Its success had depended on convincing major brokers to support the concept, but few were willing to do so. Those who might have been interested in trading by computer remained skeptical that there would be enough volume to make the market liquid. "I couldn't get the people involved who would be needed to trade here," Tattersall admitted. In the summer of 1987, negotiations with a group of potential big-time traders, including Citibank of New York, fell apart.

When that happened, AFEX was officially dead. Tattersall resigned. "I tried to find something unique . . . that would expand the liquidity in our markets," he said. "I didn't succeed. Maybe someone else will."[278]

Although Tattersall's plan to establish a viable electronic trading system failed, the basic idea was not so far-fetched. In October 1987— just a few days after Tattersall tendered his resignation—the Chicago Mercantile Exchange announced it was creating an electronic currency futures market linking more than one hundred thousand Reuters computer terminals. "Conceptually what I was trying to do was a lot like that," Tattersall said.[279] Five years later, the Mercantile Exchange

**Paul Tattersall (left) escorts Minnesota governor Rudy Perpich on a tour of the Grain Exchange, mid-1980s.**

launched Globex, the first global electronic trading platform for the trading of futures and options.

Tattersall's successor, Jim Lindau—a former mayor of Bloomington, Minnesota, and a former Pillsbury executive—did not pursue any grand, computerized trading schemes, but he did push the Grain Exchange to abandon some of its more antiquated ways. Under his direction, the exchange's trade monitoring system was overhauled. Old computers were updated and new ones installed so the exchange could reconstruct transactions with to-the-minute accuracy.[280] In 1991, the old system of clearing trades, which required staff members to sift one by one through stacks of handwritten forms, finally entered the computer age. As a result, the exchange's clearinghouse was able to process trades up to five times faster than before—an essential improvement given the explosive growth in futures trading volume.[281]

Proposals to introduce electronic trading at the Grain Exchange remained tabled until about 1998, when Lindau brought in outside consultants to revisit the issue.[282] Technology had advanced by leaps and bounds in the last decade. Lindau acknowledged that he and other policy-makers at the exchange knew little about the subject, but in a 2000 interview with the trade publication

*Prairie Grains,* he said it was clear that big changes were on the horizon:

Electronic trading should happen within two to three years. Could it replace open outcry? It's possible that the pits may eventually be replaced and I suspect everyone trading in the pits suspects that as well. Our reason for being is to provide risk management and price discovery, and it's important that the relationship between the underlying cash contract and the futures contract correlate. If that can't be done electronically, then pit trading will continue.[283]

Lindau's prediction that the Grain Exchange would enter the brave new world of electronic trading within two or three years proved to be remarkably accurate. On February 15, 2002, the exchange lifted the curtain on a new computer-based trading platform called MGEXpress. Subscribers accessed the new system through special computer terminals and were able to trade futures and options based on corn and soybean indexes. (The indexes, calculated by Data Transmission Network of Omaha, Nebraska, were based on prices reported by hundreds of country elevators around the United States.) Lindau's successor, Kent Horsager, acknowledged that many members of the exchange worried that the advent of electronic trading might signal the beginning of the end of the open outcry system, but he insisted those fears were misplaced. "We have no plans to close our one-hundred-year-old trading floor," Horsager said. "Our electronic trading plans are a completely separate initiative that is concerned with providing additional value to our membership and constituents.[284]

Despite high hopes, the corn and soybean indexes offered through MGEXpress suffered the same lack of interest that doomed the exchange's earlier experiments with pork bellies, sunflowers, shrimp, and other nontraditional futures contracts. The first seven months of trading on MGEXpress was spotty at best. On a typical day, two or three contracts changed hands. On some days there was no trading at all. "Sure, we would love to have seen more volume by this time," Horsager admitted, "but it's much too premature to say it won't work."[285] A new contract—a hard winter wheat index—introduced in the spring of 2003 attracted more interest, but the lack of liquidity remained a problem.

The concerns among some members that electronic trading might mortally wound the open outcry system came to a head in late 2003 when the exchange launched two wheat index contracts, including one based on Minneapolis's bread and butter: hard red spring wheat. Twenty-seven members went to court in an effort to stop the introduction of the

The Grain Exchange's second full-time, paid president, Jim Lindau (left), shown here with Minneapolis mayor Don Fraser, helped instill a renewed sense of professionalism at the exchange.

In 2002, with Grain Exchange president Kent Horsager at his side, Minnesota's governor Jesse Ventura rings in a new era of electronic trading in Minneapolis. The computer-based trading platform, called MGEXpress, initially allowed subscribers to trade futures and options based on corn and soybean indexes. A new contract—a hard winter wheat index—was added later.

As chair of the 125th Commemoration Committee, Martin F. (Marty) Farrell has been instrumental in the publication of *The Grain Merchants.* The committee is also responsible for organizing celebratory anniversary events, including the October 7, 2006, gala at the Depot in Minneapolis. Farrell is a twenty-five-year member of the MGEX and has served on its board of directors since 2003.

new index, claiming it would cause "irreparable injury" to their business. The challenge to the hard red spring wheat index eventually failed, but it reflected the deep reservations that many members still had about electronic trading.[286]

In 2004, the Grain Exchange abandoned its original trading platform and hitched its electronic wagon to its much larger rival to the east, the Chicago Board of Trade. By this time, the CBOT already had more than a decade of experience in the electronic trading of futures and options. Its e-cbot electronic platform provided access to all of the agricultural, mineral, and financial commodities that had once traded only in Chicago's futures pits. With the new agreement, it also offered a suite of products from Minneapolis: the existing corn, soybean, and wheat indexes, plus the old stand-by, hard red spring wheat. Open outcry trading continued as usual on the trading floor, but now traders around the world could use computers to buy and sell spring wheat futures and options when the Minneapolis market was closed. Horsager saw it as an inevitable response to the changing global marketplace. "We couldn't tell somebody from Minot or Tokyo, 'Gee, you need to call our market, and we're open for these hours,'" he said.[287]

## Past and Present

In many ways, the Minneapolis Grain Exchange of the twenty-first century bears only passing resemblance to the exchange of 1970 and earlier. The futures market, which had limped along for years under government price controls, now sets trading volume records with yawn-inducing regularity. The cash grain tables, where generations of traders had bought and sold the fruits of the region's agricultural labor, keep a relatively lonely vigil. Women are welcome; smoking is not. The blackboard that had once displayed every price fluctuation a trader might want to know has been replaced by a shimmering electronic quotations board. Colorfully clad traders still prowl the futures pit, but many wonder whether the open outcry system of buying and selling will survive the era of electronic trading.

Nearby, along the river, the city's old mills all are closed. Minneapolis's last operational mill—the majestic Pillsbury "A" Mill in the St. Anthony area—shut down for good in 2003. Yet as the millennium approached, the moribund milling district showed signs of life again as developers refurbished the structures into urban dwellings for the well-to-do. The Washburn "A" Mill, gutted by fire, has been reborn as the Mill City Museum. Even the abandoned Milwaukee Train Depot near the district has been turned into a public skating rink. Still, some things never seem to change, especially the Grain Exchange Building.

**Framed by the Stone Arch Bridge, the Washburn "A" Mill, gutted by fire in 1991, is now the Mill City Museum. Once the largest and most technologically advanced mill in the world, it ground enough flour in a single day to make twelve million loaves of bread.**

Back in 1903, the *Minneapolis Journal* called the newly completed structure at Fourth and Fourth "a building which would not only be suitable but in every way permanent."[288] Over the years, the Grain Exchange complex has undergone several major renovations, yet has retained its air of permanence. With its terra-cotta flourishes, marble floors and stairways, and brass doorknobs, it was built to inspire and to last. The buildings are, without a doubt, the Grain Exchange's greatest asset. Office rentals have always accounted for a major portion of the exchange's annual income. And while the make-up of the tenants has evolved over the years (the exchange resorted to advertising for new, non-grain-trade tenants for the first time in the early 1990s),[289] the building complex remains a reliable source of income. In 1996, for example, rentals accounted for half of the organization's total revenues. The buildings are, said President Jim Lindau, the exchange's "cash cow."[290]

**Mark Bagan joined the Grain Exchange in 1987 as a trading floor clerk. In 2005 he became its fourth paid president and CEO.**

But the Grain Exchange has always been much more than buildings. In 1881, twenty-one determined businessmen founded the organization with the goal of turning Minneapolis into one of the world's great grain markets. They succeeded in ways they never could have imagined. Thousands of people over the years have found careers within its confines. Hundreds of companies have relied on the exchange for their livelihoods. Farmers and consumers have benefited from an efficient marketplace, not to mention all of the financial, civic, and cultural impacts the exchange has had on its region.

Buyers and sellers continue to gather on the floor of what was first known as the Minneapolis Chamber of Commerce to engage in intricate rituals—many of them utterly confounding to outsiders—that determine the fair price for most of the grains grown in the rich, dark soil of the Upper Midwest. Deals are consummated with a nod or a handshake. Integrity is key. Traders who lose the trust of their colleagues don't last long on the floor. That is how Minneapolis's great grain market operated from the day it opened for business in 1881, and that is how it continues to operate 125 years later.

**Minneapolis Grain Exchange board of directors, September 29, 2005. Seated from left: Randal L. Narloch, second vice chair; Charles A. Gallup, chair; Mark G. Bagan, president and CEO; Scott A. Cordes, first vice chair. Standing, first row, from left: Michael L. Ricks; Gregory G. Konsor; Jesse Marie Bartz, assistant corporate secretary; Scott R. O'Donnell; David W. Nelson; Richard E. Cole; Layne G. Carlson, corporate secretary. Middle row from left: Mike Krueger; Richard H. Browne; Tom Miller; Martin F. Farrell. Back row from left: Richard F. Diaz; Philip J. Lindau Jr.; Randy A. Marten; Carter K. Ohrt; Christopher T. Matdorf. Not pictured: Curt Denisuik.**

# APPENDIX A

## PAST OFFICERS, CHAMBER OF COMMERCE/MINNEAPOLIS GRAIN EXCHANGE

### CHAMBER OF COMMERCE OF MINNEAPOLIS

| Year | Second Year | President | First Vice President | Second Vice President |
|---|---|---|---|---|
| 1881 | 1882 | Harrison, H. G. | Mulford, A. D. | Taylor, A. B. |
| 1882 | 1883 | White, E. V. | Hinkle, F. S. | Croswell, H.J.G. |
| 1883 | 1884 | Pillsbury, George A. | Marshall, James | Johnson, C.W. |
| 1884 | 1885 | Pillsbury, George A. | Johnson, C. W. | Marshall, James |
| 1885 | 1886 | Loring, C. M. | Marshall, James | Greenleaf, F. L. |
| 1886 | 1887 | Loring, C. M. | Greenleaf, F. L. | Marshall, James |
| 1887 | 1888 | Loring, C. M. | Marshall, James | Greenleaf, F. L. |
| 1888 | 1889 | Loring, C. M. | Greenleaf, F. L. | Pillsbury, F. C. |
| 1889 | 1890 | Greenleaf, F. L. | Pillsbury, F. C. | Kirkbride, G. B. |
| 1890 | 1891 | Greenleaf, F. L. | Kirkbride, G. B. | Pillsbury, F. C. |
| 1891 | 1892 | Greenleaf, F. L. | Pillsbury, F. C. | Martin, J. H. |
| 1892 | 1893 | Pillsbury, C. A. | Martin, J. H. | Campbell, L. W. |
| 1893 | 1894 | Pillsbury, C. A. | Campbell, L. W. | Martin, J. H. |
| 1894 | 1895 | Martin, J. H. | Brooks, L. R. | Loring, A. C. |
| 1895 | 1896 | Martin, J. H. | Loring, A. C. | Brooks, L. R. |
| 1896 | 1897 | Brooks, L. R. | Washburn, John | Harrington, C. M. |
| 1897 | 1898 | Brooks, L. R. | Harrington, C. M. | Washburn, John |
| 1898 | 1899 | Harrington, C. M. | Washburn, John | Woodworth, E. S. |
| 1899 | 1900 | Harrington, C. M. | Woodworth, E. S. | Washburn, John |
| 1900 | 1901 | Washburn, John | Commons, F. W. | Woodworth, E. S. |
| 1901 | 1902 | Washburn, John | Woodworth, E. S. | Commons, F. W. |
| 1902 | 1903 | Marshall, James | Commons, F. W. | Smith, P. B. |
| 1903 | 1904 | Marshall, James | Smith, P. B. | Piper, George F. |
| 1904 | 1905 | Woodworth, E. S. | Piper, George F. | Smith, P. B. |
| 1905 | 1906 | Smith, P. B. | Piper, George F. | McMillan, J. D. |
| 1906 | 1907 | Smith, P. B. | Piper, George F. | McMillan, J. D. |
| 1907 | 1908 | McMillan, J. D. | Douglas, H. F. | Ewe, G. F. |
| 1908 | 1909 | Douglas, H. F. | Ewe, G. F. | Marfield, J. R. |
| 1909 | 1910 | Ewe, G. F. | Marfield, J. R. | Wells, F. B. |
| 1910 | 1911 | Piper, G. F. | Marfield, J. R. | Wells, F. B. |
| 1911 | 1912 | Marfield, J. R. | Wells, F. B. | Crosby, F. M. |
| 1912 | 1913 | Wells, F. B. | Crosby, F. M. | Loring, A. C. |
| 1913 | 1914 | Crosby, F. M | Loring, A. C. | Hallet, F. A. |
| 1914 | 1915 | Loring, C. M. | Hallet, F. A. | Timmerman, W. O.* |
| 1915 | 1916 | Hallet, F. A. | Timerman, W. O. | Magnuson, C. A. |
| 1916 | 1917 | Timerman, W. O. | Magnuson, C. A. | Case, C. M. |
| 1917 | 1918 | Magnuson, C. A. | Case, C. M. | Dalrymple, William |
| 1918 | 1919 | Case, C. M. | Dalrymple, William | Benson, B. F. |
| 1919 | 1920 | Dalrymple, William | Benson, B. F. | McLeod, John |
| 1920 | 1921 | Benson, B. F. | Andrews, A. C. | MacMillan, J. H. |
| 1921 | 1922 | MacMillan, J. H. | Van Dusen, F. C. | Helm, H. S. |
| 1922 | 1923 | Van Dusen, F. C. | Helm, H. S. | Hall, T. W. |
| 1923 | 1924 | Hall, T. W. | Searle, A. L. | Moreton, H. J. |
| 1924 | 1925 | Searle, A. L. | Moreton, H. J. | Archer, Shreve M. |
| 1925 | 1926 | Moreton, H. J. | Archer, Shreve M. | Pillsbury, John S. |
| 1926 | 1927 | Archer, Shreve M. | Pillsbury, John S. | Russell, W. J. |
| 1927 | 1928 | Pillsbury, John S. | Russell, W. J. | Case, George P. |
| 1928 | 1929 | Russell, W. J. | Case, George P. | Stevenson, Charles T. |
| 1929 | 1930 | Case, George P. | Stevenson, Charles T. | Dickey, H. G. |
| 1930 | 1931 | Stevenson, Charles T. | Dickey, H. G. | Getchell, P. B. |
| 1931 | 1932 | Dickey, H. G. | Getchell, P. B. | Owen, A. F. |
| 1932 | 1933 | Getchell, P. B. | Owen, A. F. | Seidl, F. J. |
| 1933 | 1934 | Owen, A. F. | Seidl, F. C.* | Wyman, James C. |
| 1934 | 1935 | Seidl, F. J. | Wyman, James C. | Mitchell, E. E. |
| 1935 | 1936 | Wyman, James C. | Mitchell, E. E. | Helm, W. C. |
| 1936 | 1937 | Mitchell, E. E. | Smith, F. C. | Mills, Walter H. |
| 1937 | 1938 | Smith, F. C. | Mills, Walter H. | Mull, John A. |
| 1938 | 1939 | Mills, Walter H. | Mull, John A. | Ferguson, E. S. |
| 1939 | 1940 | Mull, John A. | Ferguson, E. S. | Grimes, E. J. |
| 1940 | 1941 | Ferguson, E. S. | Grimes, E. J. | Heffelfinger, F. P. |
| 1941 | 1942 | Grimes, E. J. | Heffelfinger, F. P. | Howard, Adrian M. |
| 1942 | 1943 | Howard, Adrian M. | Heffelfinger, F. P. | Mirick, Edward H. |

| 1943 | 1944 | Mirick, Edward H. | Devaney, M. R. | Tearse, Harold H. |
| 1944 | 1945 | Devaney, M. R. | Tearse, Harold H. | Culhane, John T. |
| 1945 | 1946 | Tearse, Harold H. | Culhane, John T. | Hartwell, A. M. |
| 1946 | 1947 | Tearse, Harold H. | Culhane, John T. | Hartwell, A. M. |

## MINNEAPOLIS GRAIN EXCHANGE

| Year | Second Year | President | First Vice President | Second Vice President |
| --- | --- | --- | --- | --- |
| 1947 | 1948 | Culhane, John T. | Hartwell, A. M. | Bolton, J. A. |
| 1948 | 1949 | Hartwell, A. M. | Bolton, J. A. | Woodworth, Robert C. |
| 1949 | 1950 | Bolton, J. A. | Woodworth, Robert C. | Hessburg, A. G. |
| 1950 | 1951 | Woodworth, Robert C. | Hessburg, A. G. | Higgins, Frank H. |
| 1951 | 1952 | Higgins, Frank H. | McCabe, Ben C. | Howard, Adrian M. |
| 1952 | 1953 | McCabe, Ben C. | Howard, Adrian M. | Cargill, Robert G. |
| 1953 | 1954 | Howard, Adrian M. | Cargill, Robert G. | Hicks, Percy B. |
| 1954 | 1955 | Cargill, Robert G. | Hicks, Percy B. | Mullin, James F. |
| 1955 | 1956 | Mullin, James F. | McMillan, Howard I. | Heffelfinger, George W. P. |
| 1956 | 1957 | McMillan, Howard I. | Heffelfinger, George W. P. | Duff, Philip S. |
| 1957 | 1958 | Heffelfinger, George W. P | .Duff, Philip S. | Moore, Allan Q. |
| 1958 | 1959 | Duff, Philip S. | Moore, Allan Q. | Quinn, E. E. |
| 1959 | 1960 | Moore, Allan Q. | Quinn, E. E. | Fraser, Donald E. |
| 1960 | 1961 | Quinn, E. E. | Fraser, Donald E. | Burdick, Allan L. |
| 1961 | 1962 | Fraser, Donald E. | Burdick, Allan L. | McCarthy, Charles H. |
| 1962 | 1963 | Burdick, Allan L. | McCarthy, Charles H. | Seidl, Stewart F. |
| 1963 | 1964 | Seidl, Stewart F. | Searles, Robert L. | Gage, John S. |
| 1964 | 1965 | Searles, Robert L. | Gage, John S. | Bagley, Ralph C. |
| 1965 | 1966 | Bagley, Ralph C. | P. Norman Ness | Corrigan, Fredric H. |
| 1966 | 1967 | Ness, P. Norman | Corrigan, Fredric H. | Hegman, Ralph H. |
| 1967 | 1968 | Corrigan, Fredric H. | Hegman, Ralph H. | McMillan, C. L. |
| 1968 | 1969 | Hegman, Ralph H. | McMillan, C. L. | Alexander, Gordon L. |
| 1969 | 1970 | Alexander, Gordon L. | Murrin, Francis H. | Owens, Anthony C. |
| 1970 | 1971 | Murrin, Francis H. | Owens, Anthony C. | Bolton, Robert W. |
| 1971 | 1972 | Owens, Anthony C. | Bolton, Robert W. | Whiteman, Gordon E. |
| 1972 | 1973 | Bolton, Robert W. | Whiteman, Gordon E. | Smith, Wesley B. |
| 1973 | 1974 | Smith, Wesley B. | Werner, Melvin J. | Quinn, Rupert G. |
| 1974 | 1975 | Werner, Melvin J. | Quinn, Rupert G. | McIntyre, Robert T. |
| 1975 | 1976 | Quinn, Rupert G. | McIntyre, Robert T. | Stich, Duane F. |
| 1976 | 1977 | McIntyre, Robert T. | Stich, Duane F. | Mills, Merlin W. |
| 1977 | 1978 | Stich, Duane F. | Mills, Merlin W. | Wallin, Winston R. |
| 1978 | 1979 | Mills, Merlin W. | Case, John P. | Hayenga, Ralph V. |
| 1979 | 1980 | Case, John P. | Hayenga, Ralph V. | Wallin, Winston R. |
| 1980 | 1981 | Hayenga, Ralph V. | Wallin, Winston R. | Dill, John G. Jr. |
| 1981 | 1982 | Wallin, Winston R. | Dill, John G. Jr. | Goldberg, Richard W. |

| Year | Second Year | Chair | First Vice Chair | Second Vice Chair |
| --- | --- | --- | --- | --- |
| 1982 | 1983 | Wallin, Winston R. | Dill, John G. Jr. | Goldberg, Richard W. |
| 1983 | 1984 | Dill, John G. Jr. | Mahl, Donald E. | Nedbalek, James R. |
| 1984 | 1985 | Olson, Ronald D. | Donoho, Merrill E. | Mauro, Thomas V. |
| 1985 | 1986 | Olson, Ronald D. | Donoho, Merrill E. | Mauro, Thomas V. |
| 1986 | 1987 | Olson, Ronald D. | Mauro, Thomas V. | Metz, Theodore D. |
| 1987 | 1988 | Brummer, Donald E. | Larson, Cliff W. Jr. | Hammer, Courtney R. |
| 1988 | 1989 | Brummer, Donald E. | Larson, Cliff W. Jr. | Hackett, L. Scott |
| 1989 | 1990 | Brummer, Donald E. | Larson, Cliff W. Jr. | Hackett, L. Scott |
| 1990 | 1991 | Larson, Cliff W. Jr. | Hackett, L. Scott | Gustafson, Gary R. |
| 1991 | 1992 | Larson, Cliff W. Jr. | Hackett, L. Scott | Gustafson, Gary R. |
| 1992 | 1993 | Hackett, L. Scott | Gustafson, Gary R. | Blake, Michael J. |
| 1993 | 1994 | Hackett, L. Scott | Gustafson, Gary R. | Horsager, Kent R. |
| 1994 | 1995 | Gustafson, Gary R. | Horsager, Kent R. | Miller, John C. |
| 1995 | 1996 | Gustafson, Gary R. | Horsager, Kent R. | Miller, John C. |
| 1996 | 1997 | Horsager, Kent R. | Miller, John C. | Wilson, Donald W. |
| 1997 | 1998 | Horsager, Kent R. | Miller, John C. | Wilson, Donald W. |
| 1998 | 1999 | Horsager, Kent R. | Miller, John C. | Wilson, Donald W. |
| 1999 | 2000 | Miller, John C. | Wilson, Donald W. | Lottie, Raymond F. |
| 2000 | 2001 | Miller, John C. | Wilson, Donald W. | Lottie, Raymond F. |
| 2001 | 2002 | Miller, John C. | Lottie, Raymond F. | Wilson, Donald W. |
| 2002 | 2003 | Lottie, Raymond F. | Wilson, Donald W. | Gallup, Charles A. |
| 2003 | 2004 | Lottie, Raymond F. | Gallup, Charles A. | Cordes, Scott A. |
| 2004 | 2005 | Gallup, Charles A. | Cordes, Scott A. | Narloch, Randal L. |
| 2005 | 2006 | Gallup, Charles A. | Cordes, Scott A. | Narloch, Randal L. |

# APPENDIX B

## MEMBERSHIP, MINNEAPOLIS GRAIN EXCHANGE (as of January 31, 2006)

| RECORD HOLDER | RECORD OWNER |
|---|---|
| Steven Abraham | Abraham, Steven M. |
| Albert Ambrose | CHS, Inc. |
| Andrew Anderson | Anderson, Andrew L. |
| Gary Anderson | CHS, Inc. |
| | |
| A. Edward Bailey | Bailey, A. Edward |
| Roger Baker | CHS, Inc. |
| Steven Balster | Busch Agricultural Resources |
| Roland Balthazor | Fimat USA, LLC |
| Roberto Bari | Anderson, Andrew L. |
| Andrew Bauer | Bauer, Andrew L. |
| Robert Berger | Berger, Robert |
| Natalie Berglund | Berglund, Natalie K. |
| Peter Berglund | Berglund, Peter N. |
| Douglas Binder | Helfand, Jerome M., and/or Cleary, Joan L. |
| Kimberly Bocklund | Country Hedging, Inc. |
| Keith Bronstein | Bronstein, Keith D. |
| Richard Browne | CHS, Inc. |
| Peter Brownlee | OHB Trading, LLC |
| Ralph Bruce III | ADM Investor Services, Inc. |
| Carolyn Bruhjell | Bruhjell, Carolyn A. |
| Justine Brummel | Frontier Futures, Inc. |
| Donald Brummer | Brummer, Donald E. |
| John Buboltz | Cargill, Inc. |
| Frederick Burgum | The Arthur Companies, Inc. |
| | |
| Ryan Caffrey | CHS, Inc. |
| Gordon Carlson | Carlson, Gordon W. |
| John Case | Case, John P. |
| Marc Chiodo | Chiodo, Marc A. |
| David Christofore | CHS, Inc. |
| Paul Christy | Christy, Paul E. |
| Richard Cole | General Mills Operations, Inc. |
| John Comford | AGP Grain, Ltd. |
| Patrick Commerford | Commerford, Patrick |
| Larry Conklin | Ohrt, Carter K. |
| E. James Connor | Minnesota Trading Corporation |
| Edward Connor | Connor, Edward J. |
| Jerry Cope | South Dakota Wheat Growers Association |
| Scott Cordes | Country Hedging, Inc. |
| Peter Courteau | RIS, a division of Man Financial, Inc. |
| R. Edwin Coyle | Coyle, R. Edwin |
| Leo Cress | Mayco Export, Inc. |
| Albert Cyrlin | Cyrlin, Albert |
| | |
| Daryl Dahl | Ag Processing Inc. |
| Austin Damiani | Frontier Futures, Inc. |
| Christopher Damilatis | Prudential Financial Derivatives, LLC |
| Brian Danzis | Danzis, Brian E. |
| David Darr | Darr, David P. |
| Ronald DeJongh | AGP Grain, Ltd. |
| John de Rosier | Comford, John S. |
| Thomas DeSmet | CHS, Inc. |
| Becky Deters | ADM-Benson Quinn. a division of Archer Daniels Midland |
| Richard Diaz | Diaz, Richard F. |
| Thomas Dittmer | Dittmer, Thomas H. |
| Allan Dombek | CHS, Inc. |
| James Dorn | Dorn, James Thomas |
| Mark Drangstveit | Bay State Milling Company |
| Timothy Dunn | Infinity Trading, Inc. |
| Colleen Durand | General Mills Operations, Inc. |
| Richard Dusek | CHS, Inc. |
| Jon Dye | Merrill Lynch, Pierce, Fenner, and Smith, Inc. |
| | |
| George Earl | Earl, George R. |
| April Egan | Egan, April H. |
| Jud Ellis Jr. | Ellis Jr., Jud |
| Richard Emerson | Busch Agricultural Resources |
| Douglas Erickson | Mayco Export, Inc. |
| Daniel Erz | Bunge North America, Inc. |

| RECORD HOLDER | RECORD OWNER |
|---|---|
| Martin Farrell | Farrell, Martin F. |
| Craig Fischer | ADM Milling Company |
| David Fox | Fox, David |
| Gerald Freudenthal | Oahe Grain Corporation |
| Bruce Froyum | FC Stone, LLC |
| Jack Frymire | Frymire, Jack R. |
| | |
| Timothy Gallagher | Bunge North America, Inc. |
| Charles Gallup | Charles A. Gallup Profit Sharing Plan and Trust |
| Charles Gallup | Gallup, Charles A. |
| Peter John Garratt | Garratt, Peter John |
| Marc Gordon | Gordon, Marc L. |
| Stephen Grady | Man Financial, Inc. |
| Stephen Grady | Refco, a division of Man Financial, Inc. |
| Charles Green | Wilson Trading Company |
| Harold Green | Green, Harold |
| Steven Greenberg | Greenberg, Steven A. |
| Daniel Grunewald | Farmers Elevator Company |
| | |
| Kal Hachem | Hachem, Kal |
| William Haertzen | Charles A. Gallup Profit Sharing Plan and Trust |
| Keith Hainy | North Central Farmers Elevator |
| Michael Halpert | Halpert, Michael P. |
| Gerald Handke | Handke, Gerald D. |
| George Hanley | Hanley, George |
| Carey Harrold | Jump Trading, LLC |
| T. Bradley Hays Jr. | Hays Jr., T. Bradley |
| Scott Hedin | St. Croix Commodities, Inc. |
| Ami Heesch | Country Hedging, Inc. |
| Jerome Helfand | Helfand, Jerome M., and/or Cleary, Joan L. |
| Jason Herr | Bunge North America, Inc. |
| Kevin Hilger | Hilger, Kevin C., and Teresa A. |
| Patrick Hillegass | Hillegass, Patrick S. |
| Kirsten Hoechst | The Cliff Larson Company |
| John Holliday | Smucker Foods of Canada Company |
| Kent Horsager | Horsager, Kent |
| Francis Hussian III | Hussian III, Francis D. |
| Malcolm Hutchison III | UBS Securities, LLC |
| | |
| Loren Jacobs | Country Hedging, Inc. |
| Terrence James | James Richardson International |
| Bradley John | Pound, Helen E. |
| Christine Johnson | Miller Milling Company |
| John Johnson | CHS, Inc. |
| Kent Johnson | Johnson, Kent W. |
| Theodore Johnson | Frontier Futures, Inc. |
| James Joiner | Joiner, James B. |
| Robert Jones | ABN AMRO, Inc. |
| | |
| Donald Kasbohm | Kasbohm, Donald F. |
| Ryan Kelbrants | ADM Investor Services, Inc. |
| Mary Kennedy | Minnesota Grain, Inc. |
| Paul Kim | Kim, Paul J. |
| Kevin Kjorsvik | ADM Investor Services, Inc. |
| Vincent Klueber | Klueber, Vincent A. |
| Patrick Kluempke | CHS, Inc. |
| Gregory Konsor | ConAgra Foods, Inc. |
| William Kreussling | Term Commodities, Inc. |
| Paul Krug Jr. | ADM Investor Services, Inc. |
| | |
| Craig LaBelle | ConAgra Foods, Inc. |
| Cliff Larson Jr. | Larson Jr., Cliff W. |
| Cliff Larson III | Larson III, Cliff W. |
| Reid Larson | Larson, Reid E. |
| Timothy Lee | Lee, Timothy |
| Loyal Leitgen | Leitgen, Thomas K. |
| Michael Lemke | Lansing Grain Company, LLC |
| Steve Lennartson | Lennartson, Steve N. |
| Rick Levinson | Levinson, Rick |
| Dennis Lieberg | Lieberg, Dennis |
| Philip Lindau Jr. | Commodity Specialists Company |

# APPENDIX B (continued)

| RECORD HOLDER | RECORD OWNER |
|---|---|
| Philip Lindau Sr. | Commodity Specialists Company |
| Max Lipner | Lipner, Max |
| Gary Lubben | Louis Dreyfus Corporation |
| | |
| Hitoshi Maeda | Toshoku America, Inc. |
| Thomas Malecha | CHS, Inc. |
| Travis Marier | Ohrt, Carter K. |
| Randy Marten | Miller Milling Company |
| Jason Marthaler | CHS, Inc. |
| Charles Mastel | Mastel Grain Company |
| Silas Matthies Jr. | Silas Langdon Matthies Sr. Trust |
| Silas Matthies Sr. | Silas Langdon Matthies Sr. Trust |
| Paul Mattson | ConAgra Foods, Inc. |
| Christopher Matzdorf | Matzdorf, Christopher T. |
| Shane Mayer | Country Hedging, Inc. |
| Gerard Mayerhofer | Susquehanna Clearing, LLC |
| Brian McGuire | Keystone Trading Corporation |
| Elizabeth McGuire | Keystone Trading Corporation |
| Tad McGurk | Mayport Farmers Coop |
| Timothy McWhite | McWhite, Timothy R. |
| Fred Merrill | Cereal Food Processors, Inc. |
| Harold Metzger Jr. | JP Morgan Futures, Inc. |
| O. William Mikkelson | Commodity Specialists Company |
| John Miller | Miller, John C. |
| Michael Morgan | Thompson Farmers Co-op Elevator Company |
| Robert W. Mortenson | FC Stone, LLC |
| Michael Mullin | Mullin, Michael J. |
| Thomas Murphy | Cyrlin, Albert |
| Jack Murray | Murray Commodities, Inc. |
| | |
| Scott Nagel | ADM-Benson Quinn, a division of Archer Daniels Midland |
| Randal Narloch | ADM-Benson Quinn, a division of Archer Daniels Midland |
| Thomas Neal | Neal, Thomas |
| Klaus Neitzel | Alfred C. Toepfer International, Inc. |
| Lawrence Neumann | ADM-Benson Quinn, a division of Archer Daniels Midland |
| Michael Newton | ConAgra Foods, Inc. |
| Richard Nicholson | Nicholson, Richard H. |
| Eugene Norheim | Norheim, Eugene L. |
| Bruce North | ADM-Benson Quinn, a division of Archer Daniels Midland |
| Jay Novak | Novak, Jay A. |
| | |
| Scott O'Donnell | O'Donnell, Scott R. |
| Carter Ohrt | Ohrt, Carter K. |
| Ronald Olson | General Mills Operations, Inc. |
| James Owens | Owens, James W. |
| | |
| Mark Palmquist | CHS, Inc. |
| Ryan Peterburs | AGP Grain, Ltd. |
| Donn Pikop | Bay State Milling Company |
| Helen Pound | Goldenberg, Hehmeyer, and Company |
| Robert Powers | Ohrt, Carter K. |
| | |
| Richard Quain | Quain, Richard J. |
| | |
| David Raisbeck | Cargill, Inc. |
| Mark Ramsland | General Mills Operations, Inc. |
| Martin Reagan | AGP Grain, Ltd. |
| Harold Rebne | Rebne, Harold K. |
| Bruce Reiser | Citigroup Global Markets Inc. |
| Sandie Renslow | Larson Jr., Cliff W. |
| Michael Ricks | Cargill, Inc. |
| Nathaniel Robbins Jr. | Robbins Jr., Nathaniel |
| Donald Roberts | Roberts Grain, Inc. |
| Daniel Roemer | Roemer, Daniel C. |
| Kenneth Rynda | ADM/Growmark River System, Inc. |
| | |
| David Saarela | Ohrt, Carter K. |
| Philip Safran | Safran, Philip E. |
| Kevin Sallstrom | Sallstrom, Kevin |

| RECORD HOLDER | RECORD OWNER |
|---|---|
| Robert Schachter | Schachter, Robert and Jacob |
| Robert Schachter | Schachter, Robert O. |
| Brian Schouvieller | CHS, Inc. |
| Stuart Schukei | ADM-Benson Quinn, a division of Archer Daniels Midland |
| Gary Schuld | United Harvest, LLC |
| George Schuler | Minn-Kota Ag Products |
| Stephen Schwahn | Schwahn, Stephen B. |
| Thomas Sexter | Louis Dreyfus Corporation |
| Steven Shoemaker | ADM Milling Company |
| Neil Short | Short, Neil J. |
| M. Blair Shouse | Bunge North America, Inc. |
| Jack Siljendahl | PepsiCo Beverages and Foods North America |
| Cathy Simonson | Goldenberg, Hehmeyer, and Company |
| Jonathan Sion | Norris and Associates |
| Scott Skavanger | Frontier Futures, Inc. |
| Mark Slettehaugh | Slettehaugh, Mark J. |
| Jackson Smart III | Smart III, Jackson W. |
| Howard Smith | Mayco Export, Inc. |
| David Smoot | General Mills Operations, Inc. |
| Susan Sobieck | General Mills Operations, Inc. |
| Charles Soule | Country Hedging, Inc. |
| Becky Sparrow | Country Hedging, Inc. |
| George Spisak | Frontier Futures, Inc. |
| Mark Steingas | Steingas, Mark A. |
| H. Franklin Stone | Man Financial, Inc. |
| Karl Streed | Streed, Karl E. |
| John Streicker | Streicker, John H. |
| John Streicker | The Sentinel Corporation |
| Bruce Sullivan | CHS, Inc. |
| Michael Sullivan | Swanson, Donald L. |
| | |
| Aml Joe Tadros | Frontier Futures, Inc. |
| Jason Alan Tarp | Lewis, Robert L. |
| J. Vance Taylor | North Dakota Mill and Elevator Association |
| Mark Teien | Teien, Mark E. |
| Gary Theisen | Emerado Farmers Coop Elevator Company |
| Hank Thilmony | Italgrani USA, Inc. |
| Hank Thilmony | Mayco Export, Inc. |
| Jeffrey Thomas | Cyrlin, Albert |
| Gerard Traina | Traina, Gerard |
| Jeffery Tregillis | ADM Investor Services, Inc. |
| | |
| Kent Van Gundy | Ohrt, Carter K. |
| Marc Viers | Cargill, Inc. |
| Russel Viker | CHS, Inc. |
| | |
| Bradford Wallin | Wallin, Bradford W. |
| Bradford Wallin | Wallin, Bradford W., and Cynthia R. |
| W. Shelley Walsh | Walsh Grain Company |
| Michael Walter | ConAgra Foods, Inc. |
| Michael Walter | ConAgra Trade Group, Inc. |
| Carl Wargel | Bunge North America, Inc. |
| Nicholas Warren | RIS, a division of Man Financial, Inc. |
| Michael Wedwick | Scranton Equity Exchange |
| Dennis Wendland | CHS, Inc. |
| Dale West | International Malting Company United States |
| Charles Whitman | Infinium Capital Management, LLC |
| Paul Wicklund | Wicklund, Paul E. |
| Aaron Wiegand | Bunge North America, Inc. |
| Erik Williams | The Cliff Larson Company |
| James Wilmes | Bay State Milling Company |
| Bruce Wilson | Wilson, Bruce A. |
| Donald Wilson | Wilson Trading Company |
| Mark Wilson | Wilson, Mark D. |
| John Wood | Wood, John P. |
| Donald Woodburn | AGP Grain Marketing, Inc. |
| William Wright | Wright, William A. |
| | |
| Keith Yavitt | Sparrow Trading, LLC |
| David Yost | AGP Grain, Ltd. |
| | |
| Preston Zacharias | Prudential Financial Derivatives, LLC |

## CHAPTER 1

1. Here and below: *Minneapolis Tribune,* November 16 and 18, 1881; *St. Paul and Minneapolis Pioneer Press,* November 16, 17, and 18, 1881.
2. Minneapolis Board of Trade, Annual Report, 1879.
3. Shannon Pennefeather, *Mill City* (St. Paul: Minnesota Historical Society, 2003), 26.
4. Dana W. Frear, "Early Flour Mills of Hennepin County," *Hennepin County History,* Spring 1964, 14.
5. "The Milling History of Minneapolis," *The Holiday Northwestern Miller,* 1890; Minneapolis Chamber of Commerce, *The Minneapolis Chamber of Commerce, 1881–1903* (Minneapolis: Horace B. Hudson, 1903), 20–23; Dana W. Frear, "Early Flour Mills of Hennepin County," 10–12; Alison Watts, "The Technology That Launched a City," *Minnesota History,* Summer 2000, 94.
6. Watts, "The Technology That Launched a City," 88–92.
7. Here and below: Charles B. Kuhlmann, "The Development of Flour Milling in Minneapolis" (master's thesis, University of Minnesota, 1920), 99–100; George D. Rogers, "History of Flour Manufacture in Minnesota," *Collections of the Minnesota Historical Society* 10:1, 38–45.
8. William E. Lass, *Minnesota: A History* (New York: W. W. Norton, 1998), 137–141; "Railroads in Minnesota," *Roots,* Winter 1975–76, 6; Norman K. Risjord, *A Popular History of Minnesota* (St. Paul: Minnesota Historical Society Press, 2005), 114.
9. Theodore C. Blegen, *Minnesota: A History of the State* (Minneapolis: University of Minnesota Press, 1963), 340.
10. Merrill E. Jarchow, "King Wheat," *Minnesota History,* March 1948, 3–6.
11. "Railroads in Minnesota," 10.
12. *New York Daily Graphic,* December 9, 1881, as quoted in *Minneapolis Tribune,* December 18, 1881.
13. *Northwestern Miller,* November 11, 1881.
14. *Minneapolis Tribune,* February 12, 1918.
15. Here and below: George D. Rogers, "Chamber of Commerce Keeps Minneapolis First among the Grain Markets of the World," *Minneapolis Golden Jubilee* (Minneapolis: Tribune Job Printing, 1917), 23–23.
16. Minneapolis Chamber of Commerce, *The Minneapolis Chamber of Commerce, 1881–1903,* 28; *Northwestern Miller,* December 31, 1880, 434; Charles B. Kuhlmann, "The Development of Flour Milling in Minneapolis," 102–103.
17. Minneapolis Chamber of Commerce, Annual Report, 1883, 27–28.
18. Here and below: Rogers, "Chamber of Commerce Keeps Minneapolis First among the Grain Markets of the World," 23.
19. Minneapolis Chamber of Commerce, *The Minneapolis Chamber of Commerce, 1881–1903,* 29; Rogers, "Chamber of Commerce Keeps Minneapolis First among the Grain Markets of the World," 23; Minneapolis Chamber of Commerce, Annual Report, 1883, 28.
20. Jack Cleland, "Recalls 49 Years in Chamber of Commerce," *Minneapolis Tribune,* May 14, 1933; Minneapolis Chamber of Commerce, *The Minneapolis Chamber of Commerce, 1881–1903,* 4.
21. Rogers, "Chamber of Commerce Keeps Minneapolis First among the Grain Markets of the World," 23; Minneapolis Chamber of Commerce, Annual Report, 1883, 28; *Northwestern Miller,* November 11, 1881.
22. *Minneapolis Tribune,* December 10, 1881.
23. Minneapolis Chamber of Commerce, *The Minneapolis Chamber of Commerce, 1881–1903,* 7.
24. Minneapolis Chamber of Commerce, *The Minneapolis Chamber of Commerce, 1881–1903,* 6.
25. *Northwestern Miller,* June 13, 1884; undated article from unidentified newspaper, in Charles Loring Scrapbooks, Minnesota Historical Society.
26. Minneapolis Chamber of Commerce, Annual Report, 1883, 30.
27. Minneapolis Chamber of Commerce, Annual Report, 1883, 30; Minneapolis Chamber of Commerce Minutes, October 9, 1884.
28. *Minneapolis Tribune,* June 6, 1884; *Northwestern Miller,* April 18, 1884.
29. *Northwestern Miller,* June 13, 1884.
30. *Minneapolis Tribune,* May 14, 1933; May 2, 1884.
31. *Northwestern Miller,* December 15, 1882.
32. Minneapolis Chamber of Commerce, *The Minneapolis Chamber of Commerce, 1881–1903,* 9.
33. Minneapolis Chamber of Commerce Minutes, December 6, 1882; *Northwestern Miller,* January 4, 1883; June 19, 1885.
34. *Northwestern Miller,* July 3, 1885; July 17, 1885; August 21, 1885: *Minneapolis Golden Jubilee,* 5.
35. *Northwestern Miller,* June 22, 1883; June 29, 1883; May 14, 1886; August 13, 1886; Minneapolis Chamber of Commerce, Annual Report, 1883, 32.
36. Minneapolis Chamber of Commerce, Minutes, October 13, 1886.
37. Henrietta M. Larson, *The Wheat Market and the Farmer in Minnesota, 1858–1900* (New York: Columbia University Press, 1926), 153.
38. Lucile M. Kane and Alan Ominsky, *Twin Cities: A Pictorial History of Saint Paul and Minneapolis* (St. Paul: Minnesota Historical Society Press, 1983), 102.
39. Minneapolis Chamber of Commerce, Annual Report, 1887, 120.
40. Minneapolis Chamber of Commerce, *The Minneapolis Chamber of Commerce, 1881–1903,* 33; Minneapolis Chamber of Commerce, Minutes, 1890, 92–93.
41. Larson, *The Wheat Market and the Farmer in Minnesota, 1858–1900,* 229.
42. Minneapolis Chamber of Commerce, Annual Report, 1884, 51.
43. Minneapolis Chamber of Commerce, Minutes, January 10, 1885; January 14, 1885; Minneapolis Chamber of Commerce, Annual Report, 1886, 107.
44. Larson, *The Wheat Market and the Farmer in Minnesota, 1858–1900,* 166.
45. Larson, *The Wheat Market and the Farmer in Minnesota, 1858–1900,* 155.
46. *St. Paul Globe,* October 6, 1892.
47. Minneapolis Chamber of Commerce, Annual Report, 1894, 10–11.
48. Here and below: *Minneapolis Tribune,* September 27, 1895.
49. David B. Danbom, "Flour Power: The Significance of Flour Milling at the Falls," *Minnesota History* 58:5/6 (Spring/Summer 2003), 278.
50. Dave Kenney, *Twin Cities Album: A Visual History* (St. Paul: Minnesota Historical Society Press, 2005); U.S. Census, 1880, 1890, 1900.
51. Flandrau, Charles E. *Encyclopedia of Biography of Minnesota* (Chicago: the Century Publishing and Engraving Company, 1900), 127.
52. Minneapolis Public Library, Unique Collections, Manuscripts, and Archives, Clubs and Organizations, www.mpls.lib.mn.us/ sc_orgarchives.asp
53. Minneapolis Public Library, "A History of Minneapolis: Religion, Social Services, and Medicine," www.mpls.lib.mn.us/history/rs3.asp; Dunwoody College of Technology, history, www.dunwoody.edu
54. Wilfred Bockelman, *Culture of Corporate Citizenship: Minnesota's Business Legacy for the Global Future* (Lakeville, Minnesota: Galde Press, 2000), 48.

# NOTES

## CHAPTER 2

55. *Minneapolis Times,* October 24, 1897.
56. Minneapolis Chamber of Commerce, Annual Report, 1897, 10–11.
57. Here and below: *Northwestern Miller,* March 22, 1899.
58. *Minneapolis Journal,* March 10, 1899.
59. Minneapolis Chamber of Commerce, Annual Report, 1897, 10–11.
60. Here and below: Joseph A. A. Burnquist, ed., *Minnesota and Its People* (Chicago: S. J. Clarke, 1924), 3:298-301; "Hiz Honor," *Hennepin County History* 26:1 (Summer 1966), 20–21.
61. William Henry Eustis, *Autobiography of William Henry Eustis* (New York: James T. White and Company, 1936), 60.
62. *Minneapolis Tribune,* October 24, 1897.
63. *Minneapolis Times,* October 27, 1897.
64. *Northwestern Miller,* March 22, 1899.
65. *Minneapolis Journal,* April 19, 1899.
66. Minneapolis Chamber of Commerce, Annual Report, 1899, 14.
67. William G. Ferris, *The Grain Traders: The Story of the Chicago Board of Trade* (East Lansing: Michigan State University Press, 1988), 120–121.
68. Minneapolis Chamber of Commerce, Minutes, August 30, 1897.
69. *Minneapolis Journal,* August 2, 1900.
70. Here and below: *Northwestern Miller,* May 21, 1902; *Minneapolis Journal,* March 7, 1905.
71. *Minneapolis Times,* October 29, 1902.
72. Minneapolis Chamber of Commerce, Minutes, October 16, 1902.
73. *Minneapolis Tribune,* January 19, 1903; *Minneapolis Journal,* January 19, 1903.
74. *Minneapolis Tribune,* January 20, 1903.
75. *Minneapolis Tribune,* January 20, 1903.
76. *Northwestern Miller,* April 1, 1903.
77. U.S. Supreme Court decision 198 U.S. 236.
78. Jonathan Lurie, *The Chicago Board of Trade, 1859–1905: The Dynamics of Self-Regulation* (Urbana: University of Illinois Press, 1979), 197.
79. *Minneapolis Journal,* November 1, 1906; April 7, 1907; April 11, 1907.
80. *Minneapolis Journal,* March 8, 1905.
81. *Minneapolis Journal,* July 5, 1909.
82. Lurie, *The Chicago Board of Trade, 1859–1905,* 174; *Minneapolis Journal,* June 25, 1900.
83. *Minneapolis Journal,* June 27, 1900.
84. Minneapolis Chamber of Commerce, Annual Report, 1900, 17.
85. Here and below: John G. McHugh, *Modern Grain Exchanges* (Minneapolis: Minneapolis Chamber of Commerce, 1922), 20–24.
86. *Minneapolis Journal,* June 25, 1900.

87. *Minneapolis Journal,* June 27, 1900.
88. *Minneapolis Journal,* September 7, 1900, and September 13, 1900.
89. *Minneapolis Tribune,* September 15, 1900.
90. *Minneapolis Journal,* January 23, 1901.
91. *Minneapolis Journal,* March 6, 1901.
92. Minneapolis Chamber of Commerce, Minutes, October 16, 1902.
93. *Minneapolis Journal,* September 18, 1902.
94. Minneapolis Chamber of Commerce, Annual Report, 1902.
95. *Minneapolis Journal,* September 24, 1902.
96. *Minneapolis Journal,* October 24, 1902.
97. *Minneapolis Journal,* November 3, 1902.
98. *Minneapolis Journal,* March 30, 1903.
99. Minneapolis Chamber of Commerce, Annual Report, 1902.
100. *Minneapolis Journal,* March 30, 1903.
101. Carl H. Chrislock, *The Progressive Era in Minnesota, 1899–1918* (St. Paul: Minnesota Historical Society Press, 1971), 107.
102. Chrislock, *The Progressive Era in Minnesota, 1899–1918,* 107.
103. Theodore Saloutos, "The Rise of the Equity Cooperative Exchange," *Mississippi Valley Historical Review* 32:1 (June 1945), 46–47.
104. Saloutos, "The Rise of the Equity Cooperative Exchange," 48; 50–51.
105. U.S. Federal Trade Commission, *Federal Trade Commission v. Chamber of Commerce of Minneapolis et al.* (St. Paul: Farmers Union Grain Terminal Association, 1923), 30.
106. *Duluth News Tribune,* February 28, 1913.
107. *Duluth News Tribune,* March 12, 1913.
108. *Duluth News Tribune,* March 25, 1913.
109. Saloutos, "The Rise of the Equity Cooperative Exchange," 56; *Minneapolis Tribune,* August 4, 1922.
110. *Minneapolis Journal,* March 3, 1913.
111. Saloutos, "The Rise of the Equity Cooperative Exchange," 55–56.
112. U.S. Federal Trade Commission, *Federal Trade Commission v. Chamber of Commerce of Minneapolis et al.* 7.
113. U.S. Federal Trade Commission, *Federal Trade Commission v. Chamber of Commerce of Minneapolis et al.,* 29.
114. Theodore Saloutos, "The Decline of the Equity Cooperative Exchange," *Mississippi Valley Historical Review* 34:3 (December 1947), 416.
115. "Equity Exchange Moves to St. Paul," *The Chamber of Commerce of Minneapolis* (Minneapolis: Co-operative Manager and Farmer, 1914), 51.

116. U.S. Federal Trade Commission, *Federal Trade Commission v. Chamber of Commerce of Minneapolis et al.,* 34–35.
117. U.S. Federal Trade Commission, *Federal Trade Commission v. Chamber of Commerce of Minneapolis et al.,* 35–36.
118. *Minneapolis Journal,* May 4, 1921.
119. Saloutos, "The Decline of the Equity Cooperative Exchange," 418.
120. Saloutos, "The Decline of the Equity Cooperative Exchange," 420.
121. Saloutos, "The Decline of the Equity Cooperative Exchange," 421.
122. *St. Paul Pioneer Press,* January 9, 1924; U.S. Federal Trade Commission, *Federal Trade Commission v. Chamber of Commerce of Minneapolis et al.,* 36.
123. Minneapolis Chamber of Commerce, Annual Report, 1900, 13.
124. Minneapolis Chamber of Commerce, Annual Report, 1930, 26–27.
125. Federal Trade Commission, *Report of the Federal Trade Commission on the Grain Trade* (Washington, D.C.: Government Printing Office, 1920), 5:31–37.
126. Danbom, "Flour Power: The Significance of Flour Milling at the Falls," 281–283.

## TRADING PLACES

127. Minneapolis Grain Exchange, National Register of Historic Places Registration Form, 1995.
128. *Minneapolis Journal,* March 30, 1903.
129. Minneapolis Grain Exchange, National Register of Historic Places Registration Form, 1995.
130. *Minneapolis Journal,* March 30, 1903.
131. Larry Millett, *Lost Twin Cities* (St. Paul: Minnesota Historical Society Press, 1992), 257.
132. *Minneapolis Journal,* March 30, 1903.
133. *Minneapolis Journal,* March 30, 1903.
134. *Minneapolis Journal,* March 30, 1903.
135. *Minneapolis Journal,* March 30, 1903.
136. *Minneapolis Journal,* March 30, 1903.
137. *Northwestern Miller,* March 16, 1904.
138. Minneapolis Chamber of Commerce, *The Minneapolis Chamber of Commerce, 1881–1903,* 15–16.
139. Minneapolis Grain Exchange, National Register of Historic Places Registration Form, 1995.
140. *Minneapolis Journal,* April 9, 1928.
141. Minneapolis Chamber of Commerce, Minutes, June 2, 1919.
142. McHugh, *Modern Grain Exchanges,* 2.
143. Al Gloe, interview by Dave Kenney, November 17, 2005.

## CHAPTER 3

144. Here and below: Tony Owens, interview by Deborah Morse-Kahn, August 24, 2001, transcript, Minneapolis Grain Exchange.

145. *Minneapolis Tribune,* October 25, 1929.

146. *Minneapolis Star,* November 5, 1958.

147. Don W. Larson, *Land of the Giants* (Minneapolis: Dorn Books, 1979), 137.

148. *Minneapolis Tribune,* June 27, 1965; Scott F. Anfinson, "Archaeology of the Central Minneapolis Riverfront," *Minnesota Archaeologist* 49:1-2, (p?) (1990).

149. *Farmers Union Herald,* May 1929.

150. Here and below: *Farmers Union Herald,* February 3, 1930.

151. Philip D. Jordan, "Equity, Justice, and Politics: A History of the Farmers Union Grain Terminal Association" (unpublished manuscript, 1956?), 103, Farmers Union Grain Terminal Association Papers, Minnesota Historical Society.

152. Jordan, "Equity, Justice, and Politics: A History of the Farmers Union Grain Terminal Association," 117.

153. John McHugh to Minneapolis Chamber of Commerce members, January 18, 1929.

154. John McHugh to Minneapolis Chamber of Commerce members, January 18, 1929.

155. Ferris, *The Grain Traders: The Story of the Chicago Board of Trade,* 193–204.

156. *Farmers Union Herald,* March 1940.

157. Ferris, *The Grain Traders: The Story of the Chicago Board of Trade,* 201.

158. Jordan, "Equity, Justice, and Politics: A History of the Farmers Union Grain Terminal Association," 156.

159. Luther Tweeten, "Overview of U.S. Agricultural Policy" (paper, Council of Agriculture, Taiwan, June 1998).

160. Jordan, "Equity, Justice, and Politics: A History of the Farmers Union Grain Terminal Association," 177, 183.

161. Jordan, "Equity, Justice, and Politics: A History of the Farmers Union Grain Terminal Association," 184.

162. *Farmers Union Herald,* March 1940.

163. Jordan, "Equity, Justice and Politics: A History of the Farmers Union Grain Terminal Association," 185.

164. Wayne G. Broehl Jr., *Cargill: Trading the World's Grain* (Hanover, New Hampshire: University Press of New England, 1992), 619.

165. *Northwestern Miller,* October 21, 1942.

166. *Minneapolis Star,* November 5, 1958.

167. Minneapolis Grain Exchange, Annual Report, 1970, 45–46.

168. *Grain from Farm to Market* (Minneapolis: Minneapolis Grain Exchange, 1947), 26.

169. Jordan, "Equity, Justice, and Politics: A History of the Farmers Union Grain Terminal Association," 195.

170. *Northwestern Miller,* June 30, 1943.

171. *Northwestern Miller,* February 16, 1944.

172. *Minneapolis Times,* September 4, 1946.

173. *St. Paul Pioneer Press,* September 20, 1947.

174. *Willmar Tribune,* April 4, 1944.

175. *St. Paul Pioneer Press,* September 20, 1947.

176. *Northwestern Miller,* December 13, 1944.

177. *Northwestern Miller,* December 13, 1944.

178. Jordan, "Equity, Justice, and Politics: A History of the Farmers Union Grain Terminal Association," 215.

179. *Farmers Union Herald,* July 1944.

180. *Northwestern Miller,* February 16, 1944.

181. Jordan, "Equity, Justice, and Politics: A History of the Farmers Union Grain Terminal Association," 215.

182. Jordan, "Equity, Justice, and Politics: A History of the Farmers Union Grain Terminal Association," 250S.

183. Bob McWhite, interview by Dave Kenney, August 17, 2005.

184. *Minneapolis Tribune,* May 13, 1946.

185. *Greater Minneapolis,* April 1956.

186. U.S. Federal Trade Commission, "Report of the FTC on Economic Effects of Grain Exchange Actions Affecting Futures Trading during the First Six Months of 1946," February 4, 1947.

187. *Minneapolis Star,* November 5, 1958.

188. *Minneapolis Star,* March 17, 1956.

189. *Minneapolis Star,* September 11, 1956.

190. Duane Fedje, interview by Deborah Morse-Kahn, November 29, 2001.

191. *Minneapolis Star,* November 5, 1958.

192. *Minneapolis Star,* November 5, 1958.

193. *Minneapolis Star,* November 3, 1958.

194. Here and below: *Minneapolis Star,* November 3, 1958.

195. *Minneapolis Star,* November 5, 1958.

196. *Minneapolis Star,* November 3, 1958.

197. *Minneapolis Tribune,* June 27, 1965.

198. *Northwestern Miller,* July 1965.

199. Joseph LaPray, "Terminal Elevators," *Greater Minneapolis,* November–December, 1980, 90.

200. Ralph Bagley, interview by Deborah Morse-Kahn, October 30, 2001.

201. Ralph Bagley, interview by Deborah Morse-Kahn, October 30, 2001.

202. Minneapolis Grain Exchange, Annual Report, 1969.

203. Joseph LaPray, "Terminal Elevators," 90.

204. Al Donahoo, interview by Deborah Morse-Kahn, November 2, 2001.

205. Shelley Walsh, interview with Deborah Morse-Kahn, October 11, 2001.

206. Duane Fedje, interview with Deborah Morse-Kahn, November 29, 2001.

207. Brooks Fields, interview with Deborah Morse-Kahn, October 3, 2001.

208. Bob McWhite, interview by Dave Kenney, August 17, 2005.

209. Brooks Fields, interview with Deborah Morse-Kahn, October 3, 2001.

210. Brooks Fields, interview with Deborah Morse-Kahn, October 3, 2001.

211. Mike Laurel, interview with Deborah Morse-Kahn, November 13, 2001.

212. *Duluth News-Tribune and Herald,* May 22, 1983.

213. Minneapolis Grain Exchange, Annual Report, 1970.

214. Minneapolis Grain Exchange, Annual Volume of Futures Trading, 2005.

215. *Minneapolis Grain Exchange News,* September 1963.

216. J. L. Morrill, "Milling Men Have Aided University," *Greater Minneapolis,* April 1956, 40.

## CHAPTER 4

217. *Minneapolis Tribune,* August 4, 1972.

218. Dan Morgan, *Merchants of Grain: The Power and Profits of the Five Giant Companies at the Center of the World's Food Supply* (New York: Viking Press, 1979), 8, 121.

219. Morgan, *Merchants of Grain,* 139.

220. Morgan, *Merchants of Grain,* 145.

221. "U.S.S.R. Buys 2,000,000 Tons U.S. Feed Grains," *Southwestern Miller,* November 9, 1971, 19.

222. "Palmby Clarifies Details of Russian Grain Sale," *Southwestern Miller,* December 14, 1971, 27.

223. Morgan, *Merchants of Grain,* 120.

224. Here and below: *Milling and Baking News,* October 3, 1972.

225. Mort Sosland, interview by Dave Kenney, October 4, 2005.

226. *Minneapolis Star,* August 8, 1972.

227. *St. Paul Dispatch,* August 18, 1972.

228. *Minneapolis Star,* August 11, 1972.

229. *Minneapolis Star,* August 11, 1972.

230. *St. Paul Pioneer Press,* August 18, 1972.

231. Wayne G. Broehl Jr., *Cargill: Going Global* (Hanover, New Hampshire: University Press of New England, 1998), 200.

232. *St. Paul Pioneer Press,* September 9, 1972.

233. W. Duncan MacMillan, Patricia Condon Johnston, and John Steele Gordon, *MacMillan: The American Grain Family* (Afton, Minnesota: Afton Historical Society Press, 1998), 313–314.

234. *Milling and Baking News,* October 3, 1972.

235. *St. Paul Pioneer Press,* August 29, 1972.

236. *Minneapolis Tribune,* December 23, 1972.

237. *Minneapolis Tribune,* September 19, 1972.

238. Morgan, *Merchants of Grain,* 157.

239. Leo Odden, interview by Dave Kenney, October 12, 2005.

240. *Minneapolis Tribune,* January 8, 1980.

241. *Minneapolis Tribune,* January 10, 1980.

242. *Minneapolis Tribune,* January 10, 1980.

243. John P. Case to Jimmy Carter, January 21, 1980, Minneapolis Grain Exchange.

244. *St. Paul Pioneer Press,* January 7, 1992.

245. *Minneapolis Star Tribune,* October 17, 1992.

246. *Trading Trends* (Minneapolis Grain Exchange,), September 1991.

247. Al Gloe, interview with Deborah Morse-Kahn, November 1, 2001.

248. Shelley Walsh, interview with Deborah Morse-Kahn, October 11, 2001.

249. Shelley Walsh, interview with Deborah Morse-Kahn, October 11, 2001.

250. Ralph Bagley, interview by Deborah Morse-Kahn, October 30, 2001.

251. Howard Smith, interview by Dave Kenney, October 14, 2005.

252. Ralph Hayenga, "Sunflower/1981: An Update," *Greater Minneapolis,* November– December, 1980, 32; *Minneapolis Tribune,* August 29, 1982.

253. *Minneapolis Tribune,* May 7, 1980.

254. *Minneapolis Tribune,* May 7, 1980.

255. *Minneapolis Tribune,* July 13, 1980.

256. *Minneapolis Tribune,* October 25, 1980.

257. *Minneapolis Tribune,* December 9, 1980.

258. *Minneapolis Tribune,* August 29, 1982.

259. John Dill Jr., unpublished monograph, Minneapolis Grain Exchange.

260. *Minneapolis Star Tribune,* January 19, 1993.

261. Pete Ritten, interview with Deborah Morse-Kahn, January 31, 2002.

262. *Minneapolis Journal,* July 4, 1901.

263. Minneapolis Grain Exchange, Minutes, April 15, 1966.

264. *Minneapolis Tribune,* March 26, 1971.

265. *Minneapolis Tribune,* March 26, 1971.

266. Ann Kathryn Ryan, "Women and the Exchange," *Greater Minneapolis,* November–December, 1980, 35.

267. Helen Pound, interview by Dave Kenney, October 6, 2005.

268. Howard Smith, interview by Dave Kenney, October 14, 2005.

269. Minneapolis Grain Exchange, Exchange Room Committee, Agenda, August 6, 1992.

270. Ann M. Curtin to Exchange Room Committee, September 4, 1985, Minneapolis Grain Exchange.

271. Jack Murray to Board of Directors, July 22, 1987, Minneapolis Grain Exchange.

272. Here and below: *Minneapolis Star,* April 12, 1978.

273. Johnson, Powell, and Company, "Minneapolis Grain Exchange Delphi I," April 1980, 29.

274. Johnson, Powell, and Company, "Minneapolis Grain Exchange Delphi II," July 1980, 14.

275. Johnson, Powell, and Company, "Minneapolis Grain Exchange Delphi II," 14.

276. *Minneapolis Star Tribune,* June 15, 1982.

277. "Business Plan for an Automated Futures Exchange (AFEX)," April 1985, Minneapolis Grain Exchange.

278. *St. Paul Pioneer Press,* October 14, 1987.

279. *Minneapolis Star Tribune,* November 1, 1987.

280. *Minneapolis Star Tribune,* June 25, 1990.

281. Kris Nelson, "Is This the Minneapolis Grain Exchange?" *Trading Trends,* July 1991, 2.

282. James Lindau to Glenn Windstrup, June 24, 1998, Minneapolis Grain Exchange.

283. Tracy Sayler, "Taming the Bulls and Bears," *Prairie Grains,* June 2000.

284. *Milling and Baking News,* August 28, 2001.

285. *Finance and Commerce,* October 2, 2002.

286. *Milling and Baking News,* February 10, 2004.

287. Bill Clements, "The Future of Futures Trading," *Twin Cities Business Monthly,* February 2005, 59.

288. *Minneapolis Journal,* March 30, 1903.

289. *City Business,* January 27, 1992.

290. James Lindau to Minneapolis Grain Exchange Board of Directors, July 29, 1996, Minneapolis Grain Exchange.

**ARCHER DANIELS MIDLAND COMPANY, Decatur, Illinois**
**p. 95,** ledger page from *The Nature of What's to Come: A Century of Innovation,* ADM history by Jenkins Group, 2002.

**THE BLAKE SCHOOL, Minneapolis**
**p. 46,** *The Highcroft Estate,* oil by Alexis Jean Fournier, 1897.

**BROWN CAT DESIGN (Lynne Appel), Fridley, Minnesota**
**p. 97,** Peavey Fountain, postcard, date unknown.

**CARGILL, Inc., Wayzata, Minnesota**
**p. 47,** *William W. Cargill,* oil by Edward V. Brewer, date unknown, and Sam Cargill, ca. 1898; **p. 116,** *A View of Duluth with Cargill Grain Elevator,* oil by Bela Petheo, 1986; **p. 143,** Port Cargill, Savage, Minnesota, 1976; **p. 144,** Ken McCoy, ca. 1954; **p. 151,** Cargill's *Cartasca,* Minneapolis River Terminal, 1948; **p. 164,** Cargill terminal, Albany, New York, ca. 1967; **p. 169,** "Still Pond" mansion, Cargill headquarters, Minnetonka, Minnesota, ca. 1935; **p. 180,** Cargill facility, Gibson City, Illinois, 1968.

**CONAGRA MILLS, Omaha, Nebraska**
**p. 2,** grain.

**ELMER L. ANDERSEN LIBRARY, Northwest Architectural Archives, Minneapolis, Minnesota**
**p. 101,** Frederick Kees and Serenus Coburn; **p. 105,** drawing, Grain Exchange trading room, by Kees and Coburn, ca. 1902.

**JOHN H. DANIELS COLLECTION**
**p. 94,** John William Daniels; **p. 94,** Daniels Linseed Oil Mill, Minneapolis, 1903.

**JOHN DILL COLLECTION**
**p. 189,** John Dill Jr.

**BROOKS FIELDS COLLECTION**
**p. 152,** Brooks Fields.

**GENERAL MILLS, Minneapolis**
**p. 24,** Gold Medal flour ad, 1916; **p. 28,** James Stroud Bell; **p. 29,** James Ford Bell; **p. 57,** Stevens Court, ca. 1970s.

**C. F. HAGLIN AND SONS, Edina, Minnesota**
**p. 81,** Chamber of Commerce Building, Minneapolis, ca. 1908; **p. 108,** Chamber of Commerce Building and Annex, Minneapolis, ca. 1918.

**T. BRADLEY AND PATTIE HAYS COLLECTION**
**p. 132,** "Voices from the Tomb" card.

**JIM HOWARD COLLECTION**
**p. 132,** Bob Howard, Ade Howard, and Lou Howard, late 1940s.

**KANSAS CITY BOARD OF TRADE, Kansas City, Kansas**
**p. 140,** Kansas City Board of Trade.

**DR. AND MRS. JOHN E. LARKIN COLLECTION**
**p. 21,** *The Falls of Saint Anthony,* oil on canvas by Seth Eastman, ca. 1848.

**W. DUNCAN MacMILLAN COLLECTION**
**p. 170,** W. Duncan MacMillan.

**THOMAS G. MAIRS COLLECTION**
**p. 95,** Sam Mairs.

**HOWARD McMILLAN COLLECTION**
**p. 184,** John Duncan McMillan.

**MINNEAPOLIS CLUB**
**p. 4,** *Upper Midwest Industry,* oil on canvas by John Socha, 1937, photo by Bright Star Versatile Images, Minneapolis; **p. 14,** bird's eye view of Minneapolis, 1891; **p. 23,** *The Daily Graphic,* 1878; **p. 26,** *Dakota Territory—The Great Wheat Fields in the Valley of the Red River of the North— Threshing by Steam on the Dalrymple Farm, Formerly a Barren Prairie,* engraving by Berghary based on George H. Ellsbury sketch and F. Jay Haynes photos, in *Frank Leslie's Illustrated Newspaper,* October 19, 1878; **p. 54,** "The Great Harvest at Minneapolis," in *Frank Leslie's Illustrated Newspaper,* October 10, 1891; **p. 80,** Clinton Morrison. **p. 121,** *Eagle Roller Mill Company—New Ulm, Minnesota,* pen, ink, and wash on paper, artist unknown, 1890.

**MINNEAPOLIS GRAIN EXCHANGE**
**Front cover:** trading floor, duotone by unknown photographer, circa 1970s; **p. 5,** trading floor clock, photo by Bright Star Versatile Images, Minneapolis; **p. 8,** traders, photo by Bright Star Versatile Images, Minneapolis; **p. 74,** George C. Bagley cartoon; **p. 77,** baseball poster; **p. 90,** Equity Cooperative Exchange; **p. 98,** *Grain Exchange Building,* oil on canvas, by Paul Oxborough, date unknown; **p. 100,** Grain Exchange Building complex; **p. 101-104,** Main Building; **p. 107,** metal elevator plaque; **p. 109,** North Building

construction; **p. 110 & 111,** North Building; **p. 112,** Main Building; **p. 113,** trading room restoration, 1984; **p. 114,** lobby restoration, 1984; **p. 114,** ramp construction, 1992; **p. 118,** futures pit, 1933; **p. 119,** farming; **p. 120,** General Mills; **p. 124,** public relations slide; **p. 125,** marketing photos by George Miles Ryan Studios, ca. 1940s; **p. 129,** baseball team, 1937; **p. 130,** cartoon, *The Farmers Union Herald,* 1940; **p. 133,** futures pit, 1947; **p. 133,** and cash grain tables, 1947; **p. 137,** Ben McCabe, 1952; **p. 139,** Bob McWhite; **p. 141,** board markers; **p. 141,** weather map; **p. 142,** James Mullin, ca. 1950s; **p. 142,** Hubert Humphrey, 1956; **p. 144,** Tom Gardin, August 4, 1958; **p. 147,** cartoon, *Minneapolis Tribune,* ca. 1963; **p. 149,** Ralph Bagley, 1965; **p. 150,** Al Donahoo; **p. 151,** river barge; **p. 152,** John McCaull; **p. 153,** tie contest; **p. 154,** Duluth Board of Trade, ca. 1950; **p. 156,** Grain Exchange, September 21, 1965; **p. 157,** hopper cars; **p. 163,** Clayton Moline, ca. 1972; **p. 167,** Mort Sosland; **p. 168,** cartoon by Jerry Fearing, *Pioneer Press,* September 1972; **p. 171,** suspended trading, 1973; **p. 172,** trading floor; **p. 172,** Leo Odden; **p. 174,** trading pit; **p. 174,** trading floor, January 9, 1980; **p. 177,** traders; **p. 179,** cash grain tables; **p. 180,** grain pan; **p. 181,** Shelley Walsh and Matt Walsh; **p. 185,** Win Wallin and Ralph Hayenga; **p. 186,** sunflower pit; **p. 188,** shrimp contract; **p. 190,** Marcia Hill; **p. 190,** Helen Pound; **p. 193,** dress code and trading floor; **p. 194,** board markers; **p. 195,** Jerry Johanning; **p. 195,** clearinghouse computers; **p. 197,** Paul Tattersall and Rudy Perpich, ca. 1980s; **p. 199,** Jim Lindau and Don Fraser; **p. 199,** Jesse Ventura and Kent Horsager; **p. 200,** Marty Farrell, photo by Bright Star Versatile Images, Minneapolis; **p. 202,** 2005 board of directors, photo by Craig Bares Photography; **p. 202,** Mark Bagan, photo by Bright Star Versatile Images, Minneapolis; **back cover,** traders, photos by Bright Star Versatile Images, Minneapolis.

**MINNEAPOLIS INSTITUTE OF ARTS**
**p. 16,** *Mill Pond at Minneapolis,* oil on canvas by Alexis Jean Fournier, 1888, the John R. Van Derlip Fund; **p. 52,** *Rainy Evening on Hennepin Avenue,* oil on canvas by Robert Koehler, ca. 1910; **p. 106,** *Portrait of John Scott Bradstreet,* oil on canvas by Douglas Volk, ca. 1890, gift of John Scott Bradstreet.

# ILLUSTRATION CREDITS

## MINNESOTA HISTORICAL SOCIETY, St. Paul, Minnesota

**p. 18,** Security State Bank, photo by William H. Jacoby, ca. 1885; **p. 19,** Alonzo C. Rand, photo by Floyd's Studio; **p. 20,** hauling logs to C. A. Smith's Sawmill, Minneapolis, photo by Underwood and Underwood, ca. 1885; **p. 20,** *Old Government Mills at Falls of St. Anthony*, oil by James Fairman, ca. 1890; **p. 21,** *St. Anthony Falls*, oil on canvas by Ferdinand Reichardt, ca. 1857; **p. 22,** Cadwallader Washburn, ca. 1880; **p. 22,** Washburn "A" Mill, Minneapolis, photos by William H. Jacoby, ca. 1874; **p. 25,** harvesters, G. S. Barnes and Company Farm, Glyndon, Minnesota, photo by Frank Jay Haynes, ca. 1878; **p. 27,** freight cars, Minneapolis, ca. 1890; **p. 32,** Johnson, Smith, and Harrison Printing and Lithographing building, ca. 1882; **p. 33,** *John Crosby*, oil by Leopold Seyffert, ca. 1910; **p. 34,** *William Hood Dunwoody*, engraving by W. G. Phillips, ca. 1893; **p. 35,** *George A. Pillsbury*, engraving by Samuel Sartain, 1893; **p. 39,** Chamber of Commerce Building, ca. 1885; **p. 40,** James J. Hill, photo by Ludovici's Photographic and Crayon Studios, New York, ca. 1873; **p. 40,** *Stone Arch Bridge*, Minneapolis, watercolor by Lloyd P. Hinton, date unknown; **p. 42,** *Charles M. Loring*, oil by Grace E. McKinstry, ca. 1910; **p. 44,** Atlantic Grain Elevator "A," Minneapolis, photo by William Henry Fletcher, ca. 1890; **p. 44,** *Van Dusen Elevator*, oil by Alexis Jean Fournier, 1888; **p. 46,** *Frank H. Peavey*, oil by Alexis Jean Fournier, ca. 1890; **p. 48,** experimental monolith for grain storage, St. Louis Park, Minnesota, ca. 1908; **p. 49,** Charles A. Pillsbury and Company poster by Compton-Sons Poster Collection, ca. 1890; **p. 50,** *John S. Pillsbury*, oil by John Antrobus, 1887; **p. 51,** Corn Exchange Building, Minneapolis, photo by Karker and Vanderwarker, ca. 1900; **p. 51,** Charles A. Pillsbury, ca. 1883, from *Northwestern Miller* 37: 77; **p. 53,** C. A. Pillsbury and Company "A" flour mill, drawing by L. S. Buffington, ca. 1879; **p. 53,** St. Anthony Falls and mills, Minneapolis, photo by Northwestern Photo Copying Company, ca. 1897; **p. 55,** Mahala Fisk Pillsbury with mother Mrs. Lougee, daughter Susan Pillsbury Snyder, and grandson John P. Snyder, photo by Arthur B. Rugg, ca. 1888; **p. 56,** Woman's Boarding Home, Minneapolis, ca. 1912; **p. 56,** Woman's Boarding Home, Minneapolis, photo by Lee Brothers, ca. 1918; **p. 57,** Pillsbury Settlement House, Minneapolis, ca. 1910; **p. 58,** *Lyndale Park Fountain, Minneapolis,* gouache on paper by Eric Austen Erickson, 1992; **p. 60,** Loring Park lake, Minneapolis, ca. 1905; group at Loring Park, Minneapolis, photo by T. F. Cann, 1898; **p. 61,** Chamber of Commerce Building, Minneapolis, ca. 1895; trading floor, Chamber of Commerce Building, Minneapolis, ca. 1895; **p. 63,** William H. Eustis, photo by James A. Brush, ca. 1885; **p. 64,** Thomas Lowry, ca. 1895; **p. 65,** Flour Exchange, Minneapolis, ca. 1910; **p. 67,** Northwestern Guaranty Loan Building, Minneapolis, ca. 1892; **p. 67,** Fourth Avenue South, Minneapolis, 1900; **p. 69,** political poster, ca. 1888–1896; **p. 71,** Bank of Commerce Building, Minneapolis, photo by Sweet, 1903; **p. 72,** John Washburn, ca. 1895; Gustav F. Ewe, photo by Lee Brothers, ca. 1910; **p. 79,** bird's eye view of Minneapolis, postcard, ca. 1907; **p. 80,** Minneapolis Institute of Arts, postcard, ca. 1925; **p. 83,** Chamber of Commerce Building, ca. 1905; **p. 84,** Duluth Board of Trade, 1895; **p. 87,** Samuel D. Works, 1913; Christopher Bendixen, 1909; **p. 88,** James Manahan and George Loftus, ca. 1890; **p. 89,** cartoon; **p. 93,** harvesting oats, Beltrami County, Minnesota, photo by John Krueth, ca. 1910; **p. 93,** harvesting flax, Fargo, North Dakota, photo by Sweet, ca. 1910; **p. 115,** trading floor, gelatin silver on fiber base paper by Michael Melman, 1992, gift of Mike Melman; **p. 123,** M. W. ("Bill") Thatcher, photo by Theodore J. Strasser, date unknown; **p. 126 & 127,** pages from *The Story of Grain: From Farm to You*, ca. 1950s; **p. 146,** Cavalier Room, Minneapolis Athletic Club, postcard, ca. 1950; **p. 158,** University of Minnesota Board of Regents, January 1889; **p. 159,** Pillsbury Hall, U of M, photo by Ralph D. Cleveland, ca. 1893; **p. 159,** statue of John S. Pillsbury, U of M, photo by Sweet, ca. 1904; **p. 160,** *Minneapolis Grain Exchange,* acrylic by Edwin H. Ryan, ca. 1975; **p. 163,** Minneapolis Grain Exchange quotation boards, photos by Charles Bjorgen, August 8, 1972; **p. 176,** Duane Stich and John Case; **p. 176,** Ted Metz and Ron Olson; **p. 182,** Ed Mullin and James Mullin; **p. 182,** Fritz Corrigan.

## TRUXTUN MORRISON COLLECTION
**p. 183,** Truxtun Morrison.

## NORTHEAST MINNESOTA HISTORICAL CENTER, Duluth, Minnesota
**p. 84,** Duluth Exchange floor, ca. 1920s.

## ANTHONY OWENS COLLECTION
**p. 118,** Anthony Owens, 2005.

## PRIVATE COLLECTION
**p. 37,** ads, ca. 1884–1885; **p. 86,** membership card; **p. 121,** *Mills on the Mississippi*, oil on canvas by Erie Loran, 1931; **p. 121,** *Tierney Mills,* oil on canvas by Dewey Albinson, ca. 1930s.

## STEVEN DAHLMAN PHOTOGRAPHY, Chicago, Illinois
**p. 201,** Washburn "A" Mill and Mill City Museum, 2003.

## BRADFORD WALLIN COLLECTION
**p. 41,** Minneapolis Railways, Tribune Job Rooms Print, 1883; **p. 62,** Grain Exchange Building, stereocard; **p. 70,** Chicago Board of Trade Building, postcard; **p. 83,** Chamber of Commerce Building, postcard; **p. 96,** Minneapolis milling district by moonlight, postcard; **p. 105,** trading room, Chamber of Commerce, postcard, ca. 1909; **p. 108,** Chamber of Commerce Building, postcard; **p. 146,** Club Row, postcard; **p. 154,** Peavey grain elevator, Duluth, Minnesota, postcard; **p. 187,** Win Walllin.

## WEISMAN ART MUSEUM, University of Minnesota, Minneapolis
**p. 29,** *Minneapolis from the University of Minnesota Campus,* oil on canvas by Alexis Jean Fournier, 1888, gift of Daniel S. Feidt.

## WESLEY R. HARKINS PHOTO, Duluth, Minnesota
**p. 155,** *Ramon de Larringa,* Duluth, Minnesota, 1959.

## DORIS WINTERS COLLECTION
**p. 95,** George A. Archer; **p. 96,** Shreve Archer.

## DISPLAY PAGES
**Frontispiece,** *Upper Midwest Industry,* oil on canvas, John Socha, 1937, Minneapolis Club; **Ch. 1, p. 16,** *Mill Pond at Minneapolis,* oil on canvas, Alexis Jean Fournier, 1888, Minneapolis Institute of Arts; **Ch. 2, p. 58,** *Lyndale Park Fountain, Minneapolis,* gouache on paper, Eric Austen Erickson, 1992, Minnesota Historical Society; **Trading Places, p. 98,** *Grain Exchange Building,* oil on canvas, Paul Oxborough, date unknown, Minneapolis Grain Exchange; **Ch. 3, p. 116,** *A View of Duluth with Cargill Grain Elevator,* oil, Bela Petheo, 1986, Cargill, Inc.; **Ch. 4, p. 160,** *Minneapolis Grain Exchange,* acrylic by Edwin H. Ryan, ca. 1975, Minnesota Historical Society.

# INDEX

# INDEX

*This book was designed by*

**Mary Susan Oleson**
NASHVILLE, TENNESSEE

*fonts used:*

**Universal, Scriptina**